INFORMATION RETRIEVAL SYSTEMS:
SYSTEMS:
Theory and Implementation

THE KLUWER INTERNATIONAL SERIES ON INFORMATION RETRIEVAL

Series Editor

W. Bruce Croft

University of Massachusetts
Amherst, MA 01003

Also in the Series:

MULTIMEDIA INFORMATION RETRIEVAL: *Content-Based Information Retrieval from Large Text and Audio Databases*
by Peter Schäuble
 ISBN: 0-7923-9899-8

INFORMATION RETRIEVAL SYSTEMS:
Theory and Implementation

by

Gerald Kowalski
Senior Scientist
Central Intelligence Agency
USA

KLUWER ACADEMIC PUBLISHERS
Boston / Dordrecht / London

Distributors for North, Central and South America:
Kluwer Academic Publishers
101 Philip Drive
Assinippi Park
Norwell, Massachusetts 02061 USA
Telephone (781) 871-6600
Fax (781) 871-6528
E-Mail <kluwer@wkap.com>

Distributors for all other countries:
Kluwer Academic Publishers Group
Distribution Centre
Post Office Box 322
3300 AH Dordrecht, THE NETHERLANDS
Telephone 31 78 6392 392
Fax 31 78 6546 474
E-Mail <services@wkap.nl>

 Electronic Services <http://www.wkap.nl>

Library of Congress Cataloging-in-Publication Data

Kowalski, Gerald, 1945-
    Information retrieval systems : theory and implementation / by
George Kowalski.
        p. cm. -- (The Kluwer international series on information
retrieval ; 1)
    Includes bibliographical references and index.
    ISBN 0-7923-9926-9 (alk. paper)
    1. Database management. 2. Information storage and retrieval
systems. I. Title. II. Series.
QA76.9.D3K685 1997
005.74'068--dc21   97-12568
                                           CIP

Printed on acid-free paper.

Printed in the United States of America

This book is dedicated to my parents who taught me the value of a strong work ethic and my daughters, Kris and Kara, who continue to support my taking on new challenges.

CONTENTS

PREFACE

The growth of the Internet and the availability of enormous volumes of data in digital form have necessitated intense interest in techniques to assist the user in locating data of interest. The Internet has over 350 million pages of data and is expected to reach over one billion pages by the year 2000. Buried on the Internet are both valuable nuggets to answer questions as well as a large quantity of information the average person does not care about. The Digital Library effort is also progressing, with the goal of migrating from the traditional book environment to a digital library environment.

The challenge to both authors of new publications that will reside on this information domain and developers of systems to locate information is to provide the information and capabilities to sort out the non-relevant items from those desired by the consumer. In effect, as we proceed down this path, it will be the computer that determines what we see versus the human being. The days of going to a library and browsing the new book shelf are being replaced by electronic searching the Internet or the library catalogs. Whatever the search engines return will constrain our knowledge of what information is available. An understanding of Information Retrieval Systems puts this new environment into perspective for both the creator of documents and the consumer trying to locate information.

This book provides a theoretical and practical explanation of the latest advancements in information retrieval and their application to existing systems. It takes a system approach, discussing all aspects of an Information Retrieval System. The importance of the Internet and its associated hypertext linked structure are put into perspective as a new type of information retrieval data structure. The total system approach also includes discussion of the human interface and the importance of information visualization for identification of relevant information. The theoretical metrics used to describe information systems are expanded to discuss their practical application in the uncontrolled environment of real world systems.

The primary goal of writing this book is to provide a college text on Information Retrieval Systems. But in addition to the theoretical aspects, the book maintains a theme of practicality that puts into perspective the importance and utilization of the theory in systems that are being used by anyone on the Internet. The student will gain an understanding of what is achievable using existing technologies and the deficient areas that warrant additional research. The text provides coverage of all of the major aspects of information retrieval and has sufficient detail to allow students to implement a simple Information Retrieval

System. The comparison algorithms from Chapter 10 can be used to compare how well each of the student's systems work.

The first three chapters define the scope of an Information Retrieval System. The theme, that the primary goal of an Information Retrieval System is to minimize the overhead associated in locating needed information, is carried throughout the book. Chapter 1 provides a functional overview of an Information Retrieval System and differentiates between an information system and a Database Management System (DBMS). Chapter 2 focuses on the functions available in an information retrieval system. An understanding of the functions and why they are needed help the reader gain an intuitive feeling for the application of the technical algorithms presented later. Chapter 3 provides the background on indexing and cataloging that formed the basis for early information systems and updates it with respect to the new digital data environment.

Chapter 4 provides a discussion on word stemming and its use in modern systems. It also introduces the underlying data structures used in Information Retrieval Systems and their possible applications. This is the first introduction of hypertext data structures and their applicability to information retrieval. Chapters 5, 6 and 7 go into depth on the basis for search in Information Retrieval Systems. Chapter 5 looks at the different approaches to information systems search and the extraction of information from documents that will be used during the query process. Chapter 6 describes the techniques that can be used to cluster both terms from documents for statistical thesauri and the documents themselves. Thesauri can assist searches by query term expansion while document clustering can expand the initial set of found documents to similar documents. Chapter 7 focuses on the search process as a mapping between the user's search need and the documents in the system. It introduces the importance of relevance feedback in expanding the user's query and discusses the difference between search techniques against an existing database versus algorithms that are used to disseminate newly received items to user's mail boxes.

Chapter 8 introduces the importance of information visualization and its impact on the user's ability to locate items of interest in large systems. It provides the background on cognition and perception in human beings and then how that knowledge is applied to organizing information displays to help the user locate needed information. Chapter 9 describes text scanning techniques as a special search application within information retrieval systems. It describes the hardware and software approaches to text search.

Chapter 10 describes how to evaluate Information Retrieval Systems focusing on the theoretical and standard metrics used in research to evaluate information systems. Problems with the measurement's techniques in evaluating operational systems are discussed along with possible required modifications. Existing system capabilities are highlighted by reviewing the results from the Text Retrieval Conferences (TRECs).

Although this book provides coverage of the technologies associated with Information Retrieval Systems, three areas are missing. I consider it important that students understand how to create multimedia items for the Internet because they are so ubiquitous. I recommend that one week of lecture focus on this topic using one of the many recent softback books on this topic. More advanced chapters on Optical Character Recognition (OCR), foreign language search and display, search of audio files and search of video files are planned for a future edition.

ACKNOWLEDGMENTS

I would like to thank Arnold Meltzer for his assistance in reviewing the book and providing suggestions on its contents. I especially would like to thank Nancy Kneece for her willingness to review the total text multiple times, providing invaluable suggestions on its format and contents.

1 Introduction to Information Retrieval Systems

This chapter defines an Information Storage and Retrieval System (called an Information Retrieval System for brevity) and differentiates between information retrieval and database management systems. Tied closely to the definition of an Information Retrieval System are the system objectives. It is satisfaction of the objectives that drives those areas that receive the most attention in development. For example, academia pursues all aspects of information systems, investigating new theories, algorithms and heuristics to advance the knowledge base. Academia does not worry about response time, required resources to implement a system to support thousands of users nor operations and maintenance costs associated with system delivery. On the other hand, commercial institutions are not always concerned with the optimum theoretical approach, but the approach that minimizes development costs and increases the salability of their product. This text considers both view points and technology states. Throughout this text, information retrieval is viewed from both the theoretical and practical viewpoint.

The functional view of an Information Retrieval System is introduced to put into perspective the technical areas discussed in later chapters. As detailed algorithms and architectures are discussed, they are viewed as subfunctions within a total system. They are also correlated to the major objective of an Information Retrieval System which is minimization of human resources required in the finding of needed information to accomplish a task.   As with any discipline, standard measures are identified to compare the value of different algorithms. In information systems, precision and recall are the key metrics used in evaluations. Early introduction of these concepts in this chapter will help the reader in understanding the utility of the detailed algorithms and theory introduced throughout this text.

There is a potential for confusion in the understanding of the differences between Database Management Systems (DBMS) and Information Retrieval Systems. It is easy to confuse the software that optimizes functional support of each type of system with actual information or structured data that is being stored and manipulated. The importance of the differences lies in the inability of a database management system to provide the functions needed to process "information." The opposite, an information system containing structured data, also suffers major functional deficiencies. These differences are discussed in detail in Section 1.4.

1.1 Definition of Information Retrieval System

An Information Retrieval System is a system that is capable of storage, retrieval, and maintenance of information. Information in this context can be composed of text (including numeric and date data), images, audio, video and other multi-media objects. Although the form of an object in an Information Retrieval System is diverse, the text aspect has been the only data type that lent itself to full functional processing. The other data types have been treated as highly informative sources, but are primarily linked for retrieval based upon search of the text. Techniques are beginning to emerge to search these other media types (e.g., EXCALIBUR's Visual RetrievalWare). The focus of this book is on research and implementation of search, retrieval and representation of textual sources. At the current pace of commercial development, within three years, pattern matching against other data types will be a common function integrated within the total information system. Even in today's systems, the text may only be an identifier to display another associated data type that holds the substantive information desired by the system's users. The term "user" in this book represents an end user of the information system who has minimal knowledge of computers and technical fields in general.

The term "item" is used to represent the smallest complete textual unit that is processed and manipulated by the system. The definition of item varies by how a specific source treats information. A complete document, such as a book, newspaper or magazine could be an item. At other times each chapter, or article may be defined as an item. As sources vary and systems include more complex processing, an item may address even lower levels of abstraction such as a contiguous passage of text or a paragraph. For readability, throughout this book the terms "item" and "document" are not in this rigorous definition, but interchangeably. Whichever is used, they represent the concept of an item.

An Information Retrieval System consists of a software program that facilitates a user in finding the information the user needs. The system may use standard computer hardware or specialized hardware to support the search subfunction. The gauge of success of an information system is how well it can minimize the overhead for a user to find the needed information. Overhead from a user's perspective is the time required to find the information needed, excluding the time for actually reading the relevant data. Thus search composition, search execution, and reading non-relevant items are all aspects of information retrieval overhead.

The first Information Retrieval Systems originated with the need to organize information in central repositories (e.g., libraries) (Hyman-82). Catalogues were created to facilitate the identification and retrieval of items. Chapter 3 reviews the history of cataloging and indexing. Original definitions focused on "documents" for information retrieval (or their surrogates) rather than the multi-media integrated information that is now available (Minker-77, Minker-77).

As computers became commercially available, they were obvious candidates for the storage and retrieval of text. Early introduction of Database Management Systems provided an ideal platform for electronic manipulation of the indexes to information (Rather-77). Libraries followed the paradigm of their catalogs and references by migrating the format and organization of their hardcopy information references into structured databases. These remain as a primary mechanism for researching sources of needed information and play a major role in available Information Retrieval Systems. Academic research that was pursued through the 1980s was constrained by the paradigm of the indexed structure associated with libraries and the lack of computer power to handle large (gigabyte) text databases. The Military and other Government entities have always had a requirement to store and search large textual databases. As a result they began many independent developments of textual Information Retrieval Systems. Given the large quantities of data they needed to process, they pursued both research and development of specialized hardware and unique software solutions incorporating Commercial Off The Shelf (COTS) products where possible. The Government has been the major funding source of research into Information Retrieval Systems. With the advent of inexpensive powerful personnel computer processing systems and high speed, large capacity secondary storage products, it has become commercially feasible to provide large textual information databases for the average user. The introduction and exponential growth of the Internet along with its WAIS (Wide Area Information Servers) capability has provided a new avenue for access to gigabytes of information. The algorithms and techniques to optimize the processing and access of large quantities of textual data were once the sole domain of segments of the Government, a few industries, and academics. They have now become a needed capability for large quantities of the population with significant research and development being done by the private sector.

1.2 Objectives of Information Retrieval Systems

The general objective of an Information Retrieval System is to minimize the overhead of a user locating needed information. Overhead can be expressed as the time a user spends in all of the steps leading to reading an item containing the needed information (e.g., query generation, query execution, scanning results of query to select items to read, reading non-relevant items). The success of an information system is very subjective, based upon what information is needed and the willingness of a user to accept overhead. Under some circumstances, needed information can be defined as all information that is in the system that relates to a user's need. In other cases it may be defined as sufficient information in the system to complete a task, allowing for missed data. For example, a financial advisor recommending a billion dollar purchase of another company needs to be sure that all relevant, significant information on the target company has been located and reviewed in writing the recommendation. In contrast, a student only requires sufficient references in a research paper to satisfy the expectations of the teacher, which never is all inclusive. A system that supports reasonable retrieval requires fewer features than one which requires comprehensive retrieval. In many cases comprehensive retrieval is a negative feature because it overloads the user with more information than is needed, with an overhead in absorbing information that is not needed, even though it is relevant. In information retrieval the term "relevant" item is used to represent an item containing the needed information. In reality the definition of relevance is not a binary classification but a continuous function. From a user's perspective "relevant" and "needed" are synonymous. From a system perspective, information could be relevant to a search statement (i.e., matching the criteria of the search statement) even though it is not needed/relevant to user (e.g., the user already knew the information). A discussion on relevance and the natural redundancy of relevant information is presented in Chapter 10.

The two major measures commonly associated with information systems are precision and recall. When a user decides to issue a search looking for information on a topic, the total database is logically divided into four segments shown in Figure 1.1. Relevant items are those documents that contain information that helps the searcher in answering his question. Non-relevant items are those items that do not provide any directly useful information. There are two possibilities with respect to each item: it can be retrieved or not retrieved by the user's query. Precision and recall are defined as:

$$Precision = \frac{Number\_Retrieved\_Relevant}{Number\_Total\_Retrieved}$$

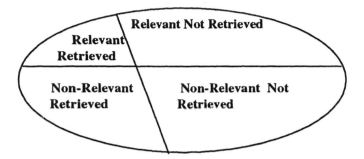

Figure 1.1 Effects of Search on Total Document Space

$$Recall = \frac{Number\_Re\,trieved\_Re\,levant}{Number\_Possible\_Re\,levant}$$

where *Number_Possible_Relevant* are the number of relevant items in the database. *Number_Total_Retieved* is the total number of items retrieved from the query. *Number_Retrieved_Relevant* is the number of items retrieved that are relevant to the user's search need. Precision measures one aspect of information retrieval overhead for a user associated with a particular search. If a search has a 85 per cent precision, then 15 per cent of the user effort is overhead reviewing non-relevant items. Recall gauges how well a system processing a particular query is able to retrieve the relevant items that the user is interested in seeing. Recall is a very useful concept, but due to the denominator, is non-calculable in operational systems. If the system knew the total set of relevant items in the database, it would have been retrieved. Figure 1.2a shows the values of precision and recall as the number of items retrieved increases, under an optimum query where every returned item is relevant. There are "N" relevant items in the database. Figures 1.2b and 1.2c show the optimal and currently achievable relationships between Precision and Recall (Harman-95). In Figure 1.2a the basic properties of precision (solid line) and recall (dashed line) can be observed. Precision starts off at 100 per cent and maintains that value as long as relevant items are retrieved. Recall starts off close to zero and increases as long as relevant items are retrieved until all possible relevant items have been retrieved. Once all "N" relevant items have been retrieved, the only items being retrieved are non-relevant. Precision is directly affected by retrieval of non-relevant items and drops to a number close to zero. Recall is not effected by retrieval of non-relevant items and thus remains at 100 per

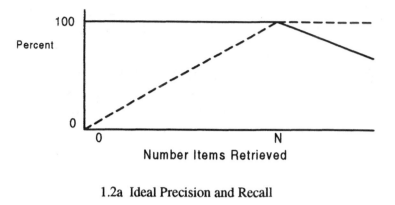

1.2a Ideal Precision and Recall

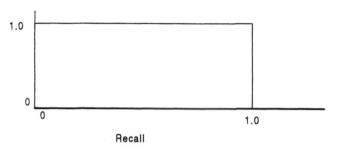

Figure 1.2b Ideal Precision/Recall Graph

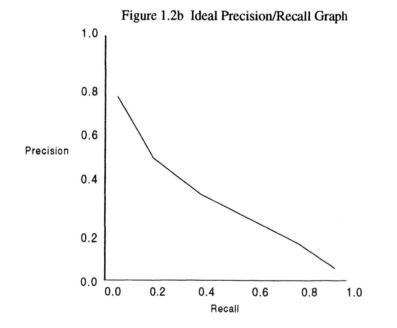

Figure 1.2c Achievable Precision/Recall Graph

cent once achieved. Precision/Recall graphs show how values for precision and recall change within a search results file (Hit file) as viewed from the most relevant to least relevant item. As with Figure 1.2a, in the ideal case every item retrieved is relevant. Thus precision stays at 100 per cent (1.0). Recall continues to increase by moving to the right on the x-axis until it also reaches the 100 per cent (1.0) point. Although Figure 1.2c stops here, continuation stays at the same x-axis location (recall never changes) but decreases down the y-axis until it gets close to the x-axis as more non-relevant are discovered and precision decreases. Figure 1.2c is from the latest TREC conference (see Chapter 10) and is representative of current capabilities.

To understand the implications of Figure 1.2c, its useful to describe the implications of a particular point on the precision/recall graph. Assume that there are 100 relevant items in the data base and from the graph at precision of .3 (i.e., 30 per cent) there is an associated recall of .5 (i.e., 50 per cent). This means there would be 50 relevant items in the Hit file from the recall value. A precision of 30 per cent means the user would likely review 167 items to find the 50 relevant items.

The first objective of an Information Retrieval System is support of user search generation. There are natural obstacles to specification of the information a user needs that come from ambiguities inherent in languages, limits to the user's ability to express what information is needed and differences between the user's vocabulary corpus and that of the authors of the items in the database. Natural languages suffer from word ambiguities such as homographs and use of acronyms that allow the same word to have multiple meanings (e.g., the word "field" or the acronym "U.S."). Disambiguation techniques exist but introduce significant system overhead in processing power and extended search times and often require interaction with the user.

Many users have trouble in generating a good search statement. The typical user does not have significant experience with nor even the aptitude for Boolean logic statements. The use of Boolean logic is a legacy from the evolution of database management systems and implementation constraints. Until recently, commercial systems were based upon databases. It is only with the introduction of Information Retrieval Systems such as RetrievalWare, TOPIC, WAIS and INQUERY that the idea of accepting natural language queries is becoming a standard system feature. This allows users to state in natural language what they are interested in finding. But the completeness of the user specification is limited by the user's willingness to construct long natural language queries.

In addition to the complexities in generating a query, quite often the user is not an expert in the area that is being searched and lacks domain specific vocabulary unique to that particular subject area. The user starts the search process with a general concept of the information required, but not have a focused definition of exactly what is needed. A limited knowledge of the vocabulary associated with a particular area along with lack of focus on exactly what information is needed leads to use of inaccurate and in some cases misleading search terms. Even when the user is an expert in the area being searched, the ability to select the proper search terms is constrained by lack of knowledge of the author's vocabulary. All writers have a vocabulary limited by their life experiences, environment where they were raised and ability to express themselves. Other than in very technical restricted information domains, the user's search vocabulary does not match the author's vocabulary.

Thus, an Information Retrieval System must provide tools to help overcome the search specification problems discussed above. In particular the search tools must assist the user automatically and through system interaction in developing a search specification that represents the need of the user and the writing style of diverse authors (see Figure 1.3).

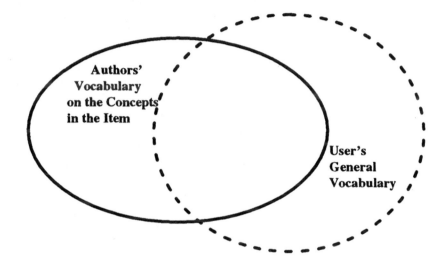

Figure 1.3 Vocabulary Domains

In addition to finding the information relevant to a user's needs, an objective of an information system is to present the search results in a format that facilitates the user in determining relevant items. Historically data has been presented in an order dictated by how it was physically stored. Typically, this is in arrival to the system order, thereby always displaying the results of a search sorted by time. For those users interested in current events this is useful. But for the majority of searches it does not filter out less useful information. The new Information Retrieval Systems provide functions that provide the results of a query in order of potential relevance to the user. This in conjunction with user search status (e.g., listing titles of highest ranked items) and item formatting options provides the user with features to assist in selection and review of the most likely relevant items first. Even more sophisticated techniques use item clustering and link analysis to provide additional item selection insights (see Chapter 8.)   Other features such as viewing only "unseen" items also help a user who can not complete the item review process in one session.

1.3 Functional Overview

A total Information Storage and Retrieval System is composed of four major functional processes: Item Normalization, Selective Dissemination of Information (i.e., "Mail"), archival Document Database Search, and an Index Database Search along with the Automatic File Build process that supports Index Files. Commercial systems have not integrated these capabilities into a single system but supply them as independent capabilities. Figure 1.4 shows the logical view of these capabilities in a single integrated Information Retrieval System. Boxes are used in the diagram to represent functions while disks represent data storage.

1.3.1 Item Normalization

The first step in any integrated system is to normalize the incoming items to a standard format. In addition to translating multiple external formats that might be received into a single consistent data structure that can be manipulated by the functional processes, item normalization provides logical restructuring of the item. Additional operations during item normalization are needed to create a searchable data structure: identification of processing tokens (e.g., words), characterization of the tokens, and stemming (e.g., removing word endings) of the tokens. The original item or any of its logical subdivisions is available for the user to display. The processing tokens and their characterization are used to define the searchable text from the total received text. Figure 1.5 shows the normalization process.

Standardizing the input takes the different external formats of input data and performs the translation to the formats acceptable to the system. A system may have a single format for all items or allow multiple formats. One example of standardization could be translation of foreign languages into Unicode. Every language has a different internal binary encoding for the characters in the language. One standard encoding that covers English, French, Spanish, etc. is ISO-Latin. The are other internal encodings for other language groups such as Russian (e.g, KOI-7, KOI-8), Japanese, Arabic, etc. Unicode is an evolving international standard based upon 16 bits (two bytes) that will be able to represent

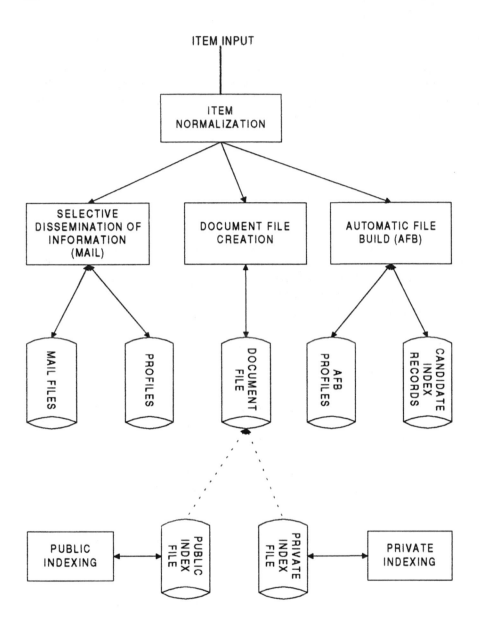

Figure 1.4 Total Information Retrieval System

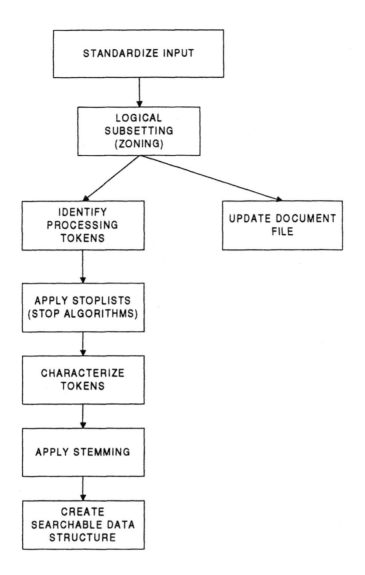

Figure 1.5 The Normalization Process

all languages. Having all of the languages encoded into a single format allows for
a single browser to display the languages and potentially a single search system to
search them.

The next process is to parse the item into logical sub-divisions that have
meaning to the user. This process, called "Zoning," is visible to the user and used
to increase the precision of a search and optimize the display. A typical item is
sub-divided into zones, which may overlap and can be hierarchical, such as Title,

Author, Abstract, Main Text, Conclusion, and References. The term "Zone" was selected over field because of the variable length nature of the data identified and because it is a logical sub-division of the total item, whereas the term "fields" has a connotation of independence. There may be other source-specific zones such as "Country" and "Keyword." The zoning information is passed to the processing token identification operation to store the information, allowing searches to be restricted to a specific zone. For example, if the user is interested in articles discussing "Einstein" then the search should not include the Bibliography, which could include references to articles written by "Einstein."

Once a search is complete, the user wants to efficiently review the results to locate the needed information. A major limitation to the user is the size of the display screen which constrains the number of items that are visible for review. To optimize the number of items reviewed per display screen, the user wants to display the minimum data required from each item to allow determination of the possible relevance of that item. Quite often the user will only display zones such as the Title or Title and Abstract. This allows multiple items to be displayed per screen. The user can expand those items of potential interest to see the complete text.

Once the standardization and zoning has been completed, information (i.e., words) that are used in the search process need to be identified in the item. The term processing token is used because a "word" is not the most efficient unit on which to base search structures. The first step in identification of a processing token consists of determining a word. Systems determine words by dividing input symbols into three classes: valid word symbols, inter-word symbols, and special processing symbols. A word is defined as a contiguous set of word symbols bounded by inter-word symbols. In many systems inter-word symbols are non-searchable and should be carefully selected. Examples of word symbols are alphabetic characters and numbers. Examples of possible inter-word symbols are blanks, periods and semicolons. The exact definition of an inter-word symbol is dependent upon the aspects of the language domain of the items to be processed by the system. For example. an apostrophe may be of little importance if only used for the possessive case in English, but might be critical to represent foreign names in the database. Based upon the required accuracy of searches and language characteristics, a trade off is made on the selection of inter-word symbols. Finally there are some symbols that may require special processing. A hyphen can be used many ways, often left to the taste and judgment of the writer (Bernstein-84). At the end of a line it is used to indicate the continuation of a word. In other places it links independent words to avoid absurdity, such as in the case of "small business men." To avoid interpreting this as short males that run businesses, it would properly be hyphenated "small-business men." Thus when a hyphen (or other special symbol) is detected a set of rules are executed to determine what action is to be taken generating one or more processing tokens.

Next, a Stop List/Algorithm is applied to the list of potential processing tokens. The objective of the Stop function is to save system resources by eliminating from the set of searchable processing tokens those that have little value to the system. Given the significant increase in available cheap memory, storage and processing power, the need to apply the Stop function to processing tokens is decreasing. Nevertheless, Stop Lists are commonly found in most systems and consist of words (processing tokens) whose frequency and/or semantic use make them of no value as a searchable token. For example, any word found in almost every item would have no discrimination value during a search. Parts of speech, such as articles (e.g., "the"), have no search value and are not a useful part of a user's query. By eliminating these frequently occurring words the system saves the processing and storage resources required to incorporate them as part of the searchable data structure. Stop Algorithms go after the other class of words, those found very infrequently.

Ziph (Ziph-49) postulated that, looking at the frequency of occurrence of the unique words across a corpus of items, the majority of unique words are found to occur a few times. The rank-frequency law of Ziph is:

Frequency * Rank = constant

where Frequency is the number of times a word occurs and rank is the rank order of the word. The law was later derived analytically using probability and information theory (Fairthorne-69). Table 1.1 shows the distribution of words in the first TREC test database (Harman-93), a database with over one billion characters and 500,000 items. In Table 1.1, WSJ is Wall Street Journal (1986-89), AP is AP Newswire (1989), ZIFF - Information from Computer Select disks, FR - Federal Register (1989), and DOE - Short abstracts from Department of Energy.

The highly precise nature of the words only found once or twice in the database reduce the probability of their being in the vocabulary of the user and the terms are almost never included in searches. Eliminating these words saves on storage and access structure (e.g., dictionary - see Chapter 4) complexities. The best technique to eliminate the majority of these words is via a Stop algorithm versus trying to list them individually. Examples of Stop algorithms are:

Stop all numbers greater than "999999" (this was selected to allow dates to be searchable)

Stop any processing token that has numbers and characters intermixed

The algorithms are typically source specific, usually eliminating unique item numbers that are frequently found in systems and have no search value.

In some systems (e.g., INQUIRE DBMS), inter-word symbols and Stop words are not included in the optimized search structure (e.g., inverted file structure, see Chapter 4) but are processed via a scanning of potential hit documents after inverted file search reduces the list of possible relevant items. Other systems never allow interword symbols to be searched.

Source	WSJ	AP	ZIFF	FR	DOE
Size in Mbytes	295	266	251	258	190
Median number terms/record	182	353	181	313	82
Average number terms/record	329	375	412	1017	89
Number Unique Terms	156,298	197,608	173,501	126,258	186,225
Number of Terms Occurring Once	64,656	89,627	85,992	58,677	95,782
Average number terms occurrences > 1	199	174	165	106	159

Table 1.1 Distribution of words in TREC Database
(from TREC-1 Conference Proceedings, Harmon-93)

The next step in finalizing on processing tokens is identification of any specific word characteristics. The characteristic is used in systems to assist in disambiguation of a particular word. Morphological analysis of the processing token's part of speech is included here. Thus, for a word such as "plane," the system understands that it could mean "level or flat" as an adjective, "aircraft or facet" as a noun, or "the act of smoothing or evening" as a verb. Other characteristics may classify a token as a member of a higher class of tokens such as "European Country" or "Financial Institution." Another example of characterization is if upper case should be preserved. In most systems upper/lower case is not preserved to avoid the system having to expand a term to cover the case where it is the first word in a sentence. But, for proper names, acronyms and organizations, the upper case represents a completely different use of the processing token versus it being found in the text. "Pleasant Grant" should be recognized as a person's name versus a "pleasant grant" that provides funding. Other characterizations that are typically treated separately from text are numbers and dates.

Once the potential processing token has been identified and characterized, most systems apply stemming algorithms to normalize the token to a standard semantic representation. The decision to perform stemming is a trade off between precision of a search (i.e., finding exactly what the query specifies) versus standardization to reduce system overhead in expanding a search term to similar token representations with a potential increase in recall. For example, the system must keep singular, plural, past tense, possessive, etc. as separate searchable tokens and potentially expand a term at search time to all its possible representations, or just keep the stem of the word, eliminating endings. The amount of stemming that is applied can lead to retrieval of many non-relevant items. The major stemming algorithms used at this time are described in Chapter 4. Some systems such as RetrievalWare, that use a large dictionary/thesaurus, looks up words in the existing dictionary to determine the stemmed version in lieu of applying a sophisticated algorithm.

Once the processing tokens have been finalized, based upon the stemming algorithm, they are used as updates to the searchable data structure. The searchable data structure is the internal representation (i.e., not visible to the user) of items that the user query searches. This structure contains the semantic concepts that represent the items in the database and limits what a user can find as a result of their search. Chapter 4 introduces the internal data structures that are used to stored the searchable data structure and Chapter 5 provides the algorithms for creating the data to be stored based upon the identified processing tokens.

1.3.2 Selective Dissemination of Information

The Selective Dissemination of Information (Mail) Process (see Figure 1.4) provides the capability to dynamically compare newly received items in the information system against standing statements of interest of users and deliver the item to those users whose statement of interest matches the contents of the item. The Mail process is composed of the search process, user statements of interest (Profiles) and user mail files. As each item is received, it is processed against every user's profile. A profile contains a typically broad search statement along with a list of user mail files that will receive the document if the search statement in the profile is satisfied. User search profiles are different than ad hoc queries in that they contain significantly more search terms (10 to 100 times more terms) and cover a wider range of interests. These profiles define all the areas in which a user is interested versus an ad hoc query which is frequently focused to answer a specific question. It has been shown in recent studies that automatically expanded user profiles perform significantly better than human generated profiles (Harman-95).

When the search statement is satisfied, the item is placed in the Mail File(s) associated with the profile. Items in Mail files are typically viewed in time of receipt order and automatically deleted after a specified time period (e.g., after one month) or upon command from the user during display. The dynamic asynchronous updating of Mail Files makes it difficult to present the results of dissemination in estimated order of likelihood of relevance to the user (ranked order). This is discussed in Chapter 2.

Very little research has focused exclusively on the Mail Dissemination process. Most systems modify the algorithms they have established for retrospective search of document (item) databases to apply to Mail Profiles.

Dissemination differs from the ad hoc search process in that thousands of user profiles are processed against one item versus the inverse and there is not a large relatively static database of items to be used in development of relevance ranking weights for an item.

Both implementers and researchers have treated the dissemination process as independent from the rest of the information system. The general assumption has been that the only knowledge available in making decisions on whether an incoming item is of interest is the user's profile and the incoming item. This restricted view has produced suboptimal systems forcing the user to receive redundant information that has little value. If a total Information Retrieval System view is taken, then the existing Mail and Index files are also potentially available during the dissemination process. This would allow the dissemination profile to be expanded to include logic against existing files. For example, assume an index file (discussed below) exists that has the price of oil from Mexico as a value in a field with a current value of $30. An analyst will be less interested in items that discuss Mexico and $30 oil prices then items that discuss Mexico and prices other than $30 (i.e., looking for changes). Similarly, if a Mail file already has many items on a particular topic, it would be useful for a profile to not disseminate additional items on the same topic, or at least reduce the relative importance that the system assigns to them (i.e., the rank value).

1.3.3 Document Database Search

The Document Database Search Process (see Figure 1.4) provides the capability for a query to search against all items received by the system. The Document Database Search process is composed of the search process, user entered queries (typically ad hoc queries) and the document database which contains all items that have been received, processed and stored by the system. It is the retrospective search source for the system. If the user is on-line, the Selective Dissemination of Information system delivers to the user items of interest as soon as they are processed into the system. Any search for information that has already been processed into the system can be considered a "retrospective" search for information. This does not preclude the search to have search statements constraining it to items received in the last few hours. But typically the searches span far greater time periods. Each query is processed against the total document database. Queries differ from profiles in that they are typically short and focused on a specific area of interest. The Document Database can be very large, hundreds of millions of items or more. Typically items in the Document Database do not change (i.e., are not edited) once received. The value of much information quickly decreases over time. These facts are often used to partition the database by time and allow for archiving by the time partitions. Some user interfaces force the user to indicate searches against items received older than a specified time, making use of the partitions of the Document database. The documents in the Mail files are also in the document database, since they logically are input to both processes.

1.3.4 Index Database Search

When an item is determined to be of interest, a user may want to save it for future reference. This is in effect filing it. In an information system this is accomplished via the index process. In this process the user can logically store an item in a file along with additional index terms and descriptive text the user wants to associate with the item. It is also possible to have index records that do not reference an item, but contain all the substantive information in the index itself. In this case the user is reading items and extracting the information of interest, never needing to go back to the original item. A good analogy to an index file is the card catalog in a library. Another perspective is to consider Index Files as structured databases whose records can optionally reference items in the Document Database. The Index Database Search Process (see Figure 1.4) provides the capability to create indexes and search them. The user may search the index and retrieve the index and/or the document it references. The system also provides the capability to search the index and then search the items referenced by the index records that satisfied the index portion of the query. This is called a combined file search. In an ideal system the index record could reference portions of items versus the total item.

There are two classes of index files: Public and Private Index files. Every user can have one or more Private Index files leading to a very large number of files. Each Private Index file references only a small subset of the total number of items in the Document Database. Public Index files are maintained by professional library services personnel and typically index every item in the Document Database. There is a small number of Public Index files. These files have access lists (i.e., lists of users and their privileges) that allow anyone to search or retrieve data. Private Index files typically have very limited access lists.

To assist the users in generating indexes, especially the professional indexers, the system provides a process called Automatic File Build shown in Figure 1.4 (also called Information Extraction). This capability processes selected incoming documents and automatically determine potential indexing for the item. The rules that govern which documents are processed for extraction of index information and the index term extraction process are stored in Automatic File Build Profiles. When an item is processed it results in creation of Candidate Index Records. As a minimum, certain citation data can be determined and extracted as part of this process assisting in creation of Public Index Files. Examples of this information are author(s), date of publication, source, and references. More complex data, such as countries an item is about or corporations referenced, have high rates of identification. The placement in an index file facilitates normalizing the terminology, assisting the user in finding items. It also provides a basis for programs that analyze the contents of systems trying to identify new information relationships (i.e., data mining). For more abstract concepts the extraction technology is not accurate and comprehensive enough to allow the created index records to automatically update the index files. Instead the candidate index record, along with the item it references, are stored in a file for review and edit by a user prior to actual update of an index file.

The capability to create Private and Public Index Files is frequently implemented via a structured Database Management System. This has introduced new challenges in developing the theory and algorithms that allow a single integrated perspective on the information in the system. For example, how to use the single instance information in index fields and free text to provide a single system value of how the index/referenced item combination satisfies the user's search statement. Usually the issue is avoided by treating the aspects of the search that apply to the structured records as a first level constraint identifying a set of items that satisfy that portion of the query. The resultant items are then searched using the rest of the query and the functions associated with information systems. The evaluation of relevance is based only on this later step. An example of how this limits the user is if part of the index is a field called "Country." This certainly allows the user to constrain his results to only those countries of interest (e.g., Peru or Mexico). But because the relevance function is only associated with the portion of the query associated with the item, there is no way for the user to ensure that Peru items have more importance to the retrieval than Mexican items.

1.4 Relationship to Database Management Systems

There are two major categories of systems available to process items: Information Retrieval Systems and Data Base Management Systems (DBMS). Confusion can arise when the software systems supporting each of these applications get confused with the data they are manipulating. An Information Retrieval System is software that has the features and functions required to manipulate "information" items versus a DBMS that is optimized to handle "structured" data. Information is fuzzy text. The term "fuzzy" is used to imply the results from the minimal standards or controls on the creators of the text items. The author is trying to present concepts, ideas and abstractions along with supporting facts. As such, there is minimal consistency in the vocabulary and styles of items discussing the exact same issue. The searcher has to be omniscient to specify all search term possibilities in the query.

Structured data is well defined data (facts) typically represented by tables. There is a semantic description associated with each attribute within a table that well defines that attribute. For example, there is no confusion between the meaning of "employee name" or "employee salary" and what values to enter in a specific database record. On the other hand, if two different people generate an abstract for the same item, they can be different. One abstract may generally discuss the most important topic in an item. Another abstract, using a different vocabulary, may specify the details of many topics. It is this diversity and ambiguity of language that causes the fuzzy nature to be associated with information items. The differences in the characteristics of the data is one reason for the major differences in functions required for the two classes of systems.

With structured data a user enters a specific request and the results returned provide the user with the desired information. The results are frequently tabulated and presented in a report format for ease of use. In contrast, a search of "information" items has a high probability of not finding all the items a user is looking for. The user has to refine his search to locate additional items of interest. This process is called "iterative search." An Information Retrieval System gives the user capabilities to assist the user in finding the relevant items, such as relevance feedback (see Chapters 2 and 7). The results from an information system search are presented in relevance ranked order. The confusion comes when DBMS software is used to store "information." This is easy to implement, but the system lacks the ranking and relevance feedback features that are critical to an information system. It is also possible to have structured data used in an information system (such as TOPIC). When this happens the user has to be very creative to get the system to provide the reports and management information that are trivially available in a DBMS.

From a practical standpoint, the integration of DBMS's and Information Retrieval Systems is very important. Commercial database companies have already integrated the two types of systems. One of the first commercial databases to integrate the two systems into a single view is the INQUIRE DBMS. This has been available for over fifteen years. A more current example is the ORACLE DBMS that now offers an imbedded capability called CONVECTIS, which is an informational retrieval system that uses a comprehensive thesaurus which provides the basis to generate "themes" for a particular item. CONVECTIS also provides standard statistical techniques that are described in Chapter 5. The INFORMIX DBMS has the ability to link to RetrievalWare to provide integration of structured data and information along with functions associated with Information Retrieval Systems.

1.5 Digital Libraries and Data Warehouses

Two other systems frequently described in the context of information retrieval are Digital Libraries and Data Warehouses (or DataMarts). There is significant overlap between these two systems and an Information Storage and Retrieval System. All three systems are repositories of information and their primary goal is to satisfy user information needs. Information retrieval easily dates back to Vannevar Bush's 1945 article on thinking (Bush-45) that set the stage for many concepts in this area. Libraries have been in existence since the beginning of writing and have served as a repository of the intellectual wealth of society. As such, libraries have always been concerned with storing and retrieving information in the media it is created on. As the quantities of information grew exponentially, libraries were forced to make maximum use of electronic tools to facilitate the storage and retrieval process. With the worldwide interneting of libraries and information sources (e.g., publishers, news agencies, wire services, radio broadcasts) via the Internet, more focus has been on the concept of an electronic library. Between 1991 and 1993 significant interest was placed on this area because of the interest in U.S. Government and private funding for making more information available in digital form (Fox-93). During this time the terminology evolved from electronic libraries to digital libraries. As the Internet continued its exponential growth and project funding became available, the topic of Digital Libraries has grown. By 1995 enough research and pilot efforts had started to support the 1ST ACM International Conference on Digital Libraries (Fox-96).

There remain significant discussions on what is a digital library. Everyone starts with the metaphor of the traditional library. The question is how do the traditional library functions change as they migrate into supporting a digital collection. Since the collection is digital and there is a worldwide communications infrastructure available, the library no longer must own a copy of information as long as it can provide access. The existing quantity of hardcopy material guarantees that we will not have all digital libraries for at least another generation of technology improvements. But there is no question that libraries have started and will continue to expand their focus to digital formats. With direct electronic access available to users the social aspects of congregating in a library and learning from librarians, friends and colleagues will be lost and new electronic collaboration equivalencies will come into existence (Wiederhold-95).

Indexing is one of the critical disciplines in library science and significant effort has gone into the establishment of indexing and cataloging standards. Migration of many of the library products to a digital format introduces both opportunities and challenges. The full text of items available for search makes the index process a value added effort as described in Section 1.3. Another important library service is a source of search intermediaries to assist users in finding information. With the proliferation of information available in electronic form, the role of search intermediary will shift from an expert in search to being an expert in source analysis. Searching will identify so much information in the global Internet information space that identification of the "pedigree" of information is required to understand its value. This will become the new refereeing role of a library.

Information Storage and Retrieval technology has addressed a small subset of the issues associated with Digital Libraries. The focus has been on the search and retrieval of textual data with no concern for establishing standards on the contents of the system. It has also ignored the issues of unique identification and tracking of information required by the legal aspects of copyright that restrict functions within a library environment. The conversion of existing hardcopy text, images (e.g., pictures, maps) and analog (e.g., audio, video) data and the storage and retrieval of the digital version is a major concern to Digital Libraries which is not considered in information systems. Other issues such as how to continue to provide access to digital information over many years as digital formats change have to be answered for the long term viability of digital libraries.

The term Data Warehouse comes more from the commercial sector than academic sources. It comes from the need for organizations to control the proliferation of digital information ensuring that it is known and recoverable. Its goal is to provide to the decision makers the critical information to answer future direction questions. Frequently a data warehouse is focused solely on structured databases. A data warehouse consists of the data, an information directory that describes the contents and meaning of the data being stored, an input function that captures data and moves it to the data warehouse, data search and manipulation tools that allow users the means to access and analyze the warehouse data and a delivery mechanism to export data to other warehouses, data marts (small warehouses or subsets of a larger warehouse), and external systems.

Data warehouses are similar to information storage and retrieval systems in that they both have a need for search and retrieval of information. But a data warehouse is more focused on structured data and decision support technologies. In addition to the normal search process, a complete system provides a flexible set of analytical tools to "mine" the data. Data mining (originally called Knowledge Discovery in Databases - KDD) is a search process that automatically analyzes data and extract relationships and dependencies that were not part of the database design. Most of the research focus is on the statistics, pattern recognition and artificial intelligence algorithms to detect the hidden relationships of data. In reality the most difficult task is in preprocessing the data from the database for processing by the algorithms. This differs from clustering in information retrieval in that clustering is based upon known characteristics of items, whereas data mining does not depend upon known relationships. For more detail on data mining see the November 1996 *Communications of the ACM* (Vol. 39, Number 11) that focuses on this topic.

1.6 Summary

Chapter 1 places into perspective a total Information Storage and Retrieval System. This perspective introduces new challenges to the problems that need to be theoretically addressed and commercially implemented. Ten years ago commercial implementation of the algorithms being developed was not realistic, allowing theoreticians to limit their focus to very specific areas. Bounding a problem is still essential in deriving theoretical results. But the commercialization and insertion of this technology into systems like the Internet that are widely being used changes the way problems are bounded. From a theoretical perspective, efficient scalability of algorithms to systems with gigabytes and terabytes of data, operating with minimal user search statement information, and making maximum use of all functional aspects of an information system need to be considered. The dissemination systems using persistent indexes or mail files to modify ranking algorithms and combining the search of structured information fields and free text into a consolidated weighted output are examples of potential new areas of investigation.

The best way for the theoretician or the commercial developer to understand the importance of problems to be solved is to place them in the context of a total vision of a complete system. Understanding the differences between Digital Libraries and Information Retrieval Systems will add an additional dimension to the potential future development of systems. The collaborative aspects of digital libraries can be viewed as a new source of information that dynamically could interact with information retrieval techniques. For example, should the weighting algorithms and search techniques discussed later in this book vary against a corpus based upon dialogue between people versus statically published material? During the collaboration, in certain states, should the system be automatically searching for reference material to support the collaboration?

EXERCISES

1.   The metric to be minimized in an Information Retrieval System from a user's perspective is user overhead. Describe the places that the user overhead is encountered from when a user has an information need until when it is satisfied. Is system complexity also part of the user overhead?

2.   Under what conditions might it be possible to achieve 100 per cent precision and 100 per cent recall in a system? What is the relationship between these measures and user overhead?

3.   Describe how the statement that "language is the largest inhibitor to good communications" applies to Information Retrieval Systems.

4.   What is the impact on precision and recall in the use of Stop Lists and Stop Algorithms?

5.   Why is the concept of processing tokens introduced and how does it relate to a word? What is the impact of searching being based on processing tokens versus the original words in an item.

6.   Can a user find the same information from a search of the Document file that is generated by a Selective Dissemination of Information process (Hint - take into consideration the potential algorithmic basis for each system)? Document database search is frequently described as a "pull" process while dissemination is described as a "push" process. Why are these terms appropriate?

7.   Does a Private Index File differ from a standard Database Management System (DBMS)? (HINT - there are both structural and functional

differences) What problems need to addressed when using a DBMS as part of an Information retrieval System?

8. What is the logical effect on the Document file when a combined file search of both a Private Index file and Document file is executed? What is returned to the user?

9. What are the problems that need resolution when the concept of dissemination profiles expands to including existing data structures (e.g., Mail files and/or Index files)?

10. What is the difference between the concept of a "Digital Library" and an Information Retrieval System? What new areas of information retrieval research may be important to support a Digital Library?

2 Information Retrieval System Capabilities

This chapter discusses the major functions that are available in an Information Retrieval System. Search and browse capabilities are crucial to assist the user in locating relevant items. The search capabilities address both Boolean and Natural Language queries. The algorithms used for searching are called Boolean, natural language processing and probabilistic. Probabilistic algorithms use frequency of occurrence of processing tokens (words) in determining similarities between queries and items and also in predictors on the potential relevance of the found item to the searcher. Chapter 4 discusses in detail the data structures used to support the algorithms, and Chapters 5 and 7 describe the algorithms. The majority of existing commercial systems are based upon Boolean query and search capabilities. The newer systems such as TOPIC, RetrievalWare, and INQUERY all allow for natural language queries.

Given the imprecise nature of the search algorithms, Browse functions to assist the user in filtering the search results to find relevant information are very important. To allow different systems to inter-operate there are evolving standards in both the language and architecture areas. Standardization of the interfaces between systems will have the same effect on information systems that acceptance of the Structured Query Language (SQL) has had in the Database Management System field. It will allow independent service providers to develop tools and augmentations that will be applicable to any Information Retrieval System accelerating the development of functions needed by the user. Examples of these functions are information visualization tools and query expansion tools.

2.1 Search Capabilities

The objective of the search capability is to allow for a mapping between a user's specified need and the items in the information database that will answer that need. The search query statement is the means that the user employs to communicate a description of the needed information to the system. It can consist of natural language text in composition style and/or query terms (referred to as terms in this book) with Boolean logic indicators between them. How the system translates the search query into processing steps to find the potential relevant items is described in later chapters. One concept that has occasionally been implemented in commercial systems (e.g., RetrievalWare), and holds significant potential for assisting in the location and ranking of relevant items, is the "weighting" of search terms. This would allow a user to indicate the importance of search terms in either a Boolean or natural language interface. Given the following natural language query statement where the importance of a particular search term is indicated by a value in parenthesis between 0.0 and 1.0 with 1.0 being the most important:

> **Find articles that discuss automobile emissions(.9) or sulfur dioxide(.3) on the farming industry.**

the system would recognize in its importance ranking and item selection process that automobile emissions are far more important than items discussing sulfur dioxide problems.

The search statement may apply to the complete item or contain additional parameters limiting it to a logical division of the item (i.e., to a zone). As discussed in Chapter 1, this restriction is useful in reducing retrieval of non-relevant items by limiting the search to those subsets of the item whose use of a particular word is consistent with the user's search objective. Finding a name in a Bibliography does not necessarily mean the item is about that person. Recent research has shown that for longer items, restricting a query statement to be satisfied within a contiguous subset of the document (passage searching) provides improved precision (Buckley-95, Wilkinson-95). Rather than allowing the search statement to be satisfied anywhere within a document it may be required to be satisfied within a 100 word contiguous subset of the item (Callan-94).

Based upon the algorithms used in a system many different functions are associated with the system's understanding the search statement. The functions define the relationships between the terms in the search statement (e.g., Boolean, Natural Language, Proximity, Contiguous Word Phrases, and Fuzzy Searches) and the interpretation of a particular word (e.g., Term Masking, Numeric and Date Range, Contiguous Word Phrases, and Concept/Thesaurus expansion).

Rather than continuing the use of the term processing token to represent the searchable units extracted from an item, the terminology "word" or "term" is also used in some contexts as an approximation that is intuitively more meaningful to the reader.

2.1.1 Boolean Logic

Boolean logic allows a user to logically relate multiple concepts together to define what information is needed. Typically the Boolean functions apply to processing tokens identified anywhere within an item. The typical Boolean operators are **AND, OR,** and **NOT.** These operations are implemented using set intersection, set union and set difference procedures. A few systems introduced the concept of "exclusive or" but it is equivalent to a slightly more complex query using the other operators and is not generally useful to users since most users do not understand it. Placing portions of the search statement in parentheses are used to overtly specify the order of Boolean operations (i.e., nesting function). If parentheses are not used, the system follows a default precedence ordering of operations (e.g., typically NOT then AND then OR). In the examples of effects of Boolean operators given in Figure 2.1, no precedence order is given to the operators and queries are processed Left to Right unless parentheses are included. Most commercial systems do not allow weighting of Boolean queries. A technique to allow weighting Boolean queries is described in Chapter 7. Some of the deficiencies of use of Boolean operators in information systems are summarized by Belkin and Croft (Belkin-89).

A special type of Boolean search is called "M of N" logic. The user lists a set of possible search terms and identifies, as acceptable, any item that contains a subset of the terms. For example, "Find any item containing any two of the following terms: "AA," "BB," "CC." This can be expanded into a Boolean search that performs an AND between all combinations of two terms and "OR"s the results together ((AA AND BB) or (AA AND CC) or (BB AND CC)). Some search examples and their meanings are given in Figure 2.1. Most Information Retrieval Systems allow Boolean operations as well as allowing for the natural language interfaces discussed in Section 2.1.8. As noted in Chapter 1, very little attention has been focused on integrating the Boolean search functions and weighted information retrieval techniques into a single search result.

SEARCH STATEMENT	SYSTEM OPERATION
COMPUTER OR PROCESSOR NOT MAINFRAME	Select all items discussing Computers and/or Processors that do not discuss Mainframes
COMPUTER OR (PROCESSOR NOT MAINFRAME)	Select all items discussing Computers and/or items that discuss Processors and do not discuss Mainframes
COMPUTER AND NOT PROCESSOR OR MAINFRAME	Select all items that discuss computers and not processors or mainframes in the item

Figure 2.1 Use of Boolean Operators

2.1.2 Proximity

Proximity is used to restrict the distance allowed within an item between two search terms. The semantic concept is that the closer two terms are

found in a text the more likely they are related in the description of a particular concept. Proximity is used to increase the precision of a search.   If the terms COMPUTER and DESIGN are found within a few words of each other then the item is more likely to be discussing the design of computers than if the words are paragraphs apart. The typical format for proximity is:

TERM1 within "m" "units" of TERM2

The distance operator "m" is an integer number and units are in Characters, Words, Sentences, or Paragraphs. Certain items may have other semantic units that would prove useful in specifying the proximity operation. For very structured items, distances in characters prove useful. For items containing imbedded images (e.g., digital photographs), text between the images could help in precision when the objective is in locating a certain image. Sometimes the proximity relationship contains a direction operator indicating the direction (before or after) that the second term must be found within the number of units specified. The default is either direction. A special case of the Proximity operator is the Adjacent (ADJ) operator that normally has a distance operator of one and a forward only direction (i.e., in WAIS). Another special case is where the distance is set to zero meaning within the same semantic unit. Some proximity search statement examples and their meanings are given in Figure 2.2.

2.1.3 Contiguous Word Phrases

A Contiguous Word Phrase (CWP) is both a way of specifying a query term and a special search operator. A Contiguous Word Phrase is two or more words that are treated as a single semantic unit. An example of a CWP is "United States of America." It is four words that specify a search term representing a

SEARCH STATEMENT	SYSTEM OPERATION
"Venetian" ADJ "Blind"	would find items that mention a Venetian Blind on a window but not items discussing a Blind Venetian
"United" within five words of "American"	would hit on "United States and American interests," "United Airlines and American Airlines" not on "United States of America and the American dream"
"Nuclear" within zero paragraphs of "clean-up"	would find items that have "nuclear" and "clean-up" in the same paragraph.

Figure 2.2 Use of Proximity

single specific semantic concept (a country) that can be used with any of the operators discussed above. Thus a query could specify "manufacturing" AND "United States of America" which returns any item that contains the word "manufacturing" and the contiguous words "United States of America."

A contiguous word phrase also acts like a special search operator that is similar to the proximity (Adjacency) operator but allows for additional specificity. If two terms are specified, the contiguous word phrase and the proximity operator using directional one word parameters or the Adjacent operator are identical. For contiguous word phrases of more than two terms the only way of creating an equivalent search statement using proximity and Boolean operators is via nested Adjacencies which are not found in most commercial systems. This is because Proximity and Boolean operators are binary operators but contiguous word phrases are an "N"ary operator where "N" is the number of words in the CWP.

Contiguous Word Phrases are called Literal Strings in WAIS and Exact Phrases in RetrievalWare. In WAIS multiple Adjacency (ADJ) operators are used to define a Literal String (e.g., "United" ADJ "States" ADJ "of" ADJ "America").

2.1.4 Fuzzy Searches

Fuzzy Searches provide the capability to locate spellings of words that are similar to the entered search term. This function is primarily used to compensate for errors in spelling of words. Fuzzy searching increases recall at the expense of decreasing precision (i.e., it can erroneously identify terms as the search term). In the process of expanding a query term fuzzy searching includes other terms that have similar spellings, giving more weight (in systems that rank output) to words in the database that have similar word lengths and position of the characters as the entered term. A Fuzzy Search on the term "computer" would automatically include the following words from the information database: "computer," "compiter," "conputer," "computter," "compute." An additional enhancement may lookup the proposed alternative spelling and if it is a valid word with a different meaning, include it in the search with a low ranking or not include it at all (e.g., "commuter"). Systems allow the specification of the maximum number of new terms that the expansion includes in the query. In this case the alternate spellings that are "closest" to the query term is included. "Closest" is a heuristic function that is system specific.

Fuzzy searching has its maximum utilization in systems that accept items that have been Optical Character Read (OCRed). In the OCR process a hardcopy item is scanned into a binary image (usually at a resolution of 300 dots per inch or more). The OCR process is a pattern recognition process that segments the scanned in image into meaningful subregions, often considering a segment the area defining a single character. The OCR process will then determine the character and translate it to an internal computer encoding (e.g., ASCII or some other standard for other than Latin based languages). Based upon the original quality of the hardcopy this process introduces errors in recognizing characters. With decent quality input, systems achieves in the 90 - 99 per cent range of accuracy. Since these are character errors throughout the text, fuzzy searching allows location of items of interest compensating for the erroneous characters.

2.1.5 Term Masking

Term masking is the ability to expand a query term by masking a portion of the term and accepting as valid any processing token that maps to the unmasked portion of the term. The value of term masking is much higher in systems that do not perform stemming or only provide a very simple stemming algorithm. There are two types of search term masking: fixed length and variable length. Sometimes they are called fixed and variable length "don't care" functions.

Fixed length masking is a single position mask. It masks out any symbol in a particular position or the lack of that position in a word. Figure 2.3 gives an example of fixed term masking. It not only allows any character in the masked position, but also accepts words where the position does not exist.   Fixed length term masking is not frequently used and typically not critical to a system.

Variable length "don't cares" allows masking of any number of characters within a processing token. The masking may be in the front, at the end, at both front and end, or imbedded. The first three of these cases are called suffix search, prefix search and imbedded character string search, respectively. The use of an imbedded variable length don't care is seldom used. Figure 2.3 provides examples of the use of variable length term masking. If "*" represents a variable length don't care then the following are examples of its use:

"*COMPUTER"	Suffix Search
"COMPUTER*"	Prefix Search
"*COMPUTER*"	Imbedded String Search

Of the options discussed, trailing "don't cares" (prefix searches) are by far the most common. In operational systems they are used in 80-90 per cent of the search terms (Kracsony-81) and in may cases are a default without the user having to specify it.

2.1.6 Numeric and Date Ranges

Term masking is useful when applied to words, but does not work for finding ranges of numbers or numeric dates. To find numbers larger than "125," using a term "125*" will not find any number except those that begin with the

SEARCH STATEMENT	SYSTEM OPERATION
multi$national	Matches"multi-national," "multiynational," "multinational" but does not match "multi national" since it is two processing tokens.
computer	Matches,"minicomputer" "microcomputer" or "computer"
comput*	Matches "computers," "computing," "computes"
comput	Matches "microcomputers" , "minicomputing," "compute"

Figure 2.3 Term Masking

digits "125." Systems, as part of their normalization process, characterizes words as numbers or dates. This allows for specialized numeric or date range processing against those words. A user could enter inclusive (e.g., "125-425" or "4/2/93-5/2/95" for numbers and dates) to infinite ranges (">125," "<=233," representing "Greater Than" or "Less Than or Equal") as part of a query.

2.1.7 Concept/Thesaurus Expansion

Associated with both Boolean and Natural Language Queries is the ability to expand the search terms via Thesaurus or Concept Class database reference tool. A Thesaurus is typically a one-level or two-level expansion of a term to other terms that are similar in meaning. A Concept Class is a tree structure that expands each meaning of a word into potential concepts that are related to the initial term (e.g., in the TOPIC system). Concept classes are sometimes implemented as a network structure that links word stems (e.g., in the RetrievalWare system). An example of Thesaurus and Concept Class structures are shown in Figure 2.4 (Thesaurus-93) and Figure 2.5. Concept class representations assist a user who has minimal knowledge of a concept domain by allowing the user to expand upon a particular concept showing related concepts. A concept based database shows associations that are not normally found in a language based thesaurus. For example, "negative advertising" may be linked to "elections" in a concept database, but are hopefully not synonyms to be found in a thesaurus. Generalization is associated with the user viewing concepts logically higher in a hierarchy that have more general meaning. Specificity is going lower in the thesaurus looking at concepts that are more specific.

Thesauri are either semantic or based upon statistics. A semantic thesaurus is a listing of words and then other words that are semantically similar. Electronic versions of thesauri are commercially available and are language based (e.g., English, Spanish, etc.). Systems such as RetrievalWare and TOPIC provide them as part of the search system. In executing a query, a term can be expanded to all related terms in the thesaurus or concept tree. Optionally, the user may display the thesaurus or concept tree and indicate which related terms should be used in a query. This function is essential to eliminate synonyms which introduce meanings that are not in the user's search statement. For example, a user searching on "pasture lands" and "fields" would not want all of the terms associated with "magnetic fields" included in the expanded search statement.

The capability usually exists to browse the thesaurus or concept trees and add additional terms and term relationships in the case of concept trees. This allows users to enhance the thesaurus or concept tree with jargon specific to their area of interest.

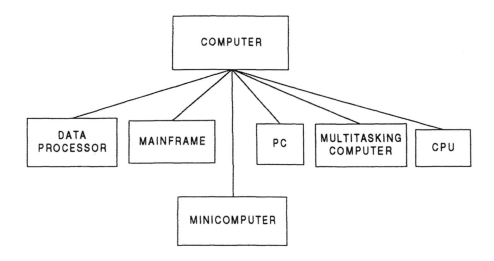

Figure 2.4 Thesaurus for term "computer"

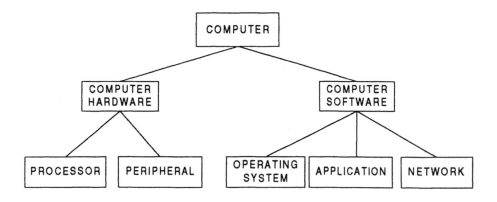

Figure 2.5 Hierarchical Concept Class Structure for "Computer"

The problem with thesauri is that they are generic to a language and can introduce many search terms that are not found in the document database. An alternative uses the database or a representative sample of it to create statistically related terms. It is conceptually a thesaurus in that words that are statistically related to other words by their frequently occurring together in the same items. This type of thesaurus is very dependent upon the database being searched and may not be portable to other databases. The statistical techniques for generating a thesaurus are discussed in detail in Chapter 6. In a statistical thesaurus it is very difficult to name a thesaurus class or understand by viewing it what caused its creation (i.e., there is not a semantic basis defining the classes). As such, statistical thesauri are frequently used as automatic expansions of user's searches without the user directly interacting with the thesaurus.

Theoretically thesauri and concept trees could be used to either expand a search statement with additional terms or make it more specific but substituting more specific terms. From this perspective expanding the terms increases the recall of the search with a possible decrease in precision. Going to more specific terms increases precision and possibly reduce recall. In most cases the generalization process is used in expanding a search statement with more terms.

2.1.8 Natural Language Queries

Rather than having the user enter a specific Boolean query by specifying search terms and the logic between them, Natural Language Queries allow a user to enter a prose statement that describes the information that the user wants to find. The longer the prose, the more accurate the results returned. The most difficult logic case associated with Natural Language Queries is the ability to specify negation in the search statement and have the system recognize it as negation. The system searches and finds those items most like the query statement entered. The techniques for locating items similar to the search statement (described in Chapters 5 and 7) are suited for finding items like other items but do not have inherent techniques to exclude items that are like a certain portion of the search statement. For many users, this type of an interface provides a natural extension to asking someone to perform a search. In this case the discourse is with the computer. An example of a Natural Language Query is:

> Find for me all the items that discuss oil reserves and current attempts to find new oil reserves. Include any items that discuss the international financial aspects of the oil production process. Do not include items about the oil industry in the United States.

The way a system uses this input for a search is described in Chapter 7. The problem with many techniques and systems is to understand the negation concept of excluding items about the oil industry in the United States.

When this capability has been made available, users have a tendency to enter sentence fragments that reflect their search need rather than complete sentences. This is predictable because the users want to minimize use of the human resource (their time). The likely input for the above example is:

oil reserves and attempts to find new oil reserves, international financial aspects of oil production, not United States oil industry

This usage pattern is important because sentence fragments make morphological analysis of the natural language query difficult and may limit the system's ability to perform term disambiguation (e.g., understand which meaning of a word is meant).

Using the same search statement, a Boolean query attempting to find the same information might appear:

("locate" AND "new" and "oil reserves") OR ("international" AND "financ*" AND "oil production") NOT ("oil industry" AND "United States")

Associated with natural language queries is a function called relevance feedback. The natural language does not have to be input by the user but just identified by the user. This introduces the concept of finding items that "are like" other items. Thus a user could identify a particular item(s) in the database or text segments within item(s) and use that as the search statement. This is discussed in detail in Chapter 7.

To accommodate the negation function and provide users with a transition to the natural language systems, most commercial systems have a user interface that provides both a natural language and Boolean logic capability. Negation is handled by the Boolean portion of a search. The integration of these two search statement types has not been achieved in Information Retrieval Systems. Natural language interfaces improve the recall of systems with a decrease in precision when negation is required.

2.2   Browse Capabilities

Once the search is complete, Browse capabilities provide the user with the capability to determine which items are of interest and select those to be displayed. There are two ways of displaying a summary of the items that are associated with a query: line item status and data visualization. From these summary displays, the user can select the specific items and zones within the items for display. The system also allows for easy transitioning between the summary displays and review of specific items. If searches resulted in high precision, then the importance of the browse capabilities would be lessened. Since searches return many items that are not relevant to the user's information need, browse capabilities can assist the user in focusing on items that have the highest likelihood in meeting his need.

2.2.1 Ranking

Under Boolean systems, the status display is a count of the number of items found by the query. Every one of the items meet all aspects of the Boolean query. The reasons why an item was selected can easily be traced to and displayed (e.g., via highlighting) in the retrieved items. Hits are retrieved in either a sorted order (e.g., sort by Title) or in time order from the newest to the oldest item. With the introduction of ranking based upon predicted relevance values, the status summary displays the relevance score associated with the item along with a brief descriptor of the item (usually both fit on one display screen line). The relevance score is an estimate of the search system on how closely the item satisfies the search statement. Typically relevance scores are normalized to a value between 0.0 and 1.0. The highest value of 1.0 is interpreted that the system is sure that the item is relevant to the search statement. This allows the user to determine at what point to stop reviewing items because of reduced likelihood of relevance. Theoretically every item in the system could be returned but many of the items will have a relevance value of 0.0 (not relevant). Practically, systems have a default minimum value which the user can modify that stops returning items that have a relevance value below the specified value.

Since one line is usually dedicated per item in a summary display, part of a zone truncated by allocated space on the display is typically displayed with the relevance weight of the item. This zone is frequently the Title and provides the user with additional information with the relevance weight to avoid selecting non-relevant items for review. Presenting the actual relevance number seems to be more confusing to the user than presenting a category that the number falls in. For example, some systems create relevance categories and indicate, by displaying items in different colors, which category an item belongs to. Other systems uses a nomenclature such as High, Medium High, Medium, Low, and Non-relevant. The color technique removes the need for written indication of an item's relevance, thereby providing additional positions in a line to display more of the title but causes problems with users that suffer from partial or total color blindness.

Rather than limiting the number of items that can be assessed by the number of lines on a screen, other graphical visualization techniques showing the relevance relationships of the hit items can be used. For example, a two or three dimensional graph can be displayed where points on the graph represent items and the location of the points represent their relative relationship between each other and the user's query. In some cases color is also used in this representation. This technique allows a user to see the clustering of items by topics and browse through a cluster or move to another topical cluster. This has an analogy of moving through the stacks at a library. In a single image the user can see the effects of his search statement rather than displaying a few items at a time.

Information visualization is also being used in displaying individual items and the terms that contributed to the item's selection. This graphical display assists the user in determining how to reformulate his query to improve finding the information the user requires. Chapter 8 describes information visualization.

2.2.2 Zoning

When the user displays a particular item, the objective of minimization of overhead still applies. The user wants to see the minimum information needed to determine if the item is relevant. Once the determination is made an item is possibly relevant, the user wants to display the complete item for detailed review. Limited display screen sizes require selectability of what portions of an item a user needs to see to make the relevance determination. For example, display of the Title and Abstract may be sufficient information for a user to predict the potential relevance of an item. Limiting the display of each item to these two zones allows multiple items to be displayed on a single display screen. This makes maximum use of the speed of the user's cognitive process in scanning the single image and understanding the potential relevance of the multiple items on the screen.

2.2.3 Highlighting

Another display aid is an indication of why an item was selected. This indication, frequently highlighting, lets the user quickly focus on the potentially relevant parts of the text to scan for item relevance. Different strengths of highlighting indicates how strongly the highlighted word participated in the selection of the item. Most systems allow the display of an item to begin with the first highlight within the item and allow subsequent jumping to the next highlight. Another capability, which is gaining strong acceptance, is for the system to determine the passage in the document most relevant to the query and position the browse to start at that passage. The DCARS system that acts as a user frontend to the RetrievalWare search system allows the user to browse an item in the order of the paragraphs or individual words that contributed most to the rank value associated with the item.

Highlighting has always been useful in Boolean systems to indicate the cause of the retrieval. This is because of the direct mapping between the terms in the search and the terms in the item. Using Natural Language Processing, automatic expansion of terms via thesauri, and the similarity ranking algorithms discussed in detail later in this book, highlighting loses some of its value The terms being highlighted that caused a particular item to be returned may not have direct or obvious mapping to any of the search terms entered. This causes frustration by the user trying to guess why a particular item was retrieved and how to use that information in reformulating the search statement to make it more exact. In a ranking system different terms can contribute to different degrees to the decision to retrieve an item. The highlighting may vary by introducing colors and intensities to indicate the relative importance of a particular word in the item in the decision to retrieve the item. Information visualization appears to be a better display process to assist in helping the user formulate his query than highlights in items.

2.3   Miscellaneous Capabilities

There are many additional functions that facilitate the user's ability to input queries, reducing the time it takes to generate the queries, and reducing *a priori* the probability of entering a poor query. Vocabulary browse provides knowledge on the processing tokens available in the searchable database and their distribution in terms of items within the database. Iterative searching and search history logs summarize previous search activities by the user allowing access to previous results from the current user session. Canned queries allow access to queries generated and saved in previous user sessions.

2.3.1 Vocabulary Browse

Vocabulary Browse provides the capability to display in alphabetical sorted order words from the document database. Logically, all unique words (processing tokens) in the database are kept in sorted order along with a count of the number of unique items in which the word is found. The user can enter a word or word fragment and the system will begin to display the dictionary around the entered text. Figure 2.6 shows what is seen in vocabulary browse if the user enters "comput." The system indicates what word fragement the user entered and then alphabetically displays other words found in the database in collating sequence on either side of the entered term. The user can continue scrolling in either direction reviewing additional terms in the database. Vocabulary browse provides information on the exact words in the database. It helps the user determine the impact of using a fixed or variable length mask on a search term and potential mis-spellings. The user can determine that entering the search term "compul*" in effect is searching for "compulsion" or "compulsive" or "compulsory." It also shows that someone probably entered the word "computen" when they really meant "computer." It provides insight on the impact of using terms in a search. By vocabulary browsing, a term may be seen to exist in a large number of documents which could make it a poor candidate as an ORed term requiring additional ANDed terms to focus on items of interest. The search term "computer" would return an excessive number of hits if used as an "OR" term.

TERM	OCCURRENCES
compromise	53
comptroller	18
compulsion	5
compulsive	22
compulsory	4
comput	
computation	265
compute	1245
computen	1
computer	10,800
computerize	18
computes	29

Figure 2.6 Vocabulary Browse List with entered term "comput"

2.3.2 Iterative Search and Search History Log

Frequently a search returns a Hit file containing many more items than the user wants to review. Rather than typing in a complete new query, the results of the previous search can be used as a constraining list to create a new query that is applied against it. This has the same effect as taking the original query and adding additional search statement against it in an AND condition. This process of refining the results of a previous search to focus on relevant items is called iterative search. This also applies when a user uses relevance feedback to enhance a previous search.

During a login session, a user could execute many queries to locate the needed information. To facilitate locating previous searches as starting points for new searches, search history logs are available. The search history log is the capability to display all the previous searches that were executed during the current session. The query along with the search completion status showing number of hits is displayed.

2.3.3 Canned Query

The capability to name a query and store it to be retrieved and executed during a later user session is called canned or stored queries. Users tend to have areas of interest within which they execute their searches on a regular basis. A canned query allows a user to create and refine a search that focuses on the user's general area of interest one time and then retrieve it to add additional search criteria to retrieve data that is currently needed. For example, a user may be responsible for European investments. Rather than always having to create a query that limits the search to European geographic search terms and then the specific question requiring resolution, a canned query can be created with all the needed geographic terms and used as a starting point for additional query specification. Significant effort can go into making the canned query into a comprehensive and focused search since it is created once but used many times with additional search terms for specific information needs. Queries that start with a canned query are significantly larger than ad hoc queries. Canned query features also allow for variables to be inserted into the query and bound to specific values at execution time.

2.4 Standards

There are two potential sources for any standard, those agreed to by an official standards organization and a de facto standard based upon high usage across a large user population. The standards organization most involved in Information Systems standards in the United States is the American National Standards Institute/ National Information Standards Organization (ANSI/NISO) in generating its Z39.50, Information Retrieval Application Service Definition and Protocol Specification. NISO is the only organization accredited by ANSI to approve and maintain standards for information services, libraries and publishers. This standard is one of many standards they generated to support interconnection of computer systems. Its relationship to other standards can be seen in the Open Systems Interconnection (OSI) basic reference model (ISO 7498). In addition to the formal standard, a second de facto standard is the WAIS standard based upon its usage in the INTERNET.

In addition to standards associated with specific language interfaces of Information Retrieval Systems, there are attempts being made to standardize the architecture of information systems. The largest de facto information system is the Internet and the Internet Engineering Task Force is focusing on how the architecture of the Internet should be modified to allow future scalability and addressability of items on the Internet. This architecture directly affects commercial information systems usage on the Internet and the integratability of future research into this environment. Additionally, the research sponsored under the guise of TREC and TIPSTER (defined in Section 2.4.2) are attempting to define certain aspects of a common information retrieval system architecture.

2.4.1 Z39.50 and WAIS Standards

The Z39.50 standard does not specify an implementation, but the capabilities within an application (Application Service) and the protocol used to communicate between applications (Information Retrieval Application Protocol). It is a computer to computer communications standard for database searching and record retrieval. Its objective is to overcome different system incompatibilities associated with multiple database searching (e.g., unique user interfaces, command language, and basic search functions). The first version of Z39.50 was approved in 1992. An international version of Z39.50, called the Search and Retrieve Standard (SR), was approved by the International Organization for Standardization (ISO) in 1991. Z39.50-1995, the latest version of Z39.50, replaces SR as the international information retrieval standard.

The standard describes eight operation types: Init (initialization), Search, Present, Delete, Scan, Sort, Resource-report, and Extended Services. There are five types of queries (Types 0, 1, 2, 100, 101, and 102). Type 101 extends previous types allowing for proximity and Type-102 is a Ranked List Query (yet to be defined). The Extended Services include saving query results, queries, and updating the database.

The client is identified as the "Origin" and performs the communications functions relating to initiating a search, translation of the query into a standardized format, sending a query, and requesting return records. The server is identified as the "Target" and interfaces to the database at the remote responding to requests from the Origin (e.g., pass query to database, return records in a standardized format and status). The end user does not have to be aware of the details of the standard since the Origin function performs the mapping from the user's query interface into Z39.50 format. This makes the dissimilarities of different database systems transparent to the user and facilitates issuing one query against multiple databases at different sites returning to the user a single integrated Hit file.

The communications between the Origin and Target utilize a dialogue known as Z39.50 association. Z39.50 not only standardizes the messages to be exchanged between the Origin and Target systems, but also the structure and the semantics of the search query, the sequence of message exchange, and the mechanism for returning records (Turner-95, Kunze-95). The 1992 version of Z39.50 was focused on library functions such as database searching, cataloguing and interlibrary loan (primarily MARC bibliographic record structure). Z39.50 version 3 (in Z39.50-1995) addresses additional functions to support non-bibliographic data such as full text documents and images. It also begins to address some of the functions being defined as necessary to information systems such as ranking values. Z39.50-1995 has just been approved by NISO and is published as the new standard (the latest information on Z39.50 is available on the WorldWide Web at http://ds.internic.net/z3950/z3950.html).

Wide Area Information Service (WAIS) is the de facto standard for many search environments on the INTERNET. WAIS was developed by a project started in 1989 by three commercial companies (Apple, Thinking Machines, and Dow Jones). The original idea was to create a program that would act as a personal librarian. It would act like a personal agent keeping track of significant amounts of data and filtering it for the information most relevant to the user. The interface concept was user entered natural language statements of topics the user had interest. In addition it provided the capability to communicate to the computer that a particular item was of interest and have the computer automatically find similar items (i.e., relevance feedback). The original corporate interest was in Apple providing the user interface, Thinking Machines providing the processing power, and Dow Jones providing the data.

The developers of WAIS pursued a generalized system of information retrieval that could access data collections all around the world (Hahn-94, Levine-94) on the Internet. Like other Internet services, free versions of WAIS were originally provided. Some of the initial products migrated to a commercial company that sells and supports a WAIS system. A free version of WAIS is still available via the Clearinghouse for Networked Information Discovery and Retrieval (CINDIR) called "FreeWAIS."

The original development of WAIS started with the 1988 Z39.50 protocol as a base following the client/server architecture concept. At that time Z39.50 was focused on a bibliographic MARC record structure against structured files. Numerous deficiencies were identified in the Z39.50 protocol forcing the developers of WAIS to vary from the Z39.50 standard (ORION-93). The developers incorporated the information retrieval concepts that allow for ranking, relevance feedback and natural language processing functions that apply to full text searchable databases. Since they were diverging from the standard, they decided to simplify their client server interface. In particular they decided to have a non-Markovian process. Thus state information is not kept between requests between clients and servers. This is one of the major differences between WAIS and Z39.50 compliant systems.

The availability of FreeWAIS in the public domain made it the method of choice for implementing databases on the INTERNET. The architecture gained significant momentum from the mandate that all U.S. Government Agencies publish their material electronically and make it accessible to the general public. WAIS and the INTERNET became the standard approach for answering the mandate. Additionally, many organizations are using WAIS as the engine to archive and access large amounts of textual information. The appeal for WAIS is that, for public domain software, it represents a well tested and documented product that can be trusted with data. A substantial community continues to test, fix and enhance the basic system. The current trend is away from WAIS and to a standard Internet interface (WEB interface) and using one of the more powerful search systems.

2.4.2 Architecture Standards

Another effort at standardization is being lead by the TIPSTER working group sponsored by the Department of Defense's Advanced Research Project Agency (DARPA). After sponsoring research on information processing technologies and associated TREC conferences, ARPA started supporting implementation of the new technologies into pilot systems. Although Z39.50 and WAIS address client/server environments that allow for searches for information systems, they view the client and server as independent systems. The TIPSTER working group is attempting to define an alternative architecture that facilitates interoperability between the various developed algorithms and systems. The draft Tipster Phase II Architecture Design Document, Version 1.52, says:

> "The primary mission of the Tipster Common Architecture is to provide a vehicle for efficiently delivering detection and extraction technology to Government agencies. The Architecture also has a secondary mission of providing a convenient and efficient environment for research in document detection and data extraction."

One of the major goals of the architecture is to "allow the interchange of modules from different suppliers ('plug and play')." It makes the existing developed capabilities available through a common interface. It focuses on standards for document management within a system. The TIPSTER architecture also includes protocols for the more advanced retrieval technologies that have yet to be incorporated into the Z39.50-1995 standard (including the advanced query standard) such as ranking and relevance feedback.

Another activity being driven by the publishing and Digital Libraries efforts is the creation of a unique way of identifying, naming and controlling documents in an information retrieval environment. It has the same paradigm as the TIPSTER architecture of separating the indexes and surrogate search structures from storing the actual item. The leader in this effort is the Center for National Research Initiatives (CNRI) that is working with the Department of Defense and also the American Association of Publishers (AAP), focusing on an Internet implementation that allows for control of electronic published and copyright material. The CNRI concept is based upon using a "handle" system where the handle is the unique network identifier of a digital object. The AAP prefers the term Digital Object Identifier over the term handle (CNRI-97). Most computer systems identify an item by the location it is stored (e.g., Uniform Resource Locators (URLs) on the Internet - see Section 4.7 for more detail). From a library and large information system perspective it is far more efficient to refer to items by name rather than location. There is still significant debate over whether the name should be just a unique identifier (e.g., a number) or also have semantic content to the user. The term "handle" refers to this unique name. A Handle server (similar to document manager in TIPSTER) ensures persistence, location independence and multiple instance management. Persistence ensures that the handle is available to locate information potentially past the life of the organization that created the item to identify any locations of the item. Location independence allows for the movement of items with a mechanism for knowing their current location. Multiple instance allows keeping track of the location of duplicates of an item. Inherent in this architecture is a unique "Handle" naming authority(s) and servers to assign names and keep track of locations. This is similar to the Domain Name Servers used in networks, but is designed to handle orders of magnitude more objects in efficient fashion.

In addition to the Handle Server architecture, CNRI is also advocating a communications protocol to retrieve items from existing systems. This protocol call Repository Archive Protocol (RAP) defines the mechanisms for Clients to use the handles to retrieve items. It also includes other administrative functions such as privilege validation. The Handle system is designed to meet the Internet Engineering Task Force (IETF) requirements for naming Internet objects via Uniform Resource Names to replace URLs as defined in the Internet's RFC-1737 (IETF-96).

2.5 Summary

Chapter 2 provides an overview of the functions commonly associated with Information Retrieval Systems. These functions define the user's view of the system versus the internal implementation that is described throughout the rest of this book. Until the early 1990s, the pressure on development of new user functions that assist the user in locating relevant items was driven by the academic community. The commercialization of information retrieval functions beingdriven by the growth of the Internet has changed the basis of development time from "academic years" (i.e., one academic year equals 18 months - the time to define the research, perform it and publish the results) to "Web years" (i.e., one Web year equals three months - demand to get new products up very quickly to be first). The test environment and test databases are changing from small scale academic environments to millions of records with millions of potential users testing new ideas. Even IBM, one of the most traditional, conservative companies, has an "alpha" site available on the Internet which contains the latest visualization and search software that is still in the process of being developing.

The areas to expect Web year changes in capabilities is in functions to assist the user in expanding his query, application of the above functions into a multilingual environment (i.e., the Internet provides information in many languages), and most importantly tools to support information visualization capabilities. The short queries that the typical user enters return too much data. The research community continues to development algorithms that is used to improve the precision and recall of the user's search. Automatic learning from user's queries coupled with large thesauri and concept dictionaries performs the query expansion process. New visualization tools have the most significant impact by allowing use of human cognitive processing to interpret the results of a user's search statement and focus on the items that most likely are relevant. Visualization tools also assist the users in enhancing their queries to find needed information. The basic search capabilities described in this chapter will not change much, but significant improvements can be expected in the browse capabilities. The underlying reason for these advancements is the need to optimize the human resource in finding needed information.

EXERCISES

1. Describe the rationale why use of proximity will improve precision versus use of just the Boolean functions. Discuss its effect on improvement of recall.

2. Show that the proximity function can not be used to provide an equivalent to a Contiguous Word Phrase.

3. What are the similarities and differences between use of fuzzy searches and term masking? What are the potentials for each to introduce errors?

4. Are thesauri a subclass of concept classes? Justify your answer.

5. Which would users prefer, Boolean queries or Natural Language queries? Why?

6. Ranking is one of the most important concepts in Information Retrieval Systems. What are the difficulties in applying ranking when Boolean queries are used?

7. What is the relationship between vocabulary browse and thesauri/concept classes?

8. Why should researchers in information retrieval care about standards?

3 Cataloging and Indexing

The first two chapters of this book presented the architecture of a total Information Storage and Retrieval System and the basic functions that apply to it. One of the most critical aspects of an information system that determines its effectiveness is how it represents concepts in items. The transformation from the received item to the searchable data structure is called Indexing. This process can be manual or automatic, creating the basis for direct search of items in the Document Database or indirect search via Index Files. Rather than trying to create a searchable data structure that directly maps to the text in the input items, some systems transform the item into a completely different representation that is concept based and use this as the searchable data structure. The concept weighting schemes have demonstrated the capability to find items that the traditional weighted and non-weighted data structures have missed. Systems that use a specialized hardware text search processor do not require the searchable data structure, but search the original standardized documents (see Chapter 9).

Once the searchable data structure has been created, techniques must be defined that correlate the user-entered query statement to the set of items in the database to determine the items to be returned to the user. This process is called Search and is often different between searches applied to the document database (called ad hoc queries) and searches against incoming items to determine the Mail File(s) the item should be delivered to (called dissemination searches). In the newer systems a by-product of the search process is a relative value for each item with respect to its correlation to the query constraints. This value is used in ranking the item. In some cases a simplified ranking algorithm is applied to the items found from the search process after it is completed.

Closely associated with the indexing process is the information extraction process. Its goal is to extract specific information to be normalized and entered into a structured database (DBMS). It is similar to the process of creating the search structure for an item in that both must locate concepts in the item. Information extraction differs because it focuses on very specific concepts and contains a transformation process that modifies the extracted information into a form compatible with the end structured database. This process was referred to in Chapter 2 as Automatic File Build. Another way information extraction can be used is in the generation of a summary of an item. The emphasis changes from extracting facts to go into index fields to extracting larger contextual constructs (e.g., sentences) that are combined to form a summary of an item.

3.1 History and Objectives of Indexing

To understand the system design associated with creation and manipulation of the searchable data structures, it is necessary to understand the objectives of the indexing process. Reviewing the history of indexing shows the dependency of information processing capabilities on manual and then automatic processing systems. Through most of the 1980's the goals of commercial Information Retrieval Systems were constrained to facilitating the manual indexing paradigm. In the 1990's, exponential growth in computer processing capabilities with a continuing decrease in cost of computer systems has allowed Information Retrieval Systems to implement the previously theoretical functions introducing, a new information retrieval paradigm.

3.1.1 History

Indexing (originally called Cataloging) is the oldest technique for identifying the contents of items to assist in their retrieval. The objective of cataloging is to give access points to a collection that are expected and most useful to the users of the information. The basic information required on an item, what is the item and what it is about, has not changed over the centuries. As early as the third-millennium, in Babylon, libraries of cuneiform tablets were arranged by subject (Hyman-89). Up to the 19th Century there was little advancement in cataloging, only changes in the methods used to represent the basic information (Norris-69). In the late 1800s subject indexing became hierarchical (e.g., Dewey Decimal System). In 1963 the Library of Congress initiated a study on the computerization of bibliographic surrogates. From 1966 - 1968 the Library of

Congress ran its MARC I pilot project. MARC (MAchine Readable Cataloging) standardizes the structure, contents and coding of bibliographic records. The system became operational in 1969 (Avram-75). The earliest commercial cataloging system is DIALOG, which was developed by Lockheed Corporation in 1965 for NASA. It became commercial in 1978 with three government files of indexes to technical publications. By 1988, when it was sold to Knight-Ridder, DIALOG contained over 320 index databases used by over 91,000 subscribers in 86 countries (Harper-81).

Indexing (cataloging), until recently, was accomplished by creating a bibliographic citation in a structured file that references the original text. These files contain citation information about the item, keywording the subject(s) of the item and, in some systems a constrained length free text field used for an abstract/summary. The indexing process is typically performed by professional indexers associated with library organizations. Throughout the history of libraries, this has been the most important and most difficult processing step. Most items are retrieved based upon what the item is about. The user's ability to find items on a particular subject is limited by the indexer creating index terms for that subject.

The initial introduction of computers to assist the cataloguing function did not change its basic operation of a human indexer determining those terms to assign to a particular item. The standardization of data structures (e.g., MARC format) did allow sharing of the indexes between libraries. It reduced the manual overhead associated with maintaining a card catalog. By not having to make physical copies of the index card for every subject index term, it also encouraged inclusion of additional index terms. But the process still required the indexer to enter index terms that are redundant with the words in the referenced item. The user, instead of searching through physical cards in a card catalog, now performed a search on a computer and electronically displayed the card equivalents.

In the 1990s, the significant reduction in cost of processing power and memory in modern computers, along with access to the full text of an item from the publishing stages in electronic form, allow use of the full text of an item as an alternative to the indexer-generated subject index. The searchable availability of the text of items has changed the role of indexers and allowed introduction of new techniques to facilitate the user in locating information of interest. The indexer is no longer required to enter index terms that are redundant with words in the text of an item. The searcher is no longer presented a list of potential item of interest, but is additionally informed of the likelihood that each item satisfies his search goal.

3.1.2 Objectives

The objectives of indexing have changed with the evolution of Information Retrieval Systems. Availability of the full text of the item in searchable form alters the objectives historically used in determining guidelines for manual indexing.   The full text searchable data structure for items in the Document File provides a new class of indexing called total document indexing. In this environment, all of the words within the item are potential index descriptors of the subject(s) of the item. Chapter 1 discusses the process of Item normalization that takes all possible words in an item and transforms them into processing tokens used in defining the searchable representation of an item.   In addition to determining the processing tokens, current systems have the ability to automatically weight the processing tokens based upon their potential importance in defining the concepts in the item.

The first reaction of many people is to question the need for manual indexing at all, given that total document indexing is available for search. If one can search on any of the words in a document why does one need to add additional index terms? Previously, indexing defined the source and major concepts of an item and provided a mechanism for standardization of index terms (i.e., use of a controlled vocabulary). A controlled vocabulary is a finite set of index terms from which all index terms must be selected (the domain of the index). In a manual indexing environment, the use of a controlled vocabulary makes the indexing process slower, but potentially simplifies the search process. The extra processing time comes from the indexer trying to determine the appropriate index terms for concepts that are not specifically in the controlled vocabulary set. Controlled vocabularies aide the user in knowing the domain of terms that the indexer had to select from and thus which terms best describe the information needed. Uncontrolled vocabularies have the opposite effect, making indexing faster but the search process much more difficult.

The availability of items in electronic form changes the objectives of manual indexing. The source information (frequently called citation data) can automatically be extracted. There is still some utility to the use of indexes for index term standardization. Modern systems, with the automatic use of thesauri and other reference databases, can account for diversity of language/vocabulary use and thus reduce the need for controlled vocabularies.   Most of the concepts discussed in the document is locatable via search of the total document index. The primary use of manual subject indexing now shifts to abstraction of concepts and judgments on the value of the information. The automatic text analysis algorithms can not consistently perform abstraction on all concepts that are in an item. They can not correlate the facts in an item in a cause/effect relationship to determine additional related concepts to be indexed. An item that is discussing the increase in water temperatures at factory discharge locations could be discussing "economic stability" of a country that has fishing as its major industry. It requires the associative capabilities of a human being to make the connection. A computer system would typically not be able to correlate the changes in temperature to economic stability. The additional index terms added under this process enhance the recall capability of the system. For certain queries it may also increase the precision. This processing deficiency indicates the potential for future enhancements of Information Retrieval Systems with Artificial Intelligence techniques.

The words used in an item do not always reflect the value of the concepts being presented. It is the combination of the words and their semantic implications that contain the value of the concepts being discussed. The utility of a concept is also determined by the user's need. The Public File indexer needs to consider the information needs of all users of the library system. Individual users of the system have their own domains of interest that bound the concepts in which they are interested. It takes a human being to evaluate the quality of the concepts being discussed in an item to determine if that concept should be indexed. The difference in "user need" between the library class of indexers and the individual users is why Private Index files are an essential part of any good information system. It allows the user to logically subset the total document file into folders of interest including only those documents that, in the user's judgment, have future value. It also allows the user to judge the utility of the concepts based upon his need versus the system need and perform concept abstraction. Selective indexing based upon the value of concepts increases the precision of searches.

Availability of full document indexing saves the indexer from entering index terms that are identical to words in the document. Users may use Public Index files as part of their search criteria to increase the recall. They may want to constrain the search by their Private Index file to increase the precision of the search. Figure 3.1 shows the potential relationship between use of the words in an item to define the concepts. Public Indexing of the concept adds additional index terms over the words in the item to achieve abstraction. The index file use fewer terms than found in the items because it only indexes the important concepts. Private Index files are even more focused, limiting the number of items indexed to those that have value to the user and within items only the concepts bounded by the specific user's interest domain. There is overlap between the Private and Public Index files, but the Private Index file is indexing fewer concepts in an item than the Public Index file and the file owner uses his specific vocabulary of index terms.

In addition to the primary objective of representing the concepts within an item to facilitate the user's finding relevant information, electronic indexes to items provide a basis for other applications to assist the user. The format of the index, in most cases, supports the ranking of the output to present the items most likely to be relevant to the user's information needs first (see Chapters 5 and 7). Also, the index can be used to cluster items by concept (see Chapter 6). The clustering of items has the effect of making an electronic system similar to a physical library. The paradigm of going to the library and browsing the book shelves in a topical area is the same as electronically browsing through items clustered by concepts.

3.2   Indexing Process

When an organization with multiple indexers decides to create a public or private index some procedural decisions on how to create the index terms assist the indexers and end users in knowing what to expect in the index file. The first decision is the scope of the indexing to define what level of detail the subject index will contain. This is based upon usage scenarios of the end users. The other decision is the need to link index terms together in a single index for a particular concept. Linking index terms is needed when there are multiple independent concepts found within an item.

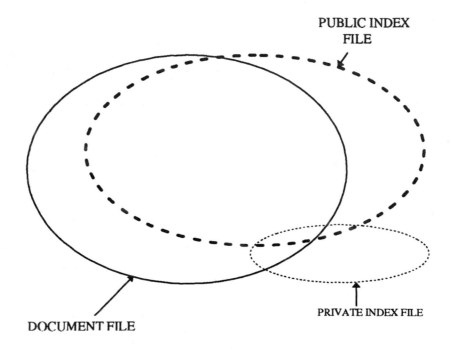

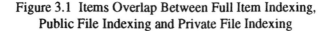

Figure 3.1 Items Overlap Between Full Item Indexing,
Public File Indexing and Private File Indexing

3.2.1   Scope of Indexing

When performed manually, the process of reliably and consistently determining the bibliographic terms that represent the concepts in an item is extremely difficult. Problems arise from interaction of two sources: the author and the indexer. The vocabulary domain of the author may be different than that of the indexer, causing the indexer to misinterpret the emphasis and possibly even the concepts being presented. The indexer is not an expert on all areas and has different levels of knowledge in the different areas being presented in the item. This results in different quality levels of indexing. The indexer must determine when to stop the indexing process.

There are two factors involved in deciding on what level to index the concepts in an item: the exhaustivity and the specificity of indexing desired. Exhaustivity of indexing is the extent to which the different concepts in the item are indexed. For example, if two sentences of a 10-page item on microprocessors discusses on-board caches, should this concept be indexed? Specificity relates to the preciseness of the index terms used in indexing. For example, whether the term "processor" or the term "microcomputer" or the term "Pentium" should be used in the index of an item is based upon the specificity decision. Indexing an item only on the most important concept in it and using general index terms yields low exhaustivity and specificity. This approach requires a minimal number of index terms per item and reduces the cost of generating the index. For example, indexing this paragraph would only use the index term "indexing."   High exhaustivity and specificity indexes almost every concept in the item using as many detailed terms as needed. Under these parameters this paragraph would have "indexing," "indexer knowledge," "exhaustivity" and "specificity" as index terms. Low exhaustivity has an adverse effect on both precision and recall. If the full text of the item is indexed, then low exhaustivity is used to index the abstract concepts not explicit in the item with the expectation that the typical query searches both the index and the full item index. Low specificity has an adverse effect on precision, but no effect to a potential increase in recall.

Another decision on indexing is what portions of an item should be indexed. The simplest case is to limit the indexing to the Title or Title and Abstract zones. This indexes the material that the author considers most important and reduces the costs associated with indexing an item. Unfortunately this leads to loss of both precision and recall.

Weighting of index terms is not common in manual indexing systems. Weighting is the process of assigning an importance to an index term's use in an item. The weight should represent the degree to which the concept associated with the index term is represented in the item. The weight should help in discriminating the extent to which the concept is discussed in items in the database. The manual process of assigning weights adds additional overhead on the indexer and requires a more complex data structure to store the weights.

3.2.2   Precoordination and Linkages

Another decision on the indexing process is whether linkages are available between index terms for an item. Linkages are used to correlate related attributes associated with concepts discussed in an item. This process of creating term linkages at index creation time is called precoordination. When index terms are not coordinated at index time, the coordination occurs at search time. This is called postcoordination, that is coordinating terms after (post) the indexing process. Postcoordination is implemented by "AND"ing index terms together, which only finds indexes that have all of the search terms.

Factors that must be determined in the linkage process are the number of terms that can be related, any ordering constraints on the linked terms, and any additional descriptors are associated with the index terms (Vickery-70). The range of the number of index terms that can be linked is not a significant implementation issue and primarily affects the design of the indexer's user interface. When multiple terms are being used, the possibility exists to have relationships between the terms. For example, the capability to link the source of a problem, the problem and who is affected by the problem may be desired. Each term must be caveated with one of these three categories along with linking the terms together into an instance of the relationships describing one semantic concept. The order of the terms is one technique for providing additional role descriptor information on the index terms. Use of the order of the index terms to implicitly define additional term descriptor information limits the number of index terms that can have a role descriptor. If order is not used, modifiers may be associated with each term linked to define its role. This technique allows any number of terms to have the associated role descriptor. Figure 3.2 shows the different types of linkages. It assumes that an item discusses the drilling of oil wells in Mexico by CITGO and the introduction of oil refineries in Peru by the U.S. When the linked capability is added, the system does not erroneously relate Peru and Mexico since they are not in the same set of linked items. It still does not have the ability to discriminate between which country is introducing oil refineries into the other country. Introducing roles in the last two examples of Figure 3.2 removes this ambiguity. Positional roles treat the data as a vector allowing only one value per position. Thus if the example is expanded so that the U.S. was introducing oil refineries in Peru, Bolivia and Argentina, then the positional role technique would require three entries, where the only difference would be in the value in the "affected country" position. When modifiers are used, only one entry would be required and all three countries would be listed with three "MODIFIER"s.

3.3 AUTOMATIC INDEXING

Automatic indexing is the capability for the system to automatically determine the index terms to be assigned to an item. The simplest case is when all words in the document are used as possible index terms (total document indexing). More complex processing is required when the objective is to emulate a human indexer and determine a limited number of index terms for the major concepts in the item. As discussed, the advantages of human indexing are the ability to determine concept abstraction and   judge the value of a concept.   The disadvantages of human indexing over automatic indexing are cost, processing

INDEX TERMS	Methodology
oil, wells, Mexico, CITGO, refineries, Peru, BP, drilling	No linking of terms
(oil wells, Mexico, drilling, CITGO)	linked (Precoordination)
(U.S.,oil refineries, Peru, introduction)	
(CITGO, drill, oil wells, Mexico) (U.S., introduction, oil refineries, Peru)	linked (Precoordination) with position indicating role

(SUBJECT: CITGO;
     ACTION: drilling;
    OBJECT: oil,wells
    MODIFIER: in Mexico)
	linked (Pre-coordination) with modifier indicating role

(SUBJECT:U.S.;
    ACTION:introduces;
    OBJECT: oil refineries;
    MODIFIER: in Peru)	

Figure 3.2 Linkage of Index Terms

time and consistency. Once the initial hardware cost is amortized, the costs of automatic indexing are absorbed as part of the normal operations and maintenance costs of the computer system. There are no additional indexing costs versus the salaries and benefits regularly paid to human indexers.

Processing time of an item by a human indexer varies significantly based upon the indexer's knowledge of the concepts being indexed, the exhaustivity and specificity guidelines and the amount and accuracy of preprocessing via Automatic File Build. Even for relatively short items (e.g., 300 - 500 words) it normally takes at least five minutes per item. A significant portion of this time is caused by the human interaction with the computer (e.g., typing speeds, cursor positioning, correcting spelling errors, taking breaks between activities). Automatic indexing requires only a few seconds or less of computer time based upon the size of the processor and the complexity of the algorithms to generate the index.

Another advantage to automatic indexing is the predictably of algorithms. If the indexing is being performed automatically, by an algorithm, there is consistency in the index term selection process. Human indexers typically generate different indexing for the same document. In an experiment on consistency in TREC-2, there was, on the average, a 20 per cent difference in judgment of the same item's topics between the original and a second independent judge of over 400 items (Harman-95). Since the judgments on relevance are different, the selection of index terms and their weighting to reflect the topics is also different. In automatic indexing, a sophisticated researcher understands the automatic process and be able to predict its utility and deficiencies, allowing for compensation for system characteristics in a search strategy. Even the end user, after interacting with the system, understands for certain classes of information and certain sources, the ability of the system to find relevant items is worse than other classes and sources. For example, the user may determine that searching for economic issues is far less precise than political issues in a particular newspaper based information system. The user may also determine that it is easier to find economic data in a information database containing *Business Weekly* than the newspaper source.

Indexes resulting from automated indexing fall into two classes: weighted and unweighted. In an unweighted indexing system, the existence of an index term in a document and sometimes its word location(s) are kept as part of the searchable data structure. No attempt is made to discriminate between the value of the index terms in representing concepts in the item. Looking at the index, it is not possible to tell the difference between the main topics in the item and a casual reference to a concept. This architecture is typical of the commercial systems through the 1980s. Queries against unweighted systems are based upon Boolean logic and the items in the resultant Hit file are considered equal in value. The last item presented in the file is as likely as the first item to be relevant to the user's information need.

In a weighted indexing system, an attempt is made to place a value on the index term's representation of its associated concept in the document. An index term's weight is based upon a function associated with the frequency of occurrence of the term in the item. Luhn, one of the pioneers in automatic indexing, introduced the concept of the "resolving power" of a term. Luhn postulated that the significance of a concept in an item is directly proportional to the frequency of use of the word associated with the concept in the document (Luhn-58, Salton-75). This is reinforced by the studies of Brookstein, Klein and Raita that show "content bearing" words are not randomly distributed (i.e., Poisson distributed), but that their occurrence "clump" within items (Brookstein-95). Typically, values for the index terms are normalized between zero and one. The higher the weight, the more the term represents a concept discussed in the item. The weight can be adjusted to account for other information such as the number of items in the database that contain the same concept (see Chapter 5).

The query process uses the weights along with any weights assigned to terms in the query to determine a scalar value (rank value) used in predicting the likelihood that an item satisfies the query. Thresholds or a parameter specifying the maximum number of items to be returned are used to bound the number of items returned to a user (see Chapter 7). The results are presented to the user in order of the rank value from highest number to lowest number.

Automatic indexing can either try to preserve the original text of an item basing the final set of searchable index values on the original text or map the item into a completely different representation, called concept indexing, and use the concepts as a basis for the final set of index values. The automatic indexing techniques are introduced in this section and later described in detail in Chapter 5.

3.3.1   Indexing by Term

When the terms of the original item are used as a basis of the index process, there are two major techniques for creation of the index: statistical and natural language. Statistical techniques can be based upon vector models and probabilistic models with a special case being Bayesian models. They are classified as statistical because their calculation of weights use statistical information such as the frequency of occurrence of words and their distributions in the searchable database. Natural language techniques also use some statistical information, but perform more complex parsing to define the final set of index concepts.

Often weighted systems are discussed as vectorized information systems. This association comes from the SMART system at Cornell University created by Dr. Gerald Salton (Salton-73, Salton-83). The system emphasizes weights as a foundation for information detection and stores these weights in a vector form. Each vector represents a document and each position in a vector represents a different unique word (processing token) in the database. The value assigned to each position is the weight of that term in the document. A value of zero indicates that the word was not in the document. The system and its associated research results have been evolving for over 30 years. Queries can be translated into the vector form. Search is accomplished by calculating the distance between the query vector and the document vectors.

In addition to a vector model, the other dominant approach uses a probabilistic model. The model that has been most successful in this area is the Bayesian approach. This approach is natural to information systems and is based upon the theories of evidential reasoning (drawing conclusions from evidence). Bayesian approaches have long been applied to information systems (Maron-60). The Bayesian approach could be applied as part of index term weighting, but usually is applied as part of the retrieval process by calculating the relationship between an item and a specific query. A Bayesian network is a directed acyclic graph in which each node represents a random variable and the arcs between the nodes represent a probabilistic dependence between the node and its parents

(Howard-81, Pearl-88). Figure 3.3 shows the basic weighting approach for index terms or associations between query terms and index terms.

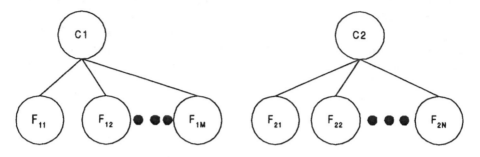

Figure 3.3 Two-level Bayesian network

The nodes C_1 and C_2 represent "the item contains concept C_i" and the F nodes represent "the item has feature (e.g., words) F_{ij}." The network could also be interpreted as C representing concepts in a query and F representing concepts in an item. The goal is to calculate the probability of C_i given F_{ij}. To perform that calculation two sets of probabilities are needed:

1. The prior probability $P(C_i)$ that an item is relevant to concept C

2. The conditional probability $P(F_{ij}/C_i)$ that the features F_{ij} where $j = 1$, m are present in an item given that the item contains topic C_i.

The automatic indexing task is to calculate the posterior probability $P(C_i/F_{i1}, \ldots, F_{im})$, the probability that the item contains concept C_i given the presence of features F_{ij}. The Bayes inference formula that is used is:

$$P(C_i/F_{i1}, \ldots, F_{im}) = P(C_i)\ P(F_{i1}, \ldots, F_{im}/C_i)\backslash P(F_{i1}, \ldots, F_{im}).$$

If the goal is to provide ranking as the result of a search by the posteriors, the Bayes rule can be simplified to a linear decision rule:

$$g(C_i/F_{i1}, \ldots, F_{im}) = \Sigma_k\ I(F_{ik})\ w(F_{ik}, C_i)$$

where $I(F_{ik})$ is an indicator variable that equals 1 only if F_{ik} is present in the item (equals zero otherwise) and w is a coefficient corresponding to a specific feature/concept pair. A careful choice of w produces a ranking in decreasing order that is equivalent to the order produced by the posterior probabilities. Interpreting the coefficients, w, as weights corresponding to each feature (e.g., index term) and the function g as the sum of the weights of the features, the result of applying the formula is a set of term weights (Fung-95).

Another approach to defining indexes to items is via use of natural language processing. The DR-LINK (Document Retrieval through Linguistic Knowledge) system processes items at the morphological, lexical, semantic, syntactic, and discourse levels (Liddy-93, Weiner-95). Each level uses information from the previous level to perform its additional analysis. The discourse level is abstracting information beyond the sentence level and can determine abstract concepts using pre-defined models of event relationships. This allows the indexing to include specific term as well as abstract concepts such as time (e.g., differentiates between a company was sold versus a company will be sold). Normal automatic indexing does a poor job at identifying and extracting "verbs" and relationships between objects based upon the verbs.

3.3.2 Indexing by Concept

The basis for concept indexing is that there are many ways to express the same idea and increased retrieval performance comes from using a single representation. Indexing by term treats each of these occurrences as a different index and then uses thesauri or other query expansion techniques to expand a query to find the different ways the same thing has been represented. Concept indexing determines a canonical set of concepts based upon a test set of terms and uses them as a basis for indexing all items This is also called Latent Semantic Indexing because it is indexing the latent semantic information in items. The determined set of concepts does not have a label associated with each concept (i.e., a word or set of words that can be used to describe it), but is a mathematical representation (e.g., a vector).

An example of a system that uses concept indexing is the MatchPlus system developed by HNC Inc. The MatchPlus system uses neural networks to facilitate machine learning of concept/word relationships and sensitivity to similarity of use (Caid-93). The systems goal is to be able to determine from the corpus of items, word relationships (e.g., synonyms) and the strength of these relationships and use that information in generating context vectors. Two neural networks are used. One neural network learning algorithm generates stem context vectors that are sensitive to similarity of use and another one performs query modification based upon user feedback.

Word stems, items and queries are represented by high dimensional (at least 300 dimensions) vectors called context vectors. Each dimension in a vector could be viewed as an abstract concept class. The approach is based upon cognitive science work by Waltz and Pollack (Waltx-85). To define context vectors, a set of n features are selected on an ad hoc basis (e.g., high frequency terms after removal of stop words). The selection of the initial features is not critical since they evolve and expand to the abstract concept classes used in the indexing process. For any word stem k, its context vector V^k is an n-dimensional vector with each component j interpreted as follows:

V^k positive if k is strongly associated with feature j
$V^k \approx 0$ if word k is not associated with feature j
V^k negative if word k contradicts feature j

The interpretation of components for concept vectors is exactly the same as weights in neural networks. Each of the n features is viewed as an abstract concept class. Then each word stem is mapped to how strongly it reflects each concept in the items in the corpus. There is overlap between the concept classes (features) providing a distributed representation and insulating against a small number of entries for context vectors that could have no representation for particular stems (Hinton-84). Once the context vectors for stems are determined, they are used to create the index for an item. A weighted sum of the context vectors for all the stems in the item is calculated and normalized to provide a vector representation of the item in terms of the n concept classes (features). Chapter 5 provides additional detail on the specific algorithms used. Queries (natural language only) go through the same analysis to determine vector representations. These vectors are then compared to the item vectors.

3.4 Information Extraction

There are two processes associated with information extraction: determination of facts to go into structured fields in a database and extraction of text that can be used to summarize an item. In the first case only a subset of the important facts in an item may be identified and extracted. In summarization all of the major concepts in the item should be represented in the summary.

The process of extracting facts to go into indexes is called Automatic File Build in Chapter 1. Its goal is to process incoming items and extract index terms that will go into a structured database. This differs from indexing in that its objective is to extract specific types of information versus understanding all of the text of the document. An Information Retrieval System's goal is to provide an in-depth representation of the total contents of an item (Sundheim-92). An Information Extraction system only analyzes those portions of a document that potentially contain information relevant to the extraction criteria. The objective of the data extraction is in most cases to update a structured database with additional facts. The updates may be from a controlled vocabulary or substrings from the item as defined by the extraction rules. The term "slot" is used to define a particular category of information to be extracted. Slots are organized into templates or semantic frames. Information extraction requires multiple levels of analysis of the text of an item. It must understand the words and their context (discourse analysis). The processing is very similar to the natural language processing described under indexing.

In establishing metrics to compare information extraction, the previously defined measures of precision and recall are applied with slight modifications to their meaning. Recall refers to how much information was extracted from an item versus how much should have been extracted from the item. It shows the amount of correct and relevant data extracted versus the correct and relevant data in the item. Precision refers to how much information was extracted accurately versus the total information extracted.

Additional metrics used are overgeneration and fallout. Overgeneration measures the amount of irrelevant information that is extracted. This could be caused by templates filled on topics that are not intended to be extracted or slots that get filled with non-relevant data. Fallout measures how much a system assigns incorrect slot fillers as the number of potential incorrect slot fillers increases (Lehnert-91).

These measures are applicable to both human and automated extraction processes. Human beings fall short of perfection in data extraction as well as automated systems. The best source of analysis of data extraction is from the Message Understanding Conference Proceedings. Conferences (similar to TREC) were held in 1991, 1992, 1993 and 1995. The conferences are sponsored by the Advanced Research Project Agency/Software and Intelligent Systems Technology Office of the Department of Defense. Large test databases are made available to any organization interested in participating in evaluation of their algorithms. In MUC-5 (1993), four experienced human analysts performed detailed extraction against 120 documents and their performance was compared against the top three information extraction systems. The humans achieved a 79 per cent recall with 82 per cent precision. That is, they extracted 79 per cent of the data they could have found and 18 per cent of what they extracted was erroneous. The automated programs achieved 53 per cent recall and 57 per cent precision. The other mediating factor is the costs associated with information extraction. The humans required between 15 and 60 minutes to process a single item versus the 30 seconds to three minutes required by the computers. Thus the existing algorithms are not operating close to what a human can achieve, but they are significantly cheaper. A combination of the two in a computer-assisted information extraction system appears the most reasonable solution in the foreseeable future.

Another related information technology is document summarization. Rather than trying to determine specific facts, the goal of document summarization is to extract a summary of an item maintaining the most important ideas while significantly reducing the size. Examples of summaries that are often part of any item are titles, table of contents, and abstracts with the abstract being the closest. The abstract can be used to represent the item for search purposes or as a way for a user to determine the utility of an item without having to read the complete item.

It is not feasible to automatically generate a coherent narrative summary of an item with proper discourse, abstraction and language usage (Sparck Jones-93). Restricting the domain of the item can significantly improve the quality of the output (Paice-93, Reimer-88). The more restricted goals for much of the research is in finding subsets of the item that can be extracted and concatenated (usually extracting at the sentence level) and represents the most important concepts in the item. There is no guarantee of readability as a narrative abstract and it is seldom achieved. It has been shown that extracts of approximately 20 per cent of the complete item can represent the majority of significant concepts (Morris-92). Different algorithms produces different summaries. Just as different humans create different abstracts for the same item, automated techniques that generate different summaries does not intrinsically imply major deficiencies between the summaries. Most automated algorithms approach summarization by calculating a score for each sentence and then extracting the sentences with the highest scores. Some examples of the scoring techniques are use of rhetorical relations (e.g., reason, direction, contrast: see Miike-94 for experiments in Japanese), contextual inference and syntactic coherence using cue words (Rush-71), term location (Salton-83), and statistical weighting properties discussed in Chapter 5. There is no overall theoretic basis for the approaches leading to many heuristic algorithms. Kupiec et al. are pursuing statistical classification approach based upon a training set reducing the heuristics by focusing on a weighted combination of criteria to produce "optimal" scoring scheme (Kupiec-95). They selected the following five feature sets as a basis for their algorithm:

> Sentence Length Feature that requires sentence to be over five words in length

> Fixed Phrase Feature that looks for the existence of phrase "cues" (e.g., "in conclusion)

> Paragraph Feature that places emphasis on the first ten and last five paragraphs in an item and also the location of the sentences within the paragraph

> Thematic Word Feature that uses word frequency

> Uppercase Word Feature that places emphasis on proper names and acronyms.

As with previous experiments by Edmundson, Kupiec et al. discovered that location based heuristics gives better results than the frequency based features (Edmundson-69).

Although there is significant overlap in the algorithms and techniques for information extraction and indexing items for information retrieval, this text does not present more detail on information extraction. For additional information, the MUC proceedings from Morgan Kaufman Publishers, Inc. in San Francisco is one source of the latest detailed information on information extraction.

3.5 Summary

This chapter introduces the concepts behind indexing. Historically, term indexing was applied to a human-generated set of terms that could be used to locate an item. With the advent of computers and the availability of text in electronic form, alternatives to human indexing are available and essential. There is too much information in electronic form to make it feasible for human indexing of each item. Thus automated indexing techniques are absolutely essential. When humans performed the indexing, there were guidelines on the scope of the indexing process. They were needed to ensure that the human indexers achieved the objectives of a particular indexing effort. The guidelines defined the level of detail to which the indexing was to be applied (i.e., exhaustivity and specificity). In automated systems there is no reason not to index to the lowest level of detail. The strength in manual indexing was the associative powers of the human indexer in consolidating many similar ideas into a small number of representative index terms and knowing when certain concepts were of such low value as to not warrant indexing. Automated indexing systems try to achieve these by using weighted and natural language systems and by concept indexing. The reliance of automated systems on statistical information alone never achieve totally accurate assignment of importance weights to the concepts being indexed. The power of language is not only in the use of words but also the elegance of their combinations.

The goal of automatic indexing is not to achieve equivalency to human processing, but to achieve sufficient interpretation of items to allow users to locate needed information with the minimum amount of wasted effort. Even the human indexing process has left much to be desired and caused significant energy by the user to locate all of the needed information.

As difficult as determining index terms is, text summarization encounters an even higher level of complexity. The focus of text summarization is still on just the location of text segments that adequately represent an item. The combining of these segments into a readable "abstract" is still an unachievable goal. In the near term, a summarization that may not be grammatically correct but adequately covers the concepts in an item can be used by user to determine if the complete item should be read in detail.

The importance of the algorithms being developed for automatic indexing can not be overstated. The original text of items is not being searched. The extracted index information is realistically the only way to find information. The

weaker the theory and implementation of the indexing algorithms is, the greater
the impact on the user in wasting energy to find needed information. The Global
Information Infrastructure (e.g., the Internet) is touching every part of our lives
from academic instruction to shopping and getting news. The indexing and search
algorithms drives the success of this new aspect of everyday life.

EXERCISES

1.   Under what circumstances is manual indexing not required to ensure finding
      information? Postulate an example where this is true.

2.   Does high specificity always imply high exhaustivity? Justify your answer.

3.   Trade off the use of precoordination versus postcoordination.

4.   What are the problems with Luhn's concept of "resolving power"?

5.   How does the process of information extraction differ from the process of
      document indexing?

4 Data Structures

Knowledge of data structures used in Information Retrieval Systems provides insights into the capabilities available to the systems that implement them. Each data structure has a set of associated capabilities that provide an insight into the objectives of the implementers by its selection. From an Information Retrieval System perspective, the two aspects of a data structure that are important are its ability to represent concepts and their relationships and how well it supports location of those concepts. This chapter discusses the major logical data structures that are used in information retrieval systems. The implementation of a data structure (e.g., as an object, linked list, array, hashed file) is discussed only as an example.

4.1 Introduction to Data Structures

There are usually two major data structures in any information system. One structure stores and manages the received items in their normalized form. The process supporting this structure is called the "document manager." The other major data structure contains the processing tokens and associated data to support search. Figure 4.1 expands the document file creation function in Figure 1.4 from Chapter 1, showing the document manager function. Details on the creation of processing tokens can be found in Section 1.3.1. The results of a search are references to the items that satisfy the search statement, which are passed to the document manager for retrieval. This chapter focuses on data structures used to support the search function. It does not address the document management function nor the data structures and other related theory associated with the parsing of queries. For that background the reader should pursue a text on finite automata and language (regular expressions).

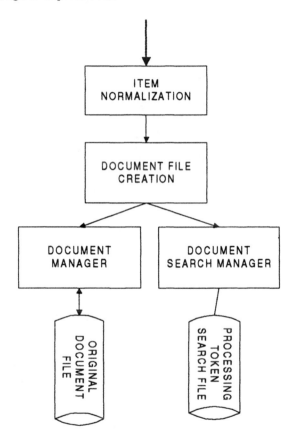

Figure 4.1 Major Data Structures

One of the first transformations often applied to data before placing it in the searchable data structure is stemming. Stemming reduces the diversity of representations of a concept (word) to a canonical morphological representation. The risk with stemming is that concept discrimination information may be lost in the process, causing a decrease in precision and the ability for ranking to be performed. On the positive side, stemming has the potential to improve recall.

The most common data structure encountered in both data base and information systems is the inverted file system (discussed in Section 4.3). It minimizes secondary storage access when multiple search terms are applied across the total database. All commercial and most academic systems use inversion as the searchable data structure. A variant of the searchable data structure is the N-gram structure that breaks processing tokens into smaller string units (which is why it is sometimes discussed under stemming) and uses the token fragments for search. N-grams have demonstrated improved efficiencies and conceptual manipulations over full word inversion. PAT trees and arrays view the text of an item as a single long stream versus a juxtaposition of words. Around this paradigm search algorithms are defined based upon text strings. Signature files are based upon the idea of fast elimination of non-relevant items reducing the searchable items to a manageable subset.   The subset can be returned to the user for review or other search algorithms may be applied to it to eliminate any false hits that passed the signature filter.

A special data structure that is becoming common place because of its use on the Internet is hypertext.   This structure allows the creator of an item to manually or automatically create imbedded links within one item to a related item.

4.2   Stemming Algorithms

The concept of stemming has been applied to information systems from their initial automation in the 1960's. The original goal of stemming was to improve performance and require less system resources by reducing the number of unique words that a system has to contain. With the continued significant increase in storage and computing power, use of stemming for performance reasons is no longer as important.   Stemming is now being reviewed for the potential improvements it can make in recall versus its associated decline in precision. A system designer can trade off the increased overhead of stemming in creating processing tokens versus reduced search time overhead of processing query terms with trailing "don't cares" (see Section 2.1.5 Term Masking) to include all of their variants. The stemming process creates one large index for the stem versus Term Masking which requires the merging (ORing) of the indexes for every term that matches the search term.

4.2.1   Introduction to the Stemming Process

Stemming algorithms are used to improve the efficiency of the information system and to improve recall. Conflation is the term frequently used to refer to mapping multiple morphological variants to a single representation (stem). The premise is that the stem carries the meaning of the concept associated with the word and the that affixes (endings) introduce subtle modifications to the concept or are used for syntactical purposes.   Languages have precise grammars that define their usage, but also evolve based upon human usage. Thus exceptions and non-consistent variants are always present in languages that typically require exception look-up tables in addition to the normal reduction rules.

At first glance, the idea of equating multiple representations of a word as a single stem term would appear to provide significant compression, with associated savings in storage and processing. For example, the stem "comput" could associate "computable, computability, computation, computational, computed, computing, computer, computerese, computerize" to one compressed word. But upon closer examination, looking at an inverted file system implementation, the savings is only in the dictionary since weighted positional information is typically needed in the inversion lists. In an architecture with stemming, the information is in the one inversion list for the stem term versus distributed across multiple inversion lists for each unstemmed term. Since the size of the inversion lists are the major storage factor, the compression of stemming does not significantly reduce storage requirements. For small test databases such as the Cranfield collection, Lennon reported savings of 32 per cent (Lennon-81). But when applied to larger databases of 1.6 Megabytes and 50 Megabytes, the compression reduced respectively to 20 percent and 13.5 percent (Harman-91). Harman also points out that misspellings and proper names reduce the compression even more. In a large text corpus, such as the TREC database, over 15 per cent of the unique words are proper nouns or acronyms that should not be stemmed.

Another major use of stemming is to improve recall. As long as a semantically consistent stem can be identified for a set of words, the generalization process of stemming does help in not missing potentially relevant items. Stemming of the words "calculate, calculates, calculation, calculations, calculating" to a single stem ("calculat") insures whichever of those terms is entered by the user, it is translated to the stem and finds all the variants in any items they exist. In contrast, stemming can not improve, but has the potential for decreasing precision. The precision value is not based on finding all relevant items but just minimizing the retrieval of non-relevant items. Any function that generalizes a user's search statement can only increase the likelihood of retrieving non-relevant items unless the expansion guarantees every item retrieved by the expansion is relevant.

It is important for a system to be able to categorize a word prior to making the decision to stem it. Certain categories such as proper names and acronyms should not have stemming applied because their morphological basis is not related to a common core concept.   Stemming can also cause problems for Natural Language Processing (NLP) systems by causing the loss of information needed for aggregate levels of natural language processing (discourse analysis). The tenses of verbs may be lost in creating a stem, but they are needed to determine if a particular concept (e.g., economic support) being indexed occurred in the past or will be occurring in the future. Time is one example of the type of relationships that are defined in Natural Language Processing systems (see Chapter 5).

The most common stemming algorithm removes suffixes and prefixes, sometimes recursively, to derive the final stem. Other techniques such as table lookup and successor stemming provide alternatives that require additional overheads. Successor stemmers determine prefix overlap as the length of a stem is increased. This information can be used to determine the optimal length for each stem from a statistical versus a linguistic perspective. Table lookup requires a large data structure. A system such as RetrievalWare that is based upon a very large thesaurus/concept network has the data structure as part of its basic product and thus uses table look-up. The Kstem algorithm used in the INQUERY System combines a set of simple stemming rules with a dictionary to determine processing tokens.

The affix removal technique removes prefixes and suffixes from terms leaving the stem. Most stemmers are iterative and attempt to remove the longest prefixes and suffixes (Lovins-68, Salton-68, Dawson-74, Porter-80 and Paice-90). The Porter algorithm is the most commonly accepted algorithm, but it leads to loss of precision and introduces some anomalies that cause the user to question the integrity of the system. Stemming is applied to the user's query as well as to the incoming text. If the transformation moves the query term to a different semantic meaning, the user will not understand why a particular item is returned and may begin questioning the integrity of the system in general.

4.2.2 Porter Stemming Algorithm

The Porter Algorithm is based upon a set of conditions of the stem, suffix and prefix and associated actions given the condition. Some examples of stem conditions are:

1. The measure, m, of a stem is a function of sequences of vowels (a, e, i, o, u, y) followed by a consonant. If V is a sequence of vowels and C is a sequence of consonants, then m is:

$$C(VC)^m V$$

where the initial C and final V are optional and m is the number VC repeats.

Measure   Example

m=0	free, why
m=1	frees, whose
m=2	prologue, compute

2. *<X>   - stem ends with letter X
3. *v*   - stem contains a vowel
4. *d   - stem ends in double consonant
5. *o   - stem ends with consonant-vowel-consonant sequence
               where the final consonant is not w, x, or y

Suffix conditions take the form current_suffix = = pattern
Actions are in the form old_suffix -> new_suffix

Rules are divided into steps to define the order of applying the rules.   The
following are some examples of the rules:

STEP	CONDITION	SUFFIX	REPLACEMENT	EXAMPLE
1a	NULL	sses	ss	stresses->stress
1b	*v*	ing	NULL	making->mak
1b1[1]	NULL	at	ate	inflat(ed)->inflate
1c	*v*	y	i	happy->happi
2	m>0	aliti	al	formaliti->formal
3	m>0	icate	ic	duplicate->duplic
4	m>1	able	NULL	adjustable->adjust
5a	m>1	e	NULL	inflate->inflat
5b	m>1 and *d and *<L>	NULL	single letter	controll->control

Given the word "duplicatable," the following are the steps in the stemming
process:

duplicat	rule 4
duplicate	rule 1b1
duplic	rule 2

The application of another rule in step 4, removing "ic," can not be applied since
only one rule from each step is allowed be applied.

---

[i]   1b1 rules are expansion rules to make correction to stems for proper conflation.
For example stemming of skies drops the es, making it ski, which is the wrong
concept and the I should be changed to y.

4.2.3 Dictionary Look-Up Stemmers

An alternative to solely relying on algorithms to determine a stem is to use a dictionary look-up mechanism. In this approach, simple stemming rules still may be applied. The rules are taken from those that have the fewest exceptions (e.g., removing pluralization from nouns). But even the most consistent rules have exceptions that need to be addressed. The original term or stemmed version of the term is looked up in a dictionary and replaced by the stem that best represents it. This technique has been implemented in the INQUERY and RetrievalWare Systems.

The INQUERY system uses a stemming technique called Kstem. Kstem is a morphological analyzer that conflates word variants to a root form (Kstem-95). It tries to avoid collapsing words with different meanings into the same root. For example, "memorial" and "memorize" reduce to "memory." But "memorial" and "memorize" are not synonyms and have very different meanings. Kstem, like other stemmers associated with Natural Language Processors and dictionaries, returns words instead of truncated word forms. Generally, Kstem requires a word to be in the dictionary before it reduces one word form to another. Some endings are always removed, even if the root form is not found in the dictionary (e.g., 'ness', 'ly'). If the word being processed is in the dictionary, it is assumed to be unrelated to the root after stemming and conflation is not performed (e.g., 'factorial' needs to be in the dictionary or it is stemmed to 'factory'). For irregular morphologies, it is necessary to explicitly map the word variant to the root desired (for example, "matrices" to "matrix").

The Kstem system uses the following six major data files to control and limit the stemming process:

Dictionary of words (lexicon)

Supplemental list of words for the dictionary

Exceptions list for those words that should retain an "e" at the end (e.g., "suites" to "suite" but "suited" to "suit")

Direct_Conflation - allows definition of direct conflation via word pairs that override the stemming algorithm

Country_Nationality - conflations between nationalities and countries ("British" maps to "Britain")

Proper Nouns - a list of proper nouns that should not be stemmed.

The strength of the RetrievalWare System lies in its Thesaurus/Semantic Network support data structure that contains over 400,000 words. The dictionaries that are used contain the morphological variants of words. New words that are not special forms (e.g., dates, phone numbers) are located in the dictionary to determine simpler forms by stripping off suffixes and respelling plurals as defined in the dictionary.

4.2.4 Successor Stemmers

Successor stemmers are based upon the length of prefixes that optimally stem expansions of additional suffixes. The algorithm is based upon an analogy in structural linguistics that investigated word and morpheme boundaries based upon the distribution of phonemes, the smallest unit of speech that distinguish one word from another (Hafer-74). The process determines the successor varieties for a word, uses this information to divide a word into segments and selects one of the segments as the stem.

The successor variety of a segment of a word in a set of words is the number of distinct letters that occupy the segment length plus one character. For example, the successor variety for the first three letters (i.e., word segment) of a five-letter word is the number of words that have the same first three letters but a different fourth letter plus one for the current word. A graphical representation of successor variety is shown in a symbol tree. Figure 4.2 shows the symbol tree for the terms bag, barn, bring, both, box, and bottle. The successor variety for any prefix of a word is the number of children that are associated with the node in the symbol tree representing that prefix. For example, the successor variety for the first letter "b" is three. The successor variety for the prefix "ba" is two.

The successor varieties of a word are used to segment a word by applying one of the following four methods :

1. Cutoff method: a cutoff value is selected to define stem length. The value varies for each possible set of words.

2. Peak and Plateau: a segment break is made after a character whose successor variety exceeds that of the character immediately preceding it and the character immediately following it.

3. Complete word method: break on boundaries of complete words.

4. Entropy method: uses the distribution of successor variety letters. Let $|D_{ak}|$ be the number of words beginning with the k length sequence of letters a. Let $|D_{akj}|$ be the number of words in D_{ak} with successor j. The

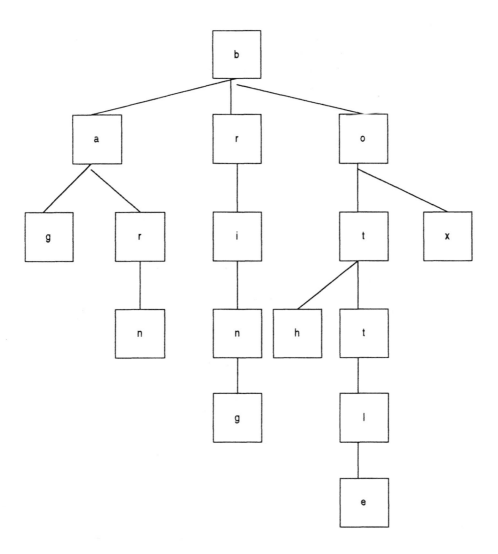

Figure 4.2 Symbol Tree for terms bag, barn, bring, box, bottle , both

probability that a member of D_{ak} has the successor j is given by $|D_{akj}|/|D_{ak}|$. The entropy (Average Information as defined by Shannon-51) of $|D_{ak}|$ is:

$$H_{ak} = \sum_{p=1}^{26} -(|D_{akj}|/|D_{ak}|) \, (\log_2(|D_{akj}|/|D_{ak}|))$$

Using this formula a set of entropy measures can be calculated for a word and its predecessors. A cutoff value is selected and a boundary is identified whenever the cutoff value is reached. Hafer and Weiss experimented with the techniques, discovering that combinations of the techniques performed best, which they used in defining their stemming process. Using the words in Figure 4.2 plus the additional word "boxer," the successor variety stemming is shown in Figure 4.3.

PREFIX	Successor Variety	Branch Letters
b	3	a,r,o
bo	2	t,x
box	1	e
boxe	1	r
boxer	1	blank

Figure 4.3 Successor Variety Stemming

If the cutoff method with value four was selected then the stem would be "boxe." The peak and plateau method can not apply because the successor variety monotonically decreases. Applying the complete word method, the stem is "box." The example given does not have enough values to apply the entropy method. The advantage of the peak and plateau and the complete word methods is that a cutoff value does not have to be selected (Frakes-92).

After a word has been segmented, the segment to be used as the stem must be selected. Hafer and Weiss used the following rule:

if (first segment occurs in <= 12 words in database)
            first segment is stem
    else (second segment is stem)

The idea is that if a segment is found in more than 12 words in the text being analyzed, it is probably a prefix. Hafer and Weiss noted that multiple prefixes in the English language do not occur often and thus selecting the first or second segment in general determines the appropriate stem.

4.2.5 Conclusions

Frakes summarized studies of various stemming studies (Frakes-92). He cautions that some of the authors failed to report test statistics, especially sizes, making interpretation difficult. Also some of the test sample sizes were so small as to make their results questionable. Frakes came to the following conclusions:

Stemming can affect retrieval (recall) and where effects were identified they were positive.   There is little difference between retrieval effectiveness of different full stemmers with the exception of the Hafer and Weiss stemmer.

Stemming is as effective as manual conflation.

Stemming is dependent upon the nature of the vocabulary.

To quantify the impact of stemmers, Paice has defined a stemming performance measure called Error Rate Relative to Truncation (ERRT) that can be used to compare stemming algorithms (Paice-94). The approach depends upon the ability to partition terms semantically and morphologically related to each other into "concept groups."   After applying a stemmer that is not perfect, concept groups may still contain multiple stems rather than one. This introduces an error reflected in the Understemming Index (UI). Also it is possible that the same stem is found in multiple groups. This error state is reflected in the Overstemming Index (OI). The worst case stemming algorithm is where words are stemmed via truncation to a word length (words shorter than the length are not truncated). UI and OI values can be calculated based upon truncated word lengths. The perfect case is where UI and OI equal zero. ERRT is then calculated as the distance from the origin to the (UI, OI) coordinate of the stemmer being evaluated (OP) versus the distance from the origin to the worst case intersection of the line generated by pure truncation (OT) (see Figure 4-4).

The values calculated are biased by the initial grouping of the test terms. Larger ERRT values occurs with looser grouping. For the particular test runs, the UI of the Porter Algorithm was greater than the UI of the Paice/Husk algorithms (Paice-90). The OI was largest for the Paice and the least for Porter. Finally, the ERRT of the Porter was greater than the Paice algorithm. These results suggest that the Paice algorithm appeared significantly better than the Porter algorithm. But the differences in objectives between the stemmers (Porter being a light stemmer - tries to avoid overstemming leaving understemming errors and Paice being the opposite, a heavy stemmer) makes comparison less meaningful. While this approach to stemmer evaluation requires additional work to remove imprecisions and provide a common comparison framework, it provides a mechanism to develop a baseline to discuss future developments.

The comparisons by Frakes and Paice support the intuitive feeling that stemming as a generalization of processing tokens for a particular concept (word) can only help in recall.   In experiments, stemming has never been proven to significantly improve recall (Harman-91). Stemming can potentially reduce

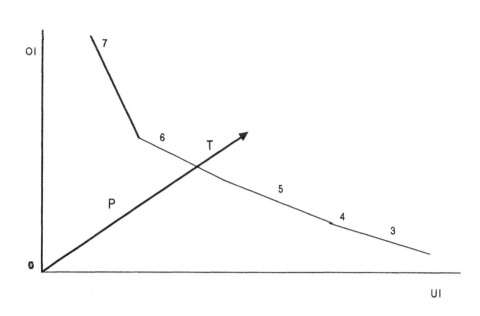

Figure 4.4 Computation of ERRT value

precision. The impact on precision can be minimized by the use of ranking items based upon all the terms in the query, categorization of terms and selective exclusion of some terms from stemming. Unless the user is very restrictive in the query , the impact of the other search terms and those expanded automatically by the system ameliorates the effects of generalization caused by stemming. Stemming in large databases should not be viewed as a significant compression technique to save on storage. Its major advantage is in the significant reduction of dictionary sizes and therefore a possible reduction in the processing time for each search term.

4.3   Inverted File Structure

The most common data structure used in both database management and Information Retrieval Systems is the inverted file structure. Inverted file structures are composed of three basic files: the document file, the inversion lists (sometimes called posting files) and the dictionary. The name "inverted file" comes from its underlying methodology of storing an inversion of the documents: inversion of the document from the perspective that, for each word, a list of documents in which the word is found in is stored (the inversion list for that word). Each document in the system is given a unique numerical identifier. It is that identifier that is stored in the inversion list. The way to locate the inversion list for a particular word is via the Dictionary. The Dictionary is typically a sorted list of all unique words (processing tokens) in the system and a pointer to the location of its inversion list (see Figure 4.5). Dictionaries can also store other information used in query optimization such as the length of inversion lists.

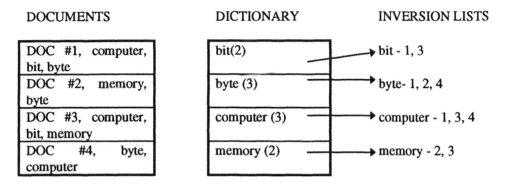

DOCUMENTS   DICTIONARY   INVERSION LISTS

DOC #1, computer, bit, byte	bit(2)	bit - 1, 3
DOC #2, memory, byte	byte (3)	byte- 1, 2, 4
DOC #3, computer, bit, memory	computer (3)	computer - 1, 3, 4
DOC #4, byte, computer	memory (2)	memory - 2, 3

Figure 4.5 Inverted File Structure

Additional information may be used from the item to increase precision and provide a more optimum inversion list file structure. For example, if zoning is used, the dictionary may be partitioned by zone. There could be a dictionary and set of inversion lists for the "Abstract" zone in an item and another dictionary and set of inversion lists for the "Main Body" zone. This increases the overhead when a user wants to search the complete item versus restricting the search to a specific zone. Another typical optimization occurs when the inversion list only contains one or two entries. Those entries can be stored as part of the dictionary. The inversion list contains the document identifier for each document in which the word is found. To support proximity, contiguous word phrases and term weighting algorithms, all occurrences of a word are stored in the inversion list along with the word position. Thus if the word "bit" was the tenth, twelfth and eighteenth word in document #1, then the inversion list would appear:

bit - 1(10), 1(12), 1(18)

Weights can also be stored in inversion lists. Words with special characteristics are frequently stored in their own dictionaries to allow for optimum internal representation and manipulation (e.g., dates which require date ranging and numbers).

When a search is performed, the inversion lists for the terms in the query are located and the appropriate logic is applied between inversion lists. The result is a final hit list of items that satisfy the query. For systems that support ranking, the list is reorganized into ranked order. The document numbers are used to retrieve the documents from the Document File. Using the inversion lists in Figure

4-5, the query (bit AND computer) would use the Dictionary to find the inversion lists for "bit" and "computer." These two lists would be logically ANDed: (1,3) AND (1,3,4) resulting in the final Hit list containing (1,3).

Rather than using a dictionary to point to the inversion list, B-trees can be used. The inversion lists may be at the leaf level or referenced in higher level pointers. Figure 4.6 shows how the words in Figure 4.5 would appear. A B-tree of order m is defined as:

A root node with between 2 and 2m keys

All other internal nodes have between m and 2m keys

All keys are kept in order from smaller to larger

All leaves are at the same level or differ by at most one level.

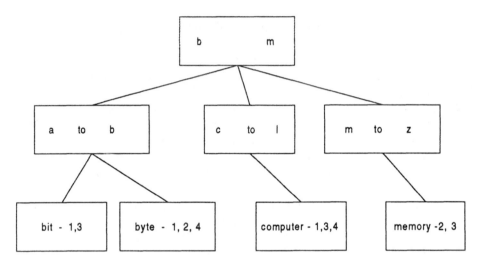

Figure 4-6 B-Tree Inversion Lists

Cutting and Pedersen described use of B-trees as an efficient inverted file storage mechanism for data that undergoes heavy updates (Cutting-90).

The nature of information systems is that items are seldom if ever modified once they are produced. Most commercial systems take advantage of this fact by allowing document files and their associated inversion lists to grow to a certain maximum size and then to freeze them, starting a new structure. Each of these databases of document file, dictionary, inversion lists is archived and made available for a user's query. This has the advantage that for queries only interested in more recent information, only the latest databases need to be searched. Since older items are seldom deleted or modified, the archived databases may be permanently backed-up, thus saving on operations overhead. Starting a new inverted database has significant overhead in adding new words and inversion lists until the frequently found words are added to the dictionary and inversion lists. Previous knowledge of archived databases can be used to establish an existing dictionary and inversion structure at the start of a new database, thus saving significant overhead during the initial adding of new documents[2].

Inversion lists structures are used because they provide optimum performance in searching large databases. The optimality comes from the minimization of data flow in resolving a query. Only data directly related to the query are retrieved from secondary storage. Also there are many techniques that can be used to optimize the resolution of the query based upon information maintained in the dictionary.

Inversion list file structures are well suited to store concepts and their relationships. Each inversion list can be thought of as representing a particular concept. The inversion list is then a concordance of all of the items that contain that concept. Finer resolution of concepts can additionally be maintained by storing locations with an item and weights of the item in the inversion lists. With this information, relationships between concepts can be determined as part of search algorithms (see Chapter 7). Location of concepts is made easy by their listing in the dictionary and inversion lists. For Natural Language Processing algorithms, other structures may be more appropriate or required in addition to inversion lists for maintaining the required semantic and syntactic information.

4.4 N-Gram Data Structures

N-Grams can be viewed as a special technique for conflation (stemming) and as a unique data structure in information systems. N-Grams are a fixed length consecutive series of "n" characters. Unlike stemming that generally tries to determine the stem of a word that represents the semantic meaning of the word, n-grams do not care about semantics. Instead they are algorithmically based upon a fixed number of characters. The searchable data structure is transformed into overlapping n-grams, which are then used to create the searchable database. Examples of bigrams, trigrams and pentagrams are given in Figure 4.7 for the word phrase "sea colony." For n-grams, with n greater than two, some systems allow interword symbols to be part of the n-gram set usually excluding the single character with interword symbol option. The symbol # is used to represent the interword symbol which is anyone of a set of symbols (e.g., blank, period, semicolon, colon, etc.). Each of the n-grams created becomes a separate

---

[2] The INQUIRE DBMS provides this feature.

processing tokens and are searchable. It is possible that the same n-gram can be created multiple times from a single word.

se ea co ol lo on ny	Bigrams (no interword symbols)
sea col olo lon ony	Trigrams (no interword symbols)
#se sea ea# #co col olo lon ony ny#	Trigrams (with interword symbol #)
#sea# #colo colon olony lony#	Pentagrams (with interword symbol #)

Figure 4.7   Bigrams, Trigrams and Pentagrams for "sea colony"

4.4.1 History

The first use of n-grams dates to World War II when it was used by cryptographers. Fletcher Pratt states that "with the backing of bigram and trigram tables any cryptographer can dismember an simple substitution cipher" (Pratt-42). Use of bigrams was described by Adamson as a method for conflating terms (Adamson-74). It does not follow the normal definition of stemming because what is produced by creating n-grams are word fragments versus semantically meaningful word stems. It is this characteristic of mapping longer words into shorter n-gram fragments that seems more appropriately classified as a data structure process than a stemming process.

Another major use of n-grams (in particular trigrams) is in spelling error detection and correction (Angell-83, McIllroy-82, Morris-75, Peterson-80, Thorelli-62, Wang-77, and Zamora-81). Most approaches look at the statistics on probability of occurrence of n-grams (trigrams in most approaches) in the English vocabulary and indicate any word that contains non-existent to seldom used n-grams as a potential erroneous word. Damerau specified four categories of spelling errors (Damerau-64) as shown in Figure 4.8. Using the classification scheme, Zamora showed trigram analysis provided a viable data structure for identifying misspellings and transposed characters. This impacts information systems as a possible basis for identifying potential input errors for correction as a procedure within the normalization process (see Chapter 1). Frequency of occurrence of n-gram patterns also can be used for identifying the language of an item (Damashek-95, Cohen-95).

Error Category	Example
Single Character Insertion	comp<u>uu</u>ter
Single Character Deletion	comp<u>t</u>er
Single Character Substitution	comp<u>i</u>ter
Transposition of two adjacent characters	comp<u>tu</u>er

Figure 4.8 Categories of Spelling Errors

In information retrieval, trigrams have been used for text compression (Wisn-87) and to manipulate the length of index terms (Will-79, Schek-78, Schuegraf-76). D'Amore and Mah (D'Amore-85) used a variety of different n-grams as index elements for inverted file systems they implemented. They have also been the core data structure to encode profiles for the Logicon LMDS system (Yochum-95) used for Selective Dissemination of Information. For retrospective search, the Acquaintance System uses n-grams to store the searchable document file (Damashek-95, Huffman-95) for retrospective search of large textual databases.

4.4.2 N-Gram Data Structure

As shown in Figure 4.7, an n-gram is a data structure that ignores words and treats the input as a continuous data, optionally limiting its processing by interword symbols. The data structure consists of fixed length overlapping symbol segments that define the searchable processing tokens. These tokens have logical linkages to all the items in which the tokens are found. Inversion lists, document vectors (described in Chapter 5) and other proprietary data structures are used to store the linkage data structure and are used in the search process. In some cases just the least frequently occurring n-gram is kept as part of a first pass search process (Yochum-85). Examples of these implementations are found in Chapter 5.

The choice of the fixed length word fragment size has been studied in many contexts. Yochum and D'Amore investigated the impacts of different values for "n." Fatah Comlekoglu (Comlekoglu-90) investigated n-gram data structures using an inverted file system for n=2 to n=26. Trigrams (n-grams of length 3) were determined to be the optimal length, trading off information versus size of data structure. The Aquaintance System uses longer n-grams, ignoring word boundaries. The advantage of n-grams is that they place a finite limit on the number of searchable tokens.

$$MaxSeg_n = (\lambda)^n$$

The maximum number of unique n-grams that can be generated, MaxSeg, can be calculated as a function of n which is the length of the n-grams, and λ which is the number of processable symbols from the alphabet (i.e., non-interword symbols).

Although there is a savings in the number of unique processing tokens and implementation techniques allow for fast processing on minimally sized machines, false hits can occur under some architectures. For example, a system that uses trigrams and does not include interword symbols or the character position of the n-gram in an item finds an item containing "retain detail" when searching for "retail" (i.e., all of the trigrams associated with "retail" are created in the processing of "retain detail"). Inclusion of interword symbols would not have helped in this example. Inclusion of character position of the n-gram would have discovered that the n-grams "ret," "eta," "tai," "ail" that define "retail" are not all consecutively starting within one character of each other. The longer the n-gram, the less likely this type error is to occur because of more information in the word fragment. But the longer the n-gram, the more it provides the same result as full word data structures since most words are included within a single n-gram. Another disadvantage of n-grams is the increased size of inversion lists (or other data structures) that store the linkage data structure. In effect, use of n-grams expands the number of processing tokens by a significant factor. The average word in the English language is between six and seven characters in length. Use of trigrams increases the number of processing tokens by a factor of five (see Figure 4.7) if interword symbols are not included. Thus the inversion lists increase by a factor of five.

Because of the processing token bounds of n-gram data structures, optimized performance techniques can be applied in mapping items to an n-gram searchable structure and in query processing. There is no semantic meaning in a particular n-gram since it is a fragment of processing token and may not represent a concept. Thus n-grams are a poor representation of concepts and their relationships. But the juxtaposition of n-grams can be used to equate to standard word indexing, achieving the same levels of recall and within 85 per cent precision levels with a significant improvement in performance (Adams-92). Vector representations of the n-grams from an item can be used to calculate the similarity between items.

4.5 PAT Data Structure

Using n-grams with interword symbols included between valid processing tokens equates to a continuous text input data structure that is being indexed in contiguous "n" character tokens. A different view of addressing a continuous text input data structure comes from PAT trees and PAT arrays. The input stream is transformed into a searchable data structure consisting of substrings. The original concepts of PAT tree data structures were described as Patricia trees (Flajolet-86, Frakes-92, Gonnet-83, Knuth-73, and Morrison-68) and have gained new momentum as a possible structure for searching text and images (Gonnet-88) and applications in genetic databases (Manber-90). The name PAT is short for PAtricia Trees (PATRICIA stands for Practical Algorithm To Retrieve Information Coded In Alphanumerics.)

In creation of PAT trees each position in the input string is the anchor point for a sub-string that starts at that point and includes all new text up to the end of the input. All substrings are unique. This view of text lends itself to many different search processing structures. It fits within the general architectures of hardware text search machines and parallel processors (see Chapter 9). A substring can start at any point in the text and can be uniquely indexed by its starting location and length. If all strings are to the end of the input, only the starting location is needed since the length is the difference from the location and the total length of the item. It is possible to have a substring go beyond the length of the input stream by adding additional null characters. These substrings are called sistring (semi-infinite string). Figure 4.9 shows some possible sistrings for an input text.

A PAT tree is an unbalanced, binary digital tree defined by the sistrings. The individual bits of the sistrings decide the branching patterns with zeros branching left and ones branching right. PAT trees also allow each node in the tree to specify which bit is used to determine the branching via bit position or the

Text	Economics for Warsaw is complex.
sistring 1	Economics for Warsaw is complex.
sistring 2	conomics for Warsaw is complex.
sistring 5	omics for Warsaw is complex.
sistring 10	for Warsaw is complex.
sistring 20	w is complex.
sistring 30	ex.

Figure 4.9 Examples of sistrings

number of bits to skip from the parent node. This is useful in skipping over levels that do not require branching.

The key values are stored at the leaf nodes (bottom nodes) in the PAT Tree. For a text input of size "n" there are "n" leaf nodes and "n-1" at most higher level nodes. It is possible to place additional constraints on sistrings for the leaf nodes. We may be interested in limiting our searches to word boundaries. Thus we could limit our sistrings to those that are immediately after an interword symbol. Figure 4.10 gives an example of the sistrings used in generating a PAT

INPUT		100110001101
	sistring 1	1001....
	sistring 2	001100...
	sistring 3	01100....
	sistring 4	11.......
	sistring 5	1000...
	sistring 6	000.....
	sistring 7	001101
	sistring 8	01101

Figure 4.10 Sistrings for input "100110001101"

tree. If the binary representations of "h" is (100), "o" is (110), "m" is (001) and "e" is (101) then the word "home" produces the input 100110001101.... Using the sistrings, the full PAT binary tree is shown in Figure 4.11. A more compact tree where skip values are in the intermediate nodes is shown in Figure 4.12. In this version the value in the intermediate nodes (indicated by rectangles) is the number of bits to skip until the next bit to compare that causes differences between similar terms. This final version saves space, but requires comparing a search value to the leaf node (in an oval) contents to ensure the skipped bits match the search term (i.e., skipped bits are not compared).

The search terms are also represented by their binary representation and the PAT trees for the sistrings are compared to the search terms looking for matches.

As noted in Chapter 2, one of the most common classes of searches is prefix searches. PAT trees are ideally constructed for this purpose because each sub-tree contains all the sistrings for the prefix defined up to that node in the tree structure. Thus all the leaf nodes after the prefix node define the sistrings that satisfy the prefix search criteria. This logically sorted order of PAT trees also facilitates range searches since it is easy to determine the sub-trees constrained by the range values. If the total input stream is used in defining the PAT tree, then suffix, imbedded string, and fixed length masked searches (see Section 2.1.5) are all easy because the given characters uniquely define the path from the root node to where the existence of sistrings need to be validated. Fuzzy searches are very difficult because large number of possible sub-trees could match the search term.

A detailed discussion on searching PAT trees and their representation as an array is provided by Gonnet, Baeza-Yates and Snider (Gonnet-92). In their comparison to Signature and Inversion files, they concluded that PAT arrays have more accuracy than Signature files and provide the ability to string searches that

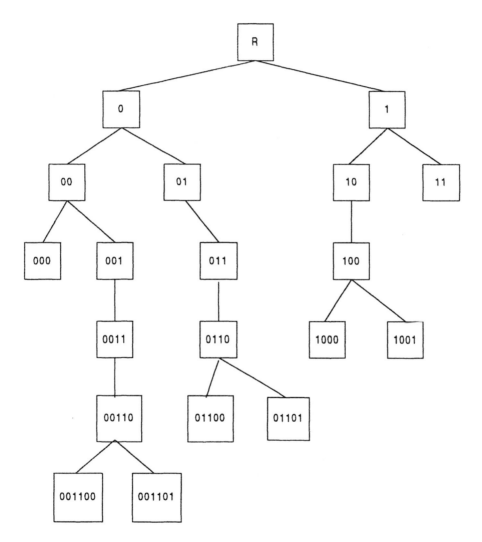

Figure 4.11 PAT Binary Tree for input "100110001101"

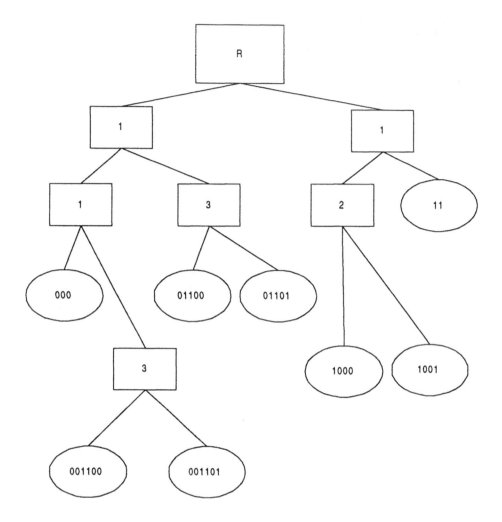

Figure 4. 12   PAT Tree skipping bits for "100110001101"

are inefficient in inverted files (e.g., suffix searches, approximate string searches, longest repetition).

Pat Trees (and arrays) provide an alternative structure if string searching is the goal. They store the text in an alternative structure supporting string manipulation. The structure does not have facilities to store more abstract concepts and their relationships associated with an item. The structure has interesting potential applications, but is not used in any major commercial products at this time.

4.6 Signature File Structure

The goal of a signature file structure is to provide a fast test to eliminate the majority of items that are not related to a query. The items that satisfy the test can either be evaluated by another search algorithm to eliminate additional false hits or delivered to the user to review. The text of the items is represented in a highly compressed form that facilitates the fast test. Because file structure is highly compressed and unordered, it requires significantly less space than an inverted file structure and new items can be concatenated to the end of the structure versus the significant inversion list update. Since items are seldom deleted from information data bases, it is typical to leave deleted items in place and mark them as deleted. Signature file search is a linear scan of the compressed version of items producing a response time linear with respect to file size.

The surrogate signature search file is created via superimposed coding (Faloutsos-85, Moders-49). The coding is based upon words in the item. The words are mapped into a "word signature." A word signature is a fixed length code with a fixed number of bits set to "1." The bit positions that are set to one are determined via a hash function of the word. The word signatures are ORed together to create the signature of an item. To avoid signatures being too dense with "1"s, a maximum number of words is specified and an item is partitioned into blocks of that size. In Figure 4.13 the block size is set at five words, the code length is 16 bits and the number of bits that are allowed to be "1" for each word is five.

TEXT: Computer Science graduate students study (assume block size is
five words)

WORD	Signature
Computer	0001 0110 0000 0110
Science	1001 0000 1110 0000
graduate	1000 0101 0100 0010
students	0000 0111 1000 0100
study	0000 0110 0110 0100
Block Signature	1001 0111 1110 0110

Figure 4.13 Superimposed Coding

The words in a query are mapped to their signature. Search is accomplished by template matching on the bit positions specified by the words in the query.

The signature file can be stored as a signature with each row representing a signature block. Associated with each row is a pointer to the original text block.

A design objective of a signature file system is trading off the size of the data structure versus the density of the final created signatures. Longer code lengths reduce the probability of collision in hashing the words (i.e., two different words hashing to the same value). Fewer bits per code reduce the effect of a code word pattern being in the final block signature even though the word is not in the item. For example, if the signature for the word "hard" is 1000 0111 0010 0000, it incorrectly matches the block signature in Figure 4.13 (false hit). In a study by Faloutous and Christodoulakis (Faloutous-87) it was shown that if compression is applied to the final data structure, the optimum number of bits per word is one. This then takes on the appearance of a binary coded vector for each item, where each position in the vector represents the existence of a word in the item. This approach requires the maximum code length but ensures that there are not any false hits unless two words hash to the same value.

Search of the signature matrix requires O(N) search time. To reduce the search time the signature matrix is partitioned horizontally. One of the earliest techniques hashes the block signature to a specific slot. If a query has less than the number of words in a block it maps to a number of possible slots rather than just one. The number of slots decreases exponentially as the number of terms increases (Gustafson-71). Another approach maps the signatures into an index sequential file, where, for example, the first "n" bits of the signature is used as the index to the block of signatures that will be compared sequentially to the query (Lee-89). Other techniques are two level signatures (Sacks-Davis-83, Sacks-Davis-88) and use of B-tree structures with similar signatures clustered at leaf nodes (Deppisch-86).

Another implementation approach takes advantage of the fact that searches are performed on the columns of the signature matrix, ignoring those columns that are not indicated by hashing of any of the search terms. Thus the signature matrix may be stored in column order versus row order (Faloutsos-88, Lin-88, Roberts-79), called vertical partitioning. This is in effect storing the signature matrix using an inverted file structure. The major overhead comes from updates, since new "1"s have to be added to each inverted column representing a signature in the new item.

Signature files provide a practical solution for storing and locating information in a number of different situations. Faloutsos summarizes the environments that signature files have been applied as medium size databases, databases with low frequency of terms, WORM devices, parallel processing machines, and distributed environments (Faloutsos-92).

4.7 Hypertext Data Structure

The advent of the Internet and its exponential growth and wide acceptance as a new global information network has introduced a new mechanism for representing information. This structure is called hypertext and differs from traditional information storage data structures in format and use. The hypertext is stored in Hypertext Markup Language (HTML). HTML is an evolving standard as new requirements for display of items on the Internet are identified and implemented.

4.7.1 Definition of Hypertext Structure

The Hypertext data structure is used extensively in the Internet environment and requires an electronic media storage for the item. Hypertext allows one item to reference another item via an imbedded pointer. Each separate item is called a node and the reference pointer is called a link. The referenced item can be of the same or a different data type than the original (e.g., a textual item references a photograph). Each node is displayed by a viewer that is defined for the file type associated with the node.

For example, Hypertext Markup Language (HTML) defines the internal structure for information exchange across the World Wide Web on the Internet. A document is composed of the text of the item along with HTML tags that describe how to display the document. Tags are formatting or structural keywords contained between less-than, greater than symbols (e.g., <title>, <strong> meaning display prominently). The HTML tag associated with hypertext linkages is <a href= ...#NAME /a> where "a" and "/a" are an anchor start tag and anchor end tag denoting the text that the user can activate. "href" is the hypertext reference containing either a file name if the referenced item is on this node or an address (Uniform Resource Locator - URL) and a file name if it is on another node. "#NAME" defines a destination point other than the top of the item to go to. The URL has three components: the access method the client used to retrieve the item, the Internet address of the server where the item is stored, and the address of the item at the server (i.e., the file including the directory it is in). For example, the URL for the HTML specification appears:

http://info.cern.ch/hypertext/WWW/MarkUp/HTML.html

"HTTP" stands for the Hypertext Transfer Protocol which is the access protocol used to retrieve the item in HTML. Other Internet protocols are used for other activities such as file transfer (ftp://), a specific text search system (gopher://), remote logon (tenet//) and collaborative newsgroups (news://). The destination point is found in "info.cern.ch" which is the name of the "info" machine at CERN with "ch" being Switzerland, and "/hypertext/WWW/MarkUP/HTML.html" defines where to find the file HTML.html. Figure 4.14 shows an example of a segment of a HTML document. Most of the formatting tags indicated by < > are not described, being out of the scope of this text, but detailed descriptions can be found in the hundreds of books available on HTML. The <a href= ... > are the previously described hypertext linkages.

An item can have many hypertext linkages. Thus, from any item there are multiple paths that can be followed in addition to skipping over the linkages to continue sequential reading of the item. This is similar to the decision a reader makes upon reaching a footnote, whether to continue reading or skip to the footnote. Hypertext is sometimes called a "generalized footnote."

In a conventional item the physical and logical structure are closely related. The item is sequential with imbedded citations to other distinct items or

```
<CENTER>
<IMG SC="/images/home_iglo.jpg" WIDTH=468 HEIGHT=107
BORDER=0 ALT="WELCOME TO NETSCAPE><BR>
<P>
<DL>
<A HREF="/comprod/mirror/index.html">
<DD>
```

The beta testing is over: please read our report <A HREF="http://www.charm.net/doc/charm/report/theme.html"> and your can find more references at HREF="http://www.charm.net/doc/charm/results/tests.html">

Figure 4.14 Example of Segment of HTML

locations in the item. From the author's perspective, the substantive semantics lie in the sequential presentation of the information. Hypertext is a non-sequential directed graph structure, where each node contains its own information. The author assumes the reader can follow the linked data as easily as following the sequential presentation. A node may have several outgoing links, each of which is then associated with some smaller part of the node called an anchor. When an anchor is activated, the associated link is followed to the destination node, thus navigating the hypertext network. The organizational and reference structure of a conventional item is fixed at printing time while hypertext nodes and links can be changed dynamically. New linkages can be added and the information at a node can change without modification to the item referencing it.

Conventional items are read sequentially by a user. In a hypertext environment, the user "navigates" through the node network by following links. This is the defining capability that allows hypertext to manage loosely structured information. Each thread through different nodes could represent a different concept with additional detail. In a small and familiar network the navigation works well, but in a large information space, it is possible for the user to become disoriented. This issue is discussed in detail in Chapters 5, 7, and 8.

Quite often hypertext references are used to include information that is other than text (e.g., graphics, audio, photograph, video) in a text item. The multiple different uses for hypertext references are evolving as more experience is gained with them. When the hypertext is logically part of the item, such as in a graphic, the referenced file is usually resident at the same physical location. When other items created by other users are referenced, they frequently are located at other physical sites. When items are deleted or moved, there is no mechanism to update other items that reference them. Linkage integrity is a major issue in use of hypertext linkages.

4.7.2 Hypertext History

Although information sciences is just starting to address the impact of the hypertext data structure, the concept of hypertext has been around for over 50 years. In 1945 an article written by Vannevar Bush in 1933 was published describing the Memex (memory extender) system (Bush-67). It was a microfilm based system that would allow the user to store much of the information from the scientific explosion of the 1940s on microfilm and retrieve it at multiple readers at the user's desk via individual links. The term "hypertext" came from Ted Nelson in 1965 (Nelson-74). Nelson's vision of all the world's literature being interlinked via hypertext references is part of his Xanadu System. The lack of cost effective computers with sufficient speed and memory to implement hypertext effectively was one of the main inhibitors to its development. One of the first commercial uses of a hypertext system was the mainframe system, Hypertext Editing System, developed at Brown University by Andres van Dam and later sold to Houston Manned Spacecraft Center where it was used for Apollo mission documentation (van Dam-88). Other systems such as the Aspen system at MIT, the KMS system at Carnegie Mellon, the Hyperties system at the University of Maryland and the Notecards system developed at Xerox PARC advanced the hypertext concepts providing hypertext (and hypermedia) systems. HyperCard, delivered with Macintosh computers, was the first widespread hypertext production product. It had a simple metalanguage (HyperTalk) that facilitated authoring hypertext items. It also provided a large number of graphical user interface elements (e.g., buttons, hands,) that facilitated the production of sophisticated items.

Hypertext became more available in the early 1990's via its use in CD-ROMs for a variety of educational and entertainment products. Its current high level of popularity originated with it being part of the specification of the World Wide Web by the CERN (the European Center for Nuclear Physics Research) in Geneva, Switzerland. The Mosaic browser, freely available from CERN on the Internet, gave everyone who had access the ability to receive and display hypertext documents.

4.8 Summary

Data structures provide the implementation basis of search techniques in Information Retrieval Systems. They may be searching the text directly, as in use of signature and possibly PAT trees, or providing the structure to hold the searchable data structure created by processing the text in items. The most important data structure to understand is the inverted file system. It has the greatest applicability in information systems. The use of n-grams has also found successes in a limited number of commercial systems. Even though n-grams have demonstrated successes in finding information, it is not a structure that lends itself to representing the concepts in an item. There is no association of an n-gram with a semantic unit (e.g., a word or word stem). Judging the relative importance (ranking) of items is much harder to accomplish under this data structure and the algorithmic options are very limited.

PAT and Signature data file structures have found successful implementations in certain bounded search domains. Both of these techniques encounter significant problems in handling very large databases of textual items. The Hypertext data structure is the newest structure to be considered from an Information Retrieval System perspective. It certainly can be mathematically mapped to linked lists and networks. But the model of how dependencies between items as hyperlinks are resolved is just being considered. The future high usage of this structure in information systems make its understanding important in finding relevant information on the Internet. Marchionini and Shneiderman believe that hypertext will be used in conjunction with full text search tools (Marchionini-88).

The stemming discussed in this chapter has the greatest effect on the human resources it takes to find relevant information. Stemming can increase the ability of the system to find relevant item by generalizing many words to a single representation. But this process reduces precision. Enough information has not been gathered to practically trade off the value of the increase in recall versus the decrease in precision for different degrees of stemming.

EXERCISES

1. Describe the similarities and differences between term stemming algorithms and n-grams. Describe how they affect precision and recall.

2. Apply the Porter stemming steps to the following words: irreplaceable, informative, activation, and triplicate.

3. Assuming the database has the following words: act, able, arch, car, court, waste, wink, write, writer, wrinkle. Show the successor variety for the word "writeable." Apply the cutoff method, peak and plateau method and complete

word method to determine possible stems for the word.   Explain your rationale for the cutoff method.

4.   Assuming a term is on the average 6 characters long, calculate the size of the inversion lists for each of the sources in Table 1.1, Distribution of words in TREC Database. Assume that 30 per cent of the words in any item are unique. What is the impact on the calculation if the system has to provide proximity versus no proximity.   Assume 4 bytes is needed for the unique number assigned to each item.

5.   Describe how a bigram data structure would be used to search for the search term "computer science"   (NOTE: the search term is a contiguous word phrase). What are the possible sources of errors that could cause non-relevant items to be retrieved?

6.   The following data structure comes from creating a PAT tree for the sentence "This is the house that Jack built." Ignoring upper and lower case and using 5 bits to represent the letters of the alphabet, explain why the tree was built in this fashion. The first word "This is called the header and is not part of the binary decisions of the PAT tree. Keep in mind that "to the right" is a 1 and "to the left" is a 0.   In general only the first characters are required to determine the direction of the next term.

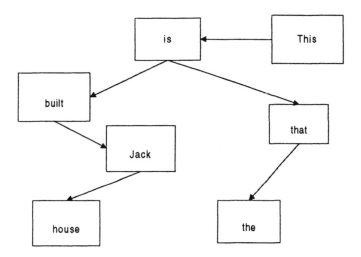

The skip value for all of the terms is 1 except for the term Jack where it is 2 and the term "that" where it is 11. Explain why the skip value for "that" is 11.

7. What is the effect of changing the number of bits that are allowed to be a one in a signature file assuming the block size and code length remain constant?

8. How are hyperlinks different from all of the other data structures described in Chapter 4? How do the differences affect their use in Information Retrieval Systems?

5 Automatic Indexing

Chapter 3 introduced the concept and objectives of indexing along with its history. This chapter focuses on the process and algorithms to perform indexing. The indexing process is a transformation of an item that extracts the semantics of the topics discussed in the item. The extracted information is used to create the processing tokens and the searchable data structure. The semantics of the item not only refers to the subjects discussed in the item but also in weighted systems, the depth to which the subject is discussed. The index can be based on the full text of the item, automatic or manual generation of a subset of terms/phrases to represent the item, natural language representation of the item or abstraction to concepts in the item. The results of this process are stored in one of the data structures (typically inverted data structure) described in Chapter 4. Distinctions, where appropriate, are made between what is logically kept in an index versus what is physically stored.

This text includes chapters on Automatic Indexing and User Search techniques. There is a major dependency between the search techniques to be implemented and the indexing process that stores the information required to execute the search. This text categorizes the indexing techniques into statistical, natural language, concept, and hypertext linkages. Insight into the rationale for this classification is presented in Section 5.1.

5.1 Classes of Automatic Indexing

Automatic indexing is the process of analyzing an item to extract the information to be permanently kept in an index. This process is associated with the generation of the searchable data structures associated with an item. Figure 1.5 Data Flow in an Information Processing System is reproduced here as Figure 5.1 to show where the indexing process is in the overall processing of an item. The figure is expanded to show where the search process relates to the indexing process. The left side of the figure including Identify Processing Tokens, Apply Stop Lists, Characterize tokens, Apply Stemming and Create Searchable Data Structure is all part of the indexing process. All systems go through an initial stage of zoning (described in Section 1.3.1) and identifying the processing tokens used to create the index. Filters, such as stop lists and stemming algorithms, are frequently applied to reduce the number of tokens to be processed. The next step depends upon the search strategy of a particular system. Search strategies can be classified as statistical, natural language, and concept. An index is the data structure created to support the search strategy.

Statistical strategies cover the broadest range of indexing techniques and are the most prevalent in commercial systems. The basis for a statistical approach is use of frequency of occurrence of events. The events usually are related to occurrences of processing tokens (words/phrases) within documents and within the database. The words/phrases are the domain of searchable values. The statistics that are applied to the event data are probabilistic, Bayesian, vector space, neural net. The static approach stores a single statistic, such as how often each word occurs in an item, that is used in generating relevance scores after a standard Boolean search. Probabilistic indexing stores the information that are used in calculating a probability that a particular item satisfies (i.e., is relevant to) a particular query. Bayesian and vector approaches store information used in generating a relative confidence level of an item's relevance to a query. It can be argued that the Bayesian approach is probabilistic, but to date the developers of this approach are more focused on a good relative relevance value than producing and absolute probability. Neural networks are dynamic learning structures that are discussed under concept indexing where they are used to determine concept classes.

Natural Language approaches perform the similar processing token identification as in statistical techniques, but then additionally perform varying levels of natural language parsing of the item. This parsing disambiguates the context of the processing tokens and generalizes to more abstract concepts within an item (e.g., present, past, future actions). This additional information is stored within the index to be used to enhance the search precision.

Concept indexing uses the words within an item to correlate to concepts discussed in the item. This is a generalization of the specific words to values used to index the item. When generating the concept classes automatically, there may not be a name applicable to the concept but just a statistical significance.

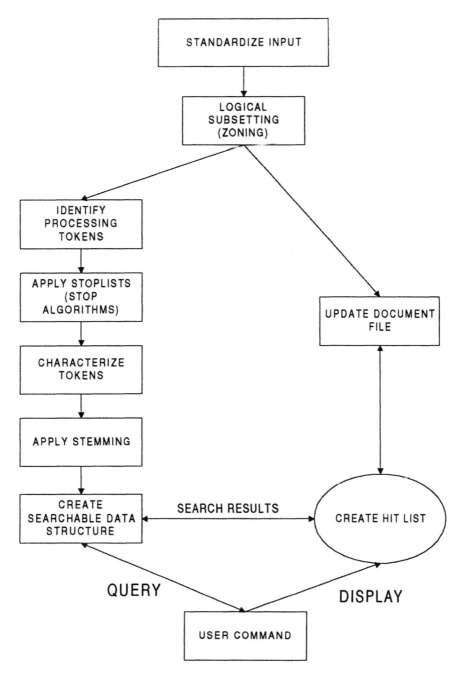

Figure 5.1 Data Flow in Information Processing System

Finally, a special class of indexing can be defined by creation of hypertext linkages. These linkages provide virtual threads of concepts between items versus directly defining the concept within an item.

Each technique has its own strengths and weaknesses. Current evaluations from TREC conferences (see Chapter 10) show that to maximize location of relevant items, applying several different algorithms to the same corpus provides the optimum results, but the storage and processing overhead is significant.

5.2 Statistical Indexing

Statistical indexing uses frequency of occurrence of events to calculate a number that is used to indicate the potential relevance of an item. One approach used in search of older systems does not use the statistics to aid in the initial selection, but uses them to assist in calculating a relevance value of each item for ranking. The documents are found by a normal Boolean search and then statistical calculations are performed on the Hit file, ranking the output (e.g., term frequency algorithms). Since the index does not contain any special data, these techniques are discussed in Chapter 7 under ranking.

Probabilistic systems attempt to calculate a probability value that should be invariant to both calculation method and text corpora. This allows easy integration of the final results when searches are performed across multiple databases and use different search algorithms. A probability of 50 per cent would mean that if enough items are reviewed, on the average one half of the reviewed items are relevant. The Bayesian and Vector approaches calculate a relative relevance value (e.g., confidence level) that a particular item is relevant. Quite often term distributions across the searchable database are used in the calculations. An issue that continues to be researched is how to merge results, even from the same search algorithm, from multiple databases. The problem is compounded when an attempt is made to merge the results from different search algorithms. This would not be a problem if true probabilities were calculated.

5.2.1 Probabilistic Weighting

The probabilistic approach is based upon direct application of the theory of probability to information retrieval systems. This has the advantage of being able to use the developed formal theory of probability to direct the algorithmic development. It also leads to an invariant result that facilitates integration of results from different databases. The use of probability theory is a natural choice because it is the basis of evidential reasoning (i.e., drawing conclusions from evidence). This is summarized by the Probability Ranking Principle (PRP) and its Plausible Corollary (Cooper-94):

HYPOTHESIS: If a reference retrieval system's response to each request is a ranking of the documents in the collection in order of decreasing probability of usefulness to the user who submitted the request, where the probabilities are estimated as accurately as possible on the basis of whatever data is available for this purpose, then the overall effectiveness of the system to its users is the best obtainable on the basis of that data.

PLAUSIBLE COROLLARY: The most promising source of techniques for estimating the probabilities of usefulness for output ranking in IR is standard probability theory and statistics.

There are several factors that make this hypothesis and its corollary difficult (Gordon-92, Gordon-91, Robertson-77). Probabilities are usually based upon a binary condition; an item is relevant or not. But in information systems the relevance of an item is a continuous function from non-relevant to absolutely useful. A more complex theory of expected utility (Cooper-78) is needed to address this characteristic. Additionally, the output ordering by rank of items based upon probabilities, even if accurately calculated, may not be as optimal as that defined by some domain specific heuristic (Stirling-77). The domains in which probabilistic ranking are suboptimal are so narrowly focused as to make this a minor issue. But these issues mentioned are not as compelling as the benefit of a good probability value for ranking that would allow integration of results from multiple sources.

The source of the problems that arise in application of probability theory come from a lack of accurate data and simplifying assumptions that are applied to the mathematical model. If nothing else, these simplifying assumptions cause the results of probabilistic approaches in ranking items to be less accurate than other approaches. The advantage of the probabilistic approach is that it can accurately identify its weak assumptions and work to strengthen them. In many other approaches, the underlying weaknesses in assumptions are less obvious and harder to identify and correct. Even with the simplifying assumption, results from comparisons of approaches in the TREC conferences have shown that the probabilistic approaches, while not scoring highest, are competitive against all other approaches.

There are many different areas in which the probabilistic approach may be applied. The method of logistic regression is described as an example of how a probabilistic approach is applied to information retrieval (Gey-94). The approach starts by defining a "Model 0" system which exists before specific probabilistic models are applied. In a retrieval system there exist query terms q_i and document terms d_i, which have a set of attributes $(v_1, \ldots, v_n)$ from the query (e.g., counts of term frequency in the query), from the document (e.g., counts of term frequency in the document) and from the database (e.g., total number of documents in the database divided by the number of documents indexed by the term).

The logistic reference model uses a random sample of query-document-term triples for which binary relevance judgments have been made from a training sample. Log O is the logarithm of the odds (logodds) of relevance for term t_k which is present in document D_j and query Q_i:

$$\log(O(R \mid Q_i, D_j, t_k)) = c_0 + c_1 v_1 + \ldots + c_n v_n$$

The logarithm that the ith Query is relevant to the jth Document is the sum of the logodds for all terms:

$$\log(O(R \mid Q_i, D_j)) = \sum_{k=1}^{q} [\log(O(R \mid Q_i, D_j, t_k)) - \log(O(R))]$$

where $O(R)$ is the odds that a document chosen at random from the database is relevant to query Q_i. The coefficients c are derived using logistic regression which fits an equation to predict a dichotomous independent variable as a function of independent variables that show statistical variation (Hosmer-89). The inverse logistic transformation is applied to obtain the probability of relevance of a document to a query:

$$P(R \mid Q_i, D_j) = 1 \backslash (1 + e^{-\log(O(R \mid Q_i, D_j))})$$

The coefficients of the equation for logodds is derived for a particular database using a random sample of query-document-term-relevance quadruples and used to predict odds of relevance for other query-document pairs.

    Gey applied this methodology to the Cranfield Collection (Gey-94). The collection has 1400 items and 225 queries with known results. Additional attributes of relative frequency in the query (QRF), relative frequency in the document (DRF) and relative frequency of the term in all the documents (RFAD) were included, producing the following logodds formula:

$$Z_j = \log(O(R \mid t_j)) = c_0 + c_1 \log(QAF) + c_2 \log(QRF) + c_3 \log(DAF) + c_4 \log(DRF)$$

$$+ c_5 \log(IDF) + c_6 \log(RFAD)$$

where QAF, DAF, and IDF were previously defined, QRF = QAF\ (total number of terms in the query), DRF = DAF\(total number of words in the document) and RFAD = (total number of term occurrences in the database)\ (total number of all words in the database). Logs are used to reduce the impact of frequency information; then smooth out skewed distributions. A higher maximum likelihood is attained for logged attributes.

    The coefficients and log $(O(R))$ were calculated creating the final formula for ranking for query vector $\bar{Q}$, which contains q terms:

$$\log(O(R \mid \vec{Q})) = -5.138 + \sum_{k=1}^{q} (Z_j + 5.138)$$

The logistic inference method was applied to the test database along with the Cornell SMART vector system which uses traditional term frequency, inverse document frequency and cosine relevance weighting formulas (see Section 5.2.2). The logistic inference method outperformed the vector method.

Thus the index that supports the calculations for the logistic reference model contains the $O(R)$ constant value (e.g., -5.138) along with the coefficients c_0 through c_6. Additionally, it needs to maintain the data to support DAF, DRF, IDF and RFAD. The values for QAF and QRF are derived from the query.

Attempts have been made to combine the results of different probabilistic techniques to get a more accurate value. The objective is have the strong points of different techniques compensate for weaknesses. To date this combination of probabilities using averages of Log-Odds has not produced better results and in many cases produced worse results (Hull-96).

5.2.2 Vector Weighting

One of the earliest systems that investigated statistical approaches to information retrieval was the SMART system at Cornell University (Buckley-95, Salton-83). The system is based upon a vector model. The semantics of every item are represented as a vector. A vector is a one-dimensional set of values, where the order/position of each value in the set is fixed and represents a particular domain. In information retrieval, each position in the vector typically represents a processing token. There are two approaches to the domain of values in the vector: binary and weighted. Under the binary approach, the domain contains the value of one or zero, with one representing the existence of the processing token in the item. In the weighted approach, the domain is typically the set of all real positive numbers. The value for each processing token represents the relative importance of that processing token in representing the semantics of the item. Figure 5.2 shows how an item that discusses petroleum refineries in Mexico would be represented . In the example, the major topics discussed are indicated by the index terms for each column (i.e., Petroleum, Mexico, Oil, Taxes, Refineries and Shipping).

Binary vectors require a decision process to determine if the degree that a particular processing token represents the semantics of an item is sufficient to include it in the vector. In the example for Figure 5.2, a five-page item may have had only one sentence like "Standard taxation of the shipment of the oil to refineries is enforced." For the binary vector, the concepts of "Tax" and "Shipment" are below the threshold of importance (e.g., assume threshold is 1.0)

	Petroleum	Mexico	Oil	Taxes	Refineries	Shipping
Binary	(1	, 1	, 1,	0 ,	1	, 0)
Weighted	(2.8	, 1.6	, 3.5,	.3 ,	3.1	, .1)

Figure 5.2 Binary and Vector Representation of an Item

and they not are included in the vector. A weighted vector acts the same as a binary vector but it provides a range of values that accommodates a variance in the value of the relative importance of a processing token in representing the semantics of the item. The use of weights also provides a basis for determining the rank of an item.

The vector approach allows for a mathematical and a physical representation using a vector space model. Each processing token can be considered another dimension in an item representation space. In Chapter 7 it is shown that a query can be represented as one more vector in the same n-dimensional space. Figure 5.3 shows a three-dimensional vector representation assuming there were only three processing tokens, Petroleum Mexico and Oil.

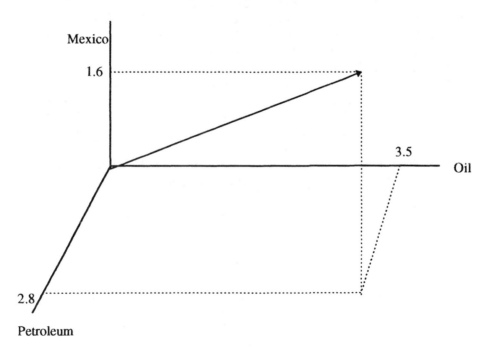

Figure 5.3 Vector Representation

There are many algorithms that can be used in calculating the weights used to represent a processing token. Part of the art in information retrieval is deriving changes to the basic algorithms to account for normalization (e.g., accounting for variances in number of words in items). The following subsections present the major algorithms starting with the most simple term frequency algorithm.

5.2.2.1 Simple Term Frequency Algorithm

In both the unweighted and weighted approaches, an automatic indexing process implements an algorithm to determine the weight to be assigned to a processing token for a particular item. In a statistical system, the data that are potentially available for calculating a weight are the frequency of occurrence of the processing token in an existing item (i.e., term frequency - TF), the frequency of occurrence of the processing token in the existing database (i.e., total frequency - TOTF) and the number of unique items in the database that contain the processing token (i.e., item frequency - IF, frequently labeled in other publications as document frequency - DF). As discussed in Chapter 3, the premises by Luhn and later Brookstein that the resolving power of content-bearing words is directly proportional to the frequency of occurrence of the word in the item is used as the basis for most automatic weighting techniques. Weighting techniques usually are based upon positive weight values.

The simplest approach is to have the weight equal to the term frequency. This approach emphasizes the use of a particular processing token within an item. Thus if the word "computer" occurs 15 times within an item it has a weight of 15. The simplicity of this technique encounters problems of normalization between items and use of the processing token within the database. The longer an item is, the more often a processing token may occur within the item. Use of the absolute value biases weights toward longer items, where a term is more likely to occur with a higher frequency. Thus, one normalization typically used in weighting algorithms compensates for the number of words in an item.

An example of this normalization in calculating term-frequency is the algorithm used in the SMART System at Cornell (Buckley-96). The term frequency weighting formula used in TREC 4 was:

$$\frac{(1 + \log(TF))/1 + \log(\text{average }(TF))}{(1 - \text{slope}) * \text{pivot} + \text{slope} * \text{number of unique terms}}$$

where slope was set at .2 and the pivot was set to the average number of unique terms occurring in the collection (Singhal-95). In addition to compensating for document length, they also want the formula to be insensitive to anomalies introduced by stemming or misspellings.

Although initially conceived of as too simple, recent experiments by the SMART system using the large databases in TREC demonstrated that use of the simpler algorithm with proper normalization factors is far more efficient in processing queries and return hits similar to more complex algorithms.

5.2.2.2 Inverse Document Frequency

The basic algorithm is improved by taking into consideration the frequency of occurrence of the processing token in the database. One of the objectives of indexing an item is to discriminate the semantics of that item from other items in the database. If the token "computer" occurs in every item in the database, its value representing the semantics of an item may be less useful compared to a processing token that occurs in only a subset of the items in the database. The term "computer" represents a concept used in an item, but it does not help a user find the specific information being sought since it returns the complete database. This leads to the general statement enhancing weighting algorithms that the weight assigned to an item should be inversely proportional to the frequency of occurrence of an item in the database. This algorithm is called inverse document frequency (IDF). The un-normalized weighting formula is:

$$WEIGHT_{ij} = TF_{ij} * [Log_2(n) - Log_2(IF_j) + 1]$$

where $WEIGHT_{ij}$ is the vector weight that is assigned to term "j" in item "i," TF_{ij} (term frequency) is the frequency of term "j" in item "i" , "n" is the number of items in the database and IF_j (item frequency or document frequency) is the number of items in the database that have term "j" in them. A negative log is the same as dividing by the log value, thus the basis for the name of the algorithm. Figure 5.4 demonstrates the impact of using this weighting algorithm. The term "refinery" has the highest frequency in the new item (10 occurrences). But it has a normalized weight of 20 which is less than the normalized weight of "Mexico." This change in relative importance between "Mexico" and "refinery" from the unnormalized to normalized vectors is due to an adjustment caused by "refinery" already existing in 50 per cent of the database versus "Mexico" which is found in 6.25 per cent of the items.

The major factor of the formula for a particular term is $Log_2(n) / Log_2(IF_j)$. The value for IF can vary from "1" to "n." At "n," the term is found in every item in the database and the factor becomes $Log_2(n)/Log_2(n) = 1$. As the number of items a term is found in decreases, the value of the denominator decreases eventually approaching the value $Log_2(1)$ which is close to 1. The weight assigned to the term in the item varies from $Tf_{i,j} * (1 + 1)$ to $Tf_{i,j} * (\sim Log_2(n))$. The effect of this factor can be too great as the number of items that a term is found in becomes small. To compensate for this, the INQUERY system at the University of Massachusetts normalizes this factor by taking an additional log value.

Assume that the term "oil" is found in 128 items, "Mexico" is found in 16 items and "refinery" is found in 1024 items. If a new item arrives with all three terms in it, "oil" found 4 times, "Mexico" found 8 times, and "refinery found 10 times and there are 2048 items in the total database, Figure 5.4 shows the weight calculations using inverse document frequency.

Using a simple unnormalized term frequency, the item vector is (4, 8, 10) Using inverse document frequency the following calculations apply:

$Weight_{oil} = 4 * (Log_2(2048) - Log_2(128) + 1) = 4 * (11 - 7 + 1) = 20$

$Weight_{Mexico} = 8 * (Log_2(2048) - Log_2(16) + 1) = 8 * (11 - 4 + 1) = 64$

$Weight_{refinery} = 10 * (Log_2(2048) - Log_2(1024) + 1) =$
$10 * (11 - 10 + 1) = 20$

with the resultant inverse document frequency item vector = (20, 64, 20)

Figure 5.4 Example of Inverse Document Frequency

The value of "n" and IF_i vary as items are added and deleted from the database. To implement this algorithm in a dynamically changing system, the physical index only stores the frequency of occurrence of the terms in an item (usually with their word location) and the IDF factor is calculated dynamically at retrieval time. The required information can easily be determined from an inversion list for a search term that is retrieved and a global variable on the number of items in the database.

5.2.2.3 Signal Weighting

Inverse document frequency adjusts the weight of a processing token for an item based upon the number of items that contain the term in the existing database. What it does not account for is the term frequency distribution of the processing token in the items that contain the term. The distribution of the frequency of processing tokens within an item can affect the ability to rank items. For example, assume the terms "SAW" and "DRILL" are found in 5 items with the following frequencies defined in Figure 5.5.

Both terms are found a total of 50 times in the five items. The term "SAW" does not give any insight into which item is more likely to be relevant to a search of "SAW". If precision is a goal (maximizing relevant items shown first), then the weighting algorithm could take into consideration the non-uniform distribution of term "DRILL" in the items that the term is found, applying even higher weights to it than "SAW." The theoretical basis for the algorithm

Item Distribution	SAW	DRILL
A	10	2
B	10	2
C	10	18
D	10	10
E	10	18

Figure 5.5 Item Distribution for SAW and DRILL

to emphasize precision is Shannon's work on Information Theory (Shannon-51).

In Information Theory, the information content value of an object is inversely proportional to the probability of occurrence of the item. An instance of an event that occurs all the time has less information value than an instance of a seldom occurring event. This is typically represented as INFORMATION $= -\text{Log}_2$ (p), where p is the probability of occurrence of event "p." The information value for an event that occurs .5 per cent of the time is:

$$\text{INFORMATION} = -\text{Log}_2(.0005)$$
$$= -(-10)$$
$$= 10$$

The information value for an event that occurs 50 per cent of the time is:

$$\text{INFORMATION} = -\text{Log}_2 (.50)$$
$$= -(-1)$$
$$= 1$$

If there are many independent occurring events then the calculation for the average information value across the events is:

$$\text{AVE\_INFO} = -\sum_{k=1}^{n} p_k \, \text{Log}_2 \, (p_k)$$

The value of AVE_INFO takes its maximum value when the values for every p_k is the same. Its value decreases proportionally to increases in variances in the values of p_k. The value of p_k can be defined as $TF_{ik}/TOTF_k$, the ratio of the frequency of occurrence of the term in an item to the total number of occurrences of the item in the data base. Using the AVE_INFO formula, the terms that have the most uniform distribution in the items that contain the term have the maximum value. To use this information in calculating a weight, the formula needs the inverse of AVE_INFO, where the minimum value is associated with uniform distributions and the maximum value is for terms that have large variances in distribution in the items containing the term. The following formula for calculating the weighting factor called **Signal** (Dennis-67) can be used:

$$Signal_k = Log_2 (TOTF) - AVE\_INFO$$

producing a final formula of:

$$Weight_{ik} = TF_{ik} * Signal_k$$

$$Weight_{ik} = TF_{ik} * [Log_2(TOTF_k) - \sum_{i=1}^{n} TF_{ik}/TOTF_k \ Log_2 \ (TF_{ik}/TOTF_k)]$$

An example of use of the weighting factor formula is given for the values in Figure 5.5:

$$Signal_{SAW} = LOG_2 (50) - [5 * \{10/50LOG_2(10/50)\} \ ]$$

$$Signal_{DRILL} = LOG_2 (50) - [2/50LOG_2(2/50) + 2/50LOG_2(2/50) + \\ 18/50LOG_2(18/50) + 10/50LOG_2(10/50) + 18/50LOG_2(18/50)$$

The weighting factor for term "DRILL" that does not have a uniform distribution is larger than that for term "SAW" and gives it a higher weight.

    This technique could be used by itself or in combination with inverse document frequency or other algorithms. The overhead of the additional data needed in an index and the calculations required to get the values have not been demonstrated to produce better results than other techniques and are not used in any systems at this time. It is a good example of use of Information Theory in developing information retrieval algorithms. Effectiveness of use of this formula can be found in results from Harman and also from Lockbaum and Streeter (Harman-86, Lochbaum-89).

5.2.2.4 Discrimination Value

    Another approach to creating a weighting algorithm is to base it upon the discrimination value of a term. To achieve the objective of finding relevant items, it is important that the index discriminates among items. The more all items appear the same, the harder it is to identify those that are needed. Salton and Yang (Salton-73) proposed a weighting algorithm that takes into consideration the ability for a search term to discriminate among items. They proposed use of a discrimination value for each term "i":

$$DISCRIM_i = AVESIM_i - AVESIM$$

where AVESIM is the average similarity between every item in the database and AVESIM$_i$ is the same calculation except that term "i" is removed from all items. There are three possibilities with the DISCRIM$_i$ value being positive, close to zero or negative. A positive value indicates that removal of term "i" has increased the similarity between items. In this case, leaving the term in the database assists in discriminating between items and is of value. A value close to zero implies that the term's removal or inclusion does not change the similarity between items. If the value of DISCRIM$_{is}$ is negative, the term's effect on the database is to make the items appear more similar since their average similarity decreased with its removal. Once the value of DISCRM$_i$ is normalized as a positive number, it can be used in the standard weighting formula as:

$$\text{Weight}_{ik} = \text{TF}_{ik} * \text{DISCRIM}_k$$

5.2.2.5 Problems With Weighting Schemes

Often weighting schemes use information that is based upon processing token distributions across the database. The two weighting schemes, inverse document frequency and signal, use total frequency and item frequency factors which makes them dependent upon distributions of processing tokens within the database. Information databases tend to be dynamic with new items always being added and to a lesser degree old items being changed or deleted. Thus these factors are changing dynamically. There are a number of approaches to compensate for the constant changing values.

a. Ignore the variances and calculate weights based upon current values, with the factors changing over time. Periodically rebuild the complete search database.

b. Use a fixed value while monitoring changes in the factors. When the changes reach a certain threshold, start using the new value and update all existing vectors with the new value.

c. Store the invariant variables (e.g., term frequency within an item) and at search time calculate the latest weights for processing tokens in items needed for search terms.

In the first approach the assumption minimizes the system overhead of maintaining currency on changing values, with the effect that term weights for the same term vary from item to item as the aggregate variables used in calculating the weights based upon changes in the database vary over time. Periodically the database and all term weights are recalculated based upon the most recent updates to the database. For large databases in the millions of items, the overhead of rebuilding the database can be significant. In the second approach, there is a recognition that for the most frequently occurring items, the aggregate values are large. As such, minor changes in the values have negligible effect on the final weight calculation. Thus, on a term basis, updates to the aggregate values are only made when sufficient changes not using the current value will have an effect on the final weights and the search/ranking process. This process also distributes the update process over time by only updating a subset of terms at any instance in time. The third approach is the most accurate. The weighted values in the database only matter when they are being used to determine items to return from a query or the rank order to return the items. This has more overhead in that database vector term weights must be calculated dynamically for every query term. If the system is using an inverted file search structure, this overhead is very minor.

An interesting side effect of maintaining currency in the database for term weights is that the same query over time returns a different ordering of items. A new word in the database undergoes significant changes in its weight structure from initial introduction until its frequency in the database reaches a level where small changes do not have significant impact on changes in weight values.

Another issue is the desire to partition an information database based upon time. The value of many sources of information vary exponentially based upon the age of an item (older items have less value). This leads to physically partitioning the database by time (e.g., starting a new database each year), allowing the user to specify the time period to search. There are issues then of how to address the aggregate variables that are different for the same processing token in each database and how to merge the results from the different databases into a single Hit file.

The best environment would allow a user to run a query against multiple different time periods and different databases that potentially use different weighting algorithms, and have the system integrate the results into a single ranked Hit file. This issue is discussed in Chapter 7.

5.2.2.6 Problems With the Vector Model

In addition to the general problem of dynamically changing databases and the effect on weighting factors, there are problems with the vector model on assignment of a weight for a particular processing token to an item. Each processing token can be viewed as a new semantic topic. A major problem comes in the vector model when there are multiple topics being discussed in a particular item. For example, assume that an item has an in-depth discussion of "oil" in "Mexico" and also "coal" in "Pennsylvania." The vector model does not have a mechanism to associate each energy source with its particular geographic area. There is no way to associate correlation factors between terms (i.e., precoordination discussed in Chapter 3) since each dimension in a vector is independent of the other dimensions. Thus the item results in a high value in a search for "coal in Mexico."

Another major limitation of a vector space is in associating positional information with a processing term. The concept of proximity searching (e.g., term "a" within 10 words of term "b") requires the logical structure to contain storage of positional information of a processing term. The concept of a vector space allows only one scalar value to be associated with each processing term for each item. Restricting searches to subsets of an item has been shown to provide increased precision (see Chapter 7). In effect this capability overcomes the multi-topical item problem by looking at subsets of an item and thus increasing the probability that the subset is discussing a particular semantic topic.

5.2.3 Bayesian Model

One way of overcoming the restrictions inherent in a vector model is to use a Bayesian approach to maintaining information on processing tokens. The Bayesian model provides a conceptually simple yet complete model for information systems. In its most general definition, the Bayesian approach is based upon conditional probabilities (e.g., Probability of Event 1 given Event 2 occurred). This general concept can be applied to the search function as well as to creating the index to the database. The objective of information systems is to return relevant items. Thus the general case, using the Bayesian formula, is P(REL/DOC$_i$, Query$_j$) which is interpreted as the probability of relevance (REL) to a search statement given a particular document and query. Interpretation of this process is discussed in detail in Chapter 7. In addition to search, Bayesian formulas can be used in determining the weights associated with a particular processing token in an item. The objective of creating the index to an item is to represent the semantic information in the item. A Bayesian network can be used to determine the final set of processing tokens (called topics) and their weights. Figure 5.6 shows a simple view of the process where T$_i$ repersents the relevance of topic "i" in a particular item and PT$_j$ represents a statistic associated with the event of processing token "j" being present in the item.

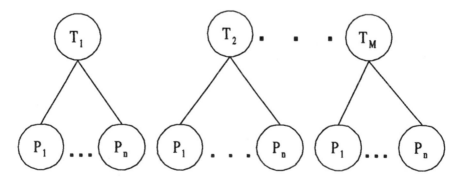

Figure 5.6 Bayesian Term Weighting

The "m" topics would be stored as the final index to the item. The statistics associated with the processing token are typically frequency of occurrence. But they can also incorporate proximity factors that are useful in items that discuss multiple topics. There is one major assumption made in this model:

> Assumption of Binary Independence : the topics and the processing token statistics are independent of each other. The existence of one topic is not related to the existence of the other topics. The existence of one processing token is not related to the existence of other processing tokens.

In most cases this assumption is not true. Some topics are related to other topics and some processing tokens related to other processing tokens. For example, the topics of "Politics" and "Economics" are in some instances related to each other (e.g., an item discussing Congress debating laws associated with balance of trade) and in many other instances totally unrelated. The same type of example would apply to processing tokens. There are two approaches to handling this problem. The first is to assume that there are dependencies, but that the errors introduced by assuming the mutual independence do not noticeably effect the determination of relevance of an item nor its relative rank associated with other retrieved items. This is the most common approach used in system implementations. A second approach can extend the network to additional layers to handle interdependencies. Thus an additional layer of Independent Topics (ITs) can be placed above the Topic layer and a layer of Independent Processing Tokens (IPs) can be placed above the processing token layer. Figure 5.7 shows the extended Bayesian network. Extending the network creates new processing tokens for those cases where there are dependencies between processing tokens. The new set of Independent Processing Tokens can then be used to define the attributes associated with the set of topics selected to represent the semantics of an item. To compensate for dependencies between topics the final layer of Independent Topics is created. The degree to which each layer is created depends upon the error that could be introduced by allowing for dependencies between Topics or Processing Tokens. Although this approach is the most mathematically correct, it suffers from losing a level of precision by reducing the number of concepts available to define the semantics of an item.

5.3 Natural Language

The goal of natural language processing is to use the semantic information in addition to the statistical information to enhance the indexing of the item. This improves the precision of searches, reducing the number of false hits a user reviews. The semantic information is extracted as a result of processing the language rather than treating each word as an independent entity. The simplest output of this process results in generation of phrases that become indexes to an item. More complex analysis generates thematic representation of events rather

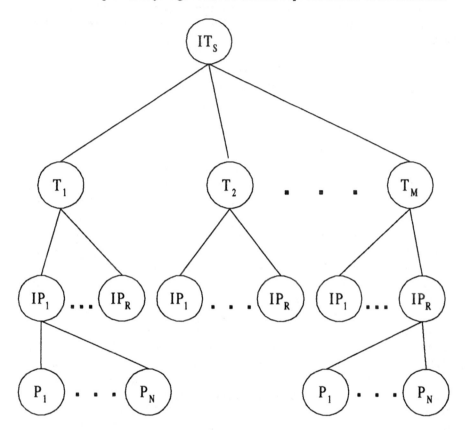

Figure 5.7 Extended Bayesian Network

than phrases. Statistical approaches use proximity as the basis behind determining the strength of word relationships in generating phrases. For example, with a proximity constraint of adjacency, the phrases "venetian blind" and "blind Venetian" may appear related and map to the same phrase. But syntactically and semantically those phrases are very different concepts. Word phrases generated by natural language processing algorithms enhance indexing specification and provide another level of disambiguation. Natural language processing can also combine the concepts into higher level concepts sometimes referred to as thematic representations. One example represents them as concept-relationship-concept triples (Liddy-93).

5.3.1 Index Phrase Generation

The goal of indexing is to represent the semantic concepts of an item in the information system to support finding relevant information. Single words have conceptual context, but frequently they are too general to help the user find the desired information. Term phrases allow additional specification and focusing of the concept to provide better precision and reduce the user's overhead of retrieving non-relevant items. Having the modifier "grass" or "magnetic" associated with the term "field" clearly disambiguates between very different concepts. One of the earliest statistical approaches to determining term phrases proposed by Salton was use of a COHESION factor between terms (Salton-83):

$$\text{COHESION}_{k,h} = \text{SIZE-FACTOR} * (\text{PAIR-FREQ}_{k,h} / \text{TOTF}_k * \text{TOTF}_H)$$

where SIZE-FACTOR is a normalization factor based upon the size of the vocabulary and $\text{PAIR-FREQ}_{k,h}$ is the total frequency of co-occurrence of the pair Term_k, Term_h in the item collection. Co-occurrence may be defined in terms of adjacency, word proximity, sentence proximity, etc. This initial algorithm has been modified in the SMART system to be based on the following guidelines (BUCKLEY-95):

> any pair of adjacent non-stop words is a potential phrase

> any pair must exist in 25 or more items

> phrase weighting uses a modified version of the SMART system single term algorithm

> normalization is achieved by dividing by the length of the single-term subvector.

Natural language processing can reduce errors in determining phrases by determining inter-item dependencies and using that information to create the term phrases used in the indexing process. Statistical approaches tend to focus on two term phrases. A major advantage of natural language approaches is their ability to produce multiple-term phrases to denote a single concept. If a phrase such as "industrious intelligent students" was used often, a statistical approach would create phrases such as "industrious intelligent" and "intelligent student." A natural language approach would create phrases such as "industrious student," "intelligent student" and "industrious intelligent student."

The first step in a natural language determination of phrases is a lexical analysis of the input. In its simplest form this is a part of speech tagger that, for example, identifies noun phrases by recognizing adjectives and nouns. Precise part of speech taggers exist that are accurate to the 99 per cent range. Additionally, proper noun identification tools exist that allow for accurate identification of names, locations and organizations since these values should be indexed as phrases and not undergo stemming. Greater gains come from identifying syntactic and semantic level dependencies creating a hierarchy of semantic concepts. For example, "nuclear reactor fusion" could produce term phrases of "nuclear reactor" and "nuclear fusion." In the ideal case all variations of a phrase would be reduced to a single canonical form that represents the semantics for a phrase. Thus, where possible the phrase detection process should output a normalized form. For example, "blind Venetian" and "Venetian who is blind" should map to the same phrase. This not only increases the precision of searches, but also increases the frequency of occurrence of the common phrase. This, in turn, improves the likelihood that the frequency of occurrence of the common phrase is above the threshold required to index the phrase. Once the phrase is indexed, it is available for search, thus participating in an item's selection for a search and the rank associated with an item in the Hit file. One solution to finding a common form is to transform the phrases into a operator-argument form or a header-modifier form. There is always a category of semantic phrases that comes from inferring concepts from an item that is non-determinable. This comes from the natural ambiguity inherent in languages that is discussed in Chapter 1.

A good example of application of natural language to phrase creation is in the natural language information retrieval system at New York University developed in collaboration with GE Corporate Research and Development (Carballo-95). The text of the item is processed by a fast syntactical process and extracted phrases are added to the index in addition to the single word terms. Statistical analysis is used to determine similarity links between phrases and identification of subphrases. Once the phrases are statistically noted as similar, a filtering process categorizes the link onto a semantic relationship (generality, specialization, antonymy, complementation, synonymy, etc.).

The Tagged Text Parser (TTP), based upon the Linguistic String Grammar (Sager-81), produces a regularized parse tree representation of each sentence reflecting the predicate-argument structure (Strzalkowski-93). The tagged text parser contains over 400 grammar production rules. Some examples of the part of speech tagger identification are given in Figure 5.8.

CLASS	EXAMPLES
determiners	a, the
singular nouns	paper, notation, structure, language
plural nouns	operations, data, processes
preposition	in, by, of, for
adjective	high, concurrent
present tense verb	presents, associates
present participal	multiprogramming

5.8 Part of Speech Tags

The TTP parse trees are header-modifier pairs where the header is the main concept and the modifiers are the additional descriptors that form the concept and eliminate ambiguities. Figure 5.9 gives an example of a regularized parse tree structure generated for the independent clause:

The former Soviet President has been a local hero ever since a Russian tank invaded Wisconsin

```
lassert
 perf[HAVE]
  verb[BE]
   subject
     np
      noun[President]
      t_pos[The]
      adj[former]
      adj[Soviet]
   object
     np
      noun[hero]
      t_pos[a]
      adj[local]
   adv[ever]
   sub_ord
     [since]
        verb[invade]
         subject
           np
            noun[tank]
            t_pos[a]
            adj[Russian]
         object
           np
            noun[Wisconsin]
```

Figure 5.9 TTP Parse Tree

This structure allows for identification of potential term phrases usually based upon noun identification. To determine if a header-modifier pair warrants indexing, Strzalkowski calculates a value for Informational Contribution (IC) for each element in the pair. Higher values of IC indicate a potentially stronger semantic relationship between terms. The basis behind the IC formula is a conditional probability between the terms. The formula for IC between two terms (x,y) is:

$$IC(x,[x,y]) = \frac{fx,y}{Nx + Dx - 1}$$

where $f_{x,y}$ is the frequency of (x,y) in the database, n_x is the number of pairs in which "x" occurs at the same position as in (x,y) and $D(x)$ is the dispersion parameter which is the number of distinct words with which x is paired. When IC=1, x occurs only with y $(f_{x,y}=n_x$ and $d_x = 1)$.

Nominal compounds are the source of many inaccurate identifications in creating header-modifier pairs. Use of statistical information on frequency of occurrence of phrases can eliminate some combinations that occur infrequently and are not meaningful.

The next challenge is to assign weights to term phrases. The most popular term weighting scheme uses term frequencies and inverse document frequencies with normalization based upon item length to calculate weights assigned to terms (see Section 5.2.2.2). Term phrases have lower frequency occurrences than the individual terms. Using natural language processing, the focus is on semantic relationships versus frequency relationships. Thus weighting schemes such as inverse document frequency require adjustments so that the weights are not overly diminished by the potential lower frequency of the phrases. For example, the weighting scheme used in the New York University system uses the following formula for weighting phrases:

$$weight(Phrase_i) = (C_i*log(termf) + C_2*\alpha(N,i))*IDF$$

where $\alpha(N,i)$ is 1 for $i<N$ and 0 otherwise and C_1 and C_2 are normalizing factors. The N assumes the phrases are sorted by IDF value and allows the top "N" highest IDF (inverse document frequency) scores to have a greater effect on the overall weight than other terms.

5.3.2 Natural Language Processing

Section 5.3.1 discussed generation of term phrases as indexes. Lexical analysis determining verb tense, plurality and part of speech is assumed to have been completed prior to the following additional processing. Natural language processing not only produces more accurate term phrases, but can provide higher level semantic information identifying relationships between concepts.

The DR-LINK system (Liddy-93) and its commercial implementation via Textwise System adds the functional processes Relationship Concept Detectors, Conceptual Graph Generators and Conceptual Graph Matchers that generate higher level linguistic relationships including semantic and discourse level relationships. This system is representative of natural language based processing systems. During the first phase of this approach, the processing tokens in the document are mapped to Subject Codes as defined by the codes in the Longman's

Dictionary of Common English (LDOCE). Disambiguation uses *a priori* statistical term relationships and the ordering of the subject codes in the LDOCE, which indicates most likely assignment of a term to a code. These codes equate to index term assignment and have some similarities to the concept-based systems discussed in Section 5.4.

The next phase is called the Text Structurer, which attempts to identify general discourse level areas within an item. Thus a news story may be subdivided into areas associated with EVALUATION (opinions), Main event (basic facts), and Expectations (Predictions). These have been updated to include Analytical Information, Cause/Effect Dimension and Attributed Quotations in the more recent versions of DR-LINK (see http://199.100.96.2 on the Internet). These areas can then be assigned higher weighting if the user includes "Preference" in a search statement. The system also attempts to determine TOPIC statement identifiers. Natural language processing is not just determining the topic statement(s) but also assigning semantic attributes to the topic such as time frame (past, present, future). To perform this type analysis, a general model of the predicted text is needed. For example, news items likely follow a model proposed by van Dijk (Dijk-88). Liddy reorganized this structure into a News Schema Components consisting of Circumstance, Consequence, Credentials, Definition, Error, Evaluation, Expectation, History, Lead, Main Event, No Comment, Previous Event, References and Verbal reaction. Each sentence is evaluated and assigned weights associated with its possible inclusion in the different components. Thus, if a query is oriented toward a future activity, then, in addition to the subject code vector mapping, it would weight higher terms associated with the Expectation component.

The next level of semantic processing is the assignment of terms to components, classifying the intent of the terms in the text and identifying the topical statements. The next level of natural language processing identifies inter-relationships between the concepts. For example, there may be two topics within an item "national elections" and "guerrilla warfare." The relationship "as a result of" is critical to link the order of these two concepts. This process clarifies if the elections were caused by the warfare or the warfare caused by the elections. Significant information is lost by not including the connector relationships. These types of linkages are generated by general linguistic cues (words in text) that are fairly general and domain independent.

The final step is to assign final weights to the established relationships. The relationships are typically envisioned as triples with two concepts and a relationship between them. Although all possible relationships are possible, constructing a system requires the selection of a subset of possible relationships and the rules to locate the relationships. The weights are based upon a combination of statistical information and values assigned to the actual words used in establishing the linkages. Passive verbs would receive less weight than active verbs.

The additional information beyond the indexing is kept in additional data structures associated with each item. This information is used whenever it is implicitly included in a search statement that is natural language based or explicitly requested by the user.

5.4 Concept Indexing

Natural language processing starts with a basis of the terms within an item and extends the information kept on an item to phrases and higher level concepts such as the relationships between concepts. In the DR-LINK system, terms within an item are replaced by an associated Subject Code. Use of subject codes or some other controlled vocabulary is one way to map from specific terms to more general terms. Often the controlled vocabulary is defined by an organization to be representative of the concepts they consider important representations of their data. Concept indexing takes the abstraction a level further. Its goal is to gain the implementation advantages of an index term system but use concepts instead of terms as the basis for the index, producing a reduced dimension vector space.

Rather than *a priori* defining a set of concepts that the terms in an item are mapped to, concept indexing can start with a number of unlabeled concept classes and let the information in the items define the concepts classes created. The process of automatic creation of concept classes is similar to the automatic generation of thesaurus classes described in Chapter 6. The process of mapping from a specific term to a concept that the term represents is complex because a term may represent multiple different concepts to different degrees. A term such as "automobile" could be associated with concepts such as "vehicle," "transportation," "mechanical device," "fuel," and "environment." The term "automobile" is strongly related to "vehicle," lesser to "transportation" and much lesser the other terms. Thus a term in an item needs to be represented by many concept codes with different weights for a particular item.

An example of applying a concept approach is the Convectis System from HNC Software Inc. (Caid-93, Carleton-95). The basis behind the generation of the concept approach is a neural network model (Waltz-85). Context vector representation and its application to textual items is described by Gallant (Gallant-91a, Gallant-91b). If a vector approach is envisioned, then there is a finite number of concepts that provide coverage over all of the significant concepts required to index a database of items. The goal of the indexing is to allow the user to find required information, minimizing the reviewing of items that are non-relevant. In an ideal environment there would be enough vectors to account for all possible concepts and thus they would be orthogonal in an "N" dimensional vector-space model. It is difficult to find a set of concepts that are orthogonal with no aspects in common. Additionally, implementation trade offs naturally limit the number of concept classes that are practical. These limitations increase the number of classes to which a processing token is mapped.

The Convectis system uses neural network algorithms and terms in a similar context (proximity) of other terms as a basis for determining which terms are related and defining a particular concept. A term can have different weights associated with different concepts as described. The definition of a similar context is typically defined by the number of non-stop words separating the terms. The farther apart terms are, the less coupled the terms are associated within a particular concept class. Existing terms already have a mapping to concept classes. New terms can be mapped to existing classes by applying the context rules to the classes that terms near the new term are mapped. Special rules must be applied to create a new concept class. Example 5.9 demonstrates how the process would work for the term "automobile."

TERM: automobile

Weights for associated concepts:

Vehicle	.65
Transportation	.60
Environment	.35
Fuel	.33
Mechanical Device	.15

Vector Representation Automobile: (.65,..., .60, ..., .35, .33, ... , .15)

Figure 5.10 Concept Vector for Automobile

Using the concept representation of a particular term, phrases and complete items can be represented as a weighted average of the concept vectors of the terms in them. The algorithms associated with vectors (e.g., inverse document frequency) can be used to perform the merging of concepts.

Another example of this process is Latent Semantic Indexing (LSI). Its assumption is that there is an underlying or "latent" structure represented by interrelationships between words (Deerwester-90, Dumais-95). The index contains representations of the "latent semantics" of the item. Like Convectis, the large term-document matrix is decomposed into a small set (e.g., 100-300) of orthogonal factors which use linear combinations of the factors (concepts) to approximate the original matrix. Latent Semantic Indexing uses singular-value decomposition to model the associative relationships between terms similar to eigenvector decomposition and factor analysis (see Cullum-85).

Any rectangular matrix can be decomposed into the product of three matrices. Let X be a mxn matrix such that:

$$X = T_0 \bullet S_0 \bullet D_0'$$

where T_0 and D_0 have orthogonal columns and are $m \times r$ and $r \times n$ matrices, S_0 is an $r \times r$ diagonal matrix and r is the rank of matrix X. This is the singular value decomposition of X. The k largest singular values of S_0 are kept along with their corresponding columns in T_0 and D_0 matrices, the resulting matrix:

$$\bar{X} = T_n \bullet S_n \bullet D_n'$$

is the unique matrix of rank k that is closest in least squares sense to X. The matrix $\bar{X}$, containing the first k independent linear components of the original X represents the major associations with noise eliminated. With so much reduction in the number of words, closeness is determined by patterns of word usage versus specific co-locations of terms. This has the effect of a thesaurus in equating many terms to the same concept. Both terms and documents (as collections of terms) can be represented as weighted vectors in the k dimensional space. The selection of k is critical to the success of this procedure. If k is too small, then there is not enough discrimination between vectors and too many false hits are returned on a search. If k is too large, the value of Latent Semantic Indexing is lost and the system equates to a standard vector model.

5.5 Hypertext Linkages

A new class of information representation, described in Chapter 4 as the hypertext data structure, is evolving on the Internet. Hypertext data structures must be generated manually although user interface tools may simplify the process. Very little research has been done on the information retrieval aspects of hypertext linkages and automatic mechanisms to use the information of item pointers in creating additional search structures. In effect, hypertext linkages are creating an additional information retrieval dimension. Traditional items can be viewed as two dimensional constructs. The text of the items is one dimension representing the information in the items. Imbedded references are a logical second dimension that has had minimal use in information search techniques. The major use of the citations has been in trying to determine the concepts within an item and clustering items (Salton-83). Hypertext, with its linkages to additional electronic items, can be view as networking between items that extends the contents. To understand the total subject of an item it is necessary to follow these additional information concept paths. The imbedding of the linkage allows the user to go immediately to the linked item for additional information. The issue is how to use this additional dimension to locate relevant information.

The easiest approach is to do nothing and let the user follow these paths to view items But this is avoiding one of the challenges in information systems on creating techniques to assist the user in finding relevant information. Looking at the Internet at the current time there are three classes of mechanisms to help find information: manually generated indexes, automatically generated indexes and web crawlers (intelligent agents). YAHOO (http://www.yahoo.com) is an example of the first case where information sources (home pages) are indexed manually into a hyperlinked hierarchy. The user can navigate through the hierarchy by expanding the hyperlink on a particular topic to see the more detailed subtopics. At some point the user starts to see the end items. LYCOS (http://www.lycos.com) and Altavista (http://www.altavista.digital.com) automatically go out to other Internet sites and return the text at the sites for automatic indexing. Lycos returns home pages from each site for automatic indexing while Altavista indexes all of the text at a site. None of these approaches use the linkages in items to enhance their indexing.

Webcrawlers (e.g., WebCrawler, OpenText, Pathfinder) and intelligent agents (Coriolis Groups' NetSeeker^{TM}) are tools that allow a user to define items of interest and they automatically go to various sites on the Internet searching for the desired information. They are better described as a search tool than an indexing tool that *a priori* analyzes items to assist in finding them via a search.

What is needed is an index algorithm for items that looks at the hypertext linkages as an extension of the concepts being presented in the item where the link exists. Some links that are for references to multi-media imbedded objects would not be part of the indexing process. The Universal Reference Locator (URL) hypertext links can map to another item or to a specific location within an item. The current concept is defined by the information within proximity of the location of the link. The concepts in the linked item, or with a stronger weight the concepts in the proximity of the location included in the link, need to be included in the index of the current item. If the current item is discussing the financial state of Louisiana and a hyperlink is included to a discussion on crop damage due to draughts in the southern states, the index should allow for a "hit" on a search statement including "draughts in Louisiana."

One approach is to view the hyperlink as an extension of the text of the item in another dimension. The index values of the hyperlinked item has a reduced weighted value from contiguous text biased by the type of linkage. The weight of processing tokens appears:

$$Weight_{i,j,k,l} = (\alpha * Weight_{i,j} + \beta * Weight_{k,l}) * (\gamma * Link_{i,k})$$

where $Weight_{i,j,k,l}$ is the Weight associated with processing token "j" in item "i" and processing token "l" in item "k" that are related via a hyperlink. $Link_{i,k}$ is the weight associated with strength of the link. It could be a one-level link that is weak or strong, or it could be a multilevel transitive link. α, β and γ are weighting/normalization factors. The values could be stored in an expanded index structure or calculated dynamically if only the hyperlink relationships between items are available.

Taking another perspective, the system could automatically generate hyperlinks between items. Attempts have been made to achieve this capability, but they suffer from as working with static versus dynamic growing databases or ignoring the efficiency needed for an operational environment (Allan-95, Furuta-89,Rearick-91). Kellog and Subhas have proposed a new solution based upon document segmentation and clustering (Kellog-96). They link at both the document and document sub-part level using the cover-coefficient based incremental clustering method (C^2ICM) to generate links between the document (document sub-parts) pairs for each cluster. (Can-95). The automatic link generation phase is performed in parallel with the clustering phase. Item pairs in the same cluster are candidates for hyperlinking (link-similarity) if they have a similarity above a given threshold. The process is completed in two phases. In the first phase the document seeds and an estimate of the number of clusters is calculated. In the second phase the items are clustered and the links are created. Rather than storing the link information within the item or storing a persistent link ID within the item and the link information externally, they store all of the link information externally. They create HTML items on demand. When analyzing links missed by their algorithm, three common problems were discovered:

> misspellings or multiple word representations (e.g., cabinet maker and cabinetmaker)

> parser problems with document segmentation caused by punctuation errors (lines were treated as paragraphs and sentences)

> problems occurred when the definition of subparts (smaller sentences) of items was attempted

A significant portion of errors came from parsing rather than algorithmic problems. This technique has maximum effectiveness for referential links which naturally have higher similarity measures.

5.6 Summary

Automatic indexing is the preprocessing stage allowing search of items in an Information Retrieval System. Its role is critical to the success of searches in finding relevant items. If the concepts within an item are not located and represented in the index during this stage, the item is not found during search. Some techniques allow for the combinations of data at search time to equate to particular concepts (i.e. postcoordination). But if the words are not properly identified at indexing time and placed in the searchable data structure, the system can not combine them to determine the concept at search time. If an inefficient data structure is selected to hold the index, the system does not scale to accommodate large numbers of items.

The steps in the identification of the processing tokens used in the index process were generally discussed in Chapter 3. Chapter 5 focuses on the specific characteristics of the processing tokens to support the different search techniques. There are many ways of defining the techniques. All of the techniques have statistical algorithmic properties. But looking at the techniques from a conceptual level, the approaches are classified as statistical, natural language and concept indexing. Hypertext linkages are placed in a separate class because an algorithm to search items that include linkages has to address dependencies between items. Normally the processing for processing tokens is restricted to an item. The next item may use some corpus statistics that changed by previous items, but does not consider a tight coupling between items. In effect, one item may be considered an extension of another, which should effect the concept identification and representation process.

Of all the statistical techniques, an accurate probabilistic technique would have the greatest benefit in the search process. Unfortunately, identification of consistent statistical values used in the probabilistic formulas has proven to be a formidable task. The assumptions that must be made significantly reduce the accuracy of the search process. Vector techniques have very powerful representations and have been shown to be successful. But they lack the flexibility to represent items that contain many distinct but overlapping concepts. Bayesian techniques are a way to relax some of the constraints inherent in a pure vector approach, allowing dependencies between concepts within the same item to be represented. Most commercial systems do not try to calculate weighted values at index time. It is easier and more flexible to store the basic word data for each item and calculate the statistics at search time. This allows tuning the algorithms without having to re-index the database. It also allows the combination of statistical and traditional Boolean techniques within the same system.

Natural language systems attempt to introduce a higher level of abstraction indexing on top of the statistical processes. Making use of rules associated with language assist in the disambiguation of terms and provide an additional layer of concepts that are not found in purely statistical systems. Use of natural language processing provides the additional data that could focus searches, reducing the retrieval of non-relevant items. The tendency of users to enter short queries may reduce the benefits of this approach.

Concept indexing is a statistical technique whose goal is to determine a canonical representation of the concepts. It has been shown to find relevant items that other techniques miss. In its transformation process, some level of precision is lost. The analysis of enhanced recall over potential reduced precision is still under investigation.

EXERCISES

1.   What are the trade offs in use of Zoning as part of the indexing process?

2.   What are the benefits of a weighted index system over a Binary index system? Are there benefits that the binary system can provide over a weighted system?

3.   How do the concepts underlying Discrimination Value indexing provide a good or poor basis for searching items? What is the major problem with the weight formula?

4.   Given the following Item collection of 10 items, where the numbers reflect the frequency of occurrence of each term in each item, calculate the Inverse Document Frequency and Signal weights for documents D1 and D2.

	Term1	Term2	Term3	Term4	Term5	Term6	Term7	Term8
DOC1	0	3	4	0	0	2	4	0
DOC2	5	5	0	0	4	0	4	3
DOC3	3	0	4	3	4	0	0	5
DOC4	0	7	0	3	2	0	4	3
DOC5	0	1	0	0	0	5	4	2
DOC6	2	0	2	0	0	4	0	1
DOC7	3	5	3	4	0	0	4	2
DOC8	0	3	0	0	0	4	4	2
DOC9	0	0	3	3	3	0	0	1
DOC10	0	5	0	0	0	4	4	2

5.   Under what conditions would the Bayesian and the Vector approach be the same?

6.   Describe how use of Natural Language Processing will assist in the disambiguation process. What is the impact on index structure and the user search interface to take advantage of the results of disambiguation?

7.   What information is available in a natural language based indexing system that is not available in normal statistical systems? What effect does this have on the search process?

8.   What is the effect of Latent Semantic Indexing on the characteristics of the searchable data structure (i.e., the index)? Which user functions described in Chapter 2 have significant problems or are impossible to provide when using LSI?

9.   Conceptually, what role does Hypertext play in indexing and the definition of an item? What is the major problem with URLs as a basis for hypertext links?

10.   Discuss how the decisions on the use of different techniques can affect the user's ability to find information. Frame your answer in the context of an overall system objective of maximizing recall or maximizing precision.

6 Document and Term Clustering

Chapter 5 introduced indexing associated with representation of the semantics of an item. In all of the techniques discussed in Chapter 5, our information database can be viewed as being composed of a number of independent items indexed by a series of index terms. This model lends itself to two types of clustering: clustering index terms to create a statistical thesaurus and clustering items to create document clusters. In the first case clustering is used to increase recall by expanding searches with related terms. In document clustering the search can retrieve items similar to an item of interest, even if the query would not have retrieved the item. The clustering process is not precise and care must be taken on use of clustering techniques to minimize the negative impact misuse can have. These issues are discussed in Section 6.1 along with some general guidelines of clustering.

Section 6.2 discusses a variety of specific techniques to create thesaurus clusters. The techniques can be categorized as those that use the complete database to perform the clustering and those that start with some initial structure. Section 6.3 looks at the same techniques as they apply to item (document) clustering. A class of clustering algorithms creates a hierarchical output. The hierarchy of clusters usually reflects more abstract concepts in the higher levels and more detailed specific items in the lower levels. Given the large data sets in information retrieval systems, it is essential to optimize the clustering process in terms of time and required processing power. Hierarchical clustering and its associated performance improvements are described in Section 6.4.

6.1 Introduction to Clustering

The concept of clustering has been around as long as there have been libraries. One of the first uses of clustering was an attempt to cluster items discussing the same subject. The goal of the clustering was to assist in the location of information. This eventually lead to indexing schemes used in organization of items in libraries and standards associated with use of electronic indexes. Clustering of words originated with the generation of thesauri. Thesaurus, coming from the Latin word meaning "treasure," is similar to a dictionary in that it stores words. Instead of definitions, it provides the synonyms and antonyms for the words. Its primary purpose is to assist authors in selection of vocabulary. The goal of clustering is to provide a grouping of similar objects (e.g., terms or items) into a "class" under a more general title. Clustering also allows linkages between clusters to be specified. The term class is frequently used as a synonym for the term cluster. They are used interchangeably in this chapter.

The process of clustering follows the following steps:

a. Define the domain for the clustering effort. If a thesaurus is being created, this equates to determining the scope of the thesaurus such as "medical terms." If document clustering is being performed, it is determination of the set of items to be clustered. This can be a subset of the database or the complete database. Defining the domain for the clustering identifies those objects to be used in the clustering process and reduce the potential for erroneous data that could induce errors in the clustering process.

b. Once the domain is determined, determine the attributes of the objects to be clustered. If a thesaurus is being generated, determine the specific words in the objects to be used in the clustering process. Similarly, if documents are being clustered, the clustering process may focus on specific zones within the items (e.g., Title and abstract only, main body of the item but not the references, etc.) that are to be used to determine similarity. The objective, as with the first step (a.) is to reduce erroneous associations.

c. Determine the strength of the relationships between the attributes whose co-occurrence in objects suggest those objects should be in the same class. For thesauri this is determining which words are synonyms and the strength of their term relationships. For documents it may be defining a similarity function based upon word co-occurrences that determine the similarity between two items.

d.   At this point, the total set of objects and the strengths of the relationships between the objects have been determined. The final step is applying some algorithm to determine the class(s) to which each item will be assigned.

There are guidelines (not hard constraints) on the characteristics of the classes:

A well-defined semantic definition should exist for each class. There is a risk that the name assigned to the semantic definition of the class could also be misleading. In some systems numbers are assigned to classes to reduce the misinterpretation that a name attached to each class could have. A clustering of items into a class called "computer" could mislead a user into thinking that it includes items on main memory that may actually reside in another class called "hardware."

The size of the classes should be within the same order of magnitude. One of the primary uses of the classes is to expand queries or expand the resultant set of retrieved items. If a particular class contains 90 per cent of the objects, that class is not useful for either purpose. It also places in question the utility of the other classes that are distributed across 10 per cent of the remaining objects.

Within a class, one object should not dominate the class. For example, assume a thesaurus class called "computer" exists and it contains the objects (words/word phrases) "microprocessor," "286-processor," "386-processor" and "pentium." If the term "microprocessor" is found 85 per cent of the time and the other terms are used 5 per cent each, there is a strong possibility that using "microprocessor" as a synonym for "286-processor" will introduce too many errors. It may be better to place "microprocessor" into its own class.

Whether an object can be assigned to multiple classes or just one must be decided at creation time. This is a tradeoff based upon the specificity and partitioning capability of the semantics of the objects. Given the ambiguity of language in general, it is better to allow an object to be in multiple classes rather than constrained to one. This added flexibility comes at a cost of additional complexity in creating and maintaining the classes.

There are additional important decisions associated with the generation of thesauri that are not part of item clustering (Aitchison-72):

Word coordination approach: specifies if phrases as well as individual terms are to be clustered (see discussion on precoordination and postcoordination in Chapter 3).

Word relationships: when the generation of a thesaurus includes a human interface (versus being totally automated), a variety of relationships between words are possible. Aitchison and Gilchrist (Aitchison-72) specified three types of relationships: equivalence, hierarchical and non-hierarchical. Equivalence relationships are the most common and represent synonyms. The definition of a synonym allows for some discretion in the thesaurus creation, allowing for terms that have significant overlap but differences. Thus the terms photograph and print may be defined as synonyms even though prints also include lithography. The definition can even be expanded to include words that have the same "role" but not necessarily the same meaning. Thus the words "genius" and "moron" may be synonyms in a class called "intellectual capability." A very common technique is hierarchical relationships where the class name is a general term and the entries are specific examples of the general term. The previous example of "computer" class name and "microprocessor," "pentium," etc. is an example of this case. Non-hierarchical relationships cover other types of relationships such as "object"-"attribute" that would contain "employee" and "job title."

A more recent word relationship scheme (Wang-85) classified relationships as Parts-Wholes, Collocation, Paradigmatic, Taxonomy and Synonymy, and Antonymy. The only two of these classes that require further amplification are collocation and paradigmatic. Collocation is a statistical measure that relates words that co-occur in the same proximity (sentence, phrase, paragraph). Paradigmatic relates words with the same semantic base such as "formula" and "equation."

In the expansion to semantic networks other relationships are included such as contrasted words, child-of (sphere is a child-of geometric volume), parent-of, part-of (foundation is part of a building), and contains part-of (bicycle contains parts-of wheel, handlebars) (RetrievalWare-95).

Homograph resolution: a homograph is a word that has multiple, completely different meanings. For example, the term "field" could mean a electronic field, a field of grass, etc. It is difficult to eliminate homographs by supplying a unique meaning for every homograph (limiting the thesaurus domain helps). Typically the system allows for homographs and requires that the user interact with the system to select the desired meaning. It is possible to determine the correct meaning of the homograph when a user enters multiple search terms by analyzing the other terms entered (hay, crops, and field suggest the agricultural meaning for field).

Vocabulary constraints: this includes guidelines on the normalization and specificity of the vocabulary. Normalization may constrain the thesaurus to stems versus complete words. Specificity may eliminate specific words or use general terms for class identifiers. The previous discussion in Chapter 3 on these topics applies to their use in the thesauri.

As is evident in these guidelines, clustering is as much an arcane art as it is a science. Good clustering of terms or items assists the user by improving recall. But typically an increase in recall has an associated decrease in precision. Automatic clustering has the imprecision of information retrieval algorithms, compounding the natural ambiguities that come from language. Care must be taken to ensure that the increases in recall are not associated with such decreases in precision as to make the human processing (reading) of the retrieved items unmanageable. The key to successful clustering lies in steps c. and d., selection of a good measure of similarity and selection of a good algorithm for placing items in the same class. When hierarchical item clustering is used, there is a possibility of a decrease in recall discussed in Section 6.4. The only solution to this problem is to make minimal use of the hierarchy.

6.2 Thesaurus Generation

Manual generation of clusters usually focuses on generating a thesaurus (i.e., clustering terms versus items) and has been used for hundreds of years. As items became available in electronic form, automated term statistical clustering techniques became available. Automatically generated thesauri contain classes that reflect the use of words in the corpora. The classes do not naturally have a name, but are just a groups of statistically similar terms. The optimum technique for generating the classes requires intensive computation. Other techniques starting with existing clusters can reduce the computations required but may not produce optimum classes.

6.2.1 Manual Clustering

The manual clustering process follows the steps described in Section 6.1 in the generation of a thesaurus. The first step is to determine the domain for the clustering. Defining the domain assists in reducing ambiguities caused by homographs and helps focus the creator. Usually existing thesauri, concordances from items that cover the domain and dictionaries are used as starting points for generating the set of potential words to be included in the new thesaurus. A concordance is an alphabetical listing of words from a set of items along with their frequency of occurrence and references of which items in which they are found. The art of manual thesaurus construction resides in the selection of the set of words to be included. Care is taken to not include words that are unrelated to the domain of the thesaurus or those that have very high frequency of occurrence and thus hold no information value (e.g., the term Computer in a thesaurus focused on data processing machines). If a concordance is used, other tools such as KWOC, KWIC or KWAC may help in determining useful words. A Key Word Out of Context (KWOC) is another name for a concordance. Key Word In Context (KWIC) displays a possible term in its phrase context. It is structured to identify easily the location of the term under consideration in the sentence. Key Word And Context (KWAC) displays the keywords followed by their context. Figure 6.1 shows the various displays for "computer design contains memory chips" (NOTE: the phrase is assumed to be from doc4; the other frequency and document ids for KWOC were created for this example.) In the Figure 6.1 the character "/" is used in KWIC to indicate the end of the phrase. The KWIC and KWAC are useful in determining the meaning of homographs. The term "chips" could be wood chips or memory chips. In both the KWIC and KWAC displays, the editor of the thesaurus can read the sentence fragment associated with the term and determine its meaning. The KWOC does not present any information that would help in resolving this ambiguity.

KWOC

TERM	FREQ	ITEM Ids
chips	2	doc2, doc4
computer	3	doc1, doc4, doc10
design	1	doc4
memory	3	doc3, doc4, doc8, doc12

KWIC

chips/	computer design contains memory
computer	design contains memory chips/
design	contains memory chips/ computer
memory	chips/ computer design contains

KWAC

chips	computer design contains memory chips
computer	computer design contains memory chips
design	computer design contains memory chips
memory	computer design contains memory chips

Figure 6.1 Example of KWOC, KWIC and KWAC

Once the terms are selected they are clustered based upon the word relationship guidelines and the interpretation of the strength of the relationship. This is also part of the art of manual creation of the thesaurus, using the judgment of the human analyst. The resultant thesaurus undergoes many quality assurance reviews by additional editors using some of the guidelines already suggested before it is finalized.

6.2.2 Automatic Term Clustering

There are many techniques for the automatic generation of term clusters to create statistical thesauri. They all use as their basis the concept that the more frequently two terms co-occur in the same items, the more likely they are about the same concept. They differ by the completeness with which terms are correlated. The more complete the correlation, the higher the time and computational overhead to create the clusters. The most complete process computes the strength of the relationships between all combinations of the "n" unique words with an overhead of $O(n^2)$. Other techniques start with an arbitrary set of clusters and iterate on the assignment of terms to these clusters. The simplest case employs one pass of the data in creation of the clusters. When the number of clusters created is very large, the initial clusters may be used as a starting point to generate more abstract clusters creating a hierarchy.

The steps described in Section 6.1 apply to the automatic generation of thesauri. The basis for automatic generation of a thesaurus is a set of items that represents the vocabulary to be included in the thesaurus. Selection of this set of items is the first step of determining the domain for the thesaurus. The processing tokens (words) in the set of items are the attributes to be used to create the clusters. Implementation of the other steps differs based upon the algorithms being applied. In the following sections a term is usually restricted to be included in only one class. It is also possible to use a threshold instead of choosing the highest value, allowing a term to be assigned to all of the classes that it could be included in above the threshold.

6.2.2.1 Complete Term Relation Method

In the complete term relation method, the similarity between every term pair is calculated as a basis for determining the clusters. The easiest way to understand this approach is to consider the vector model. The vector model is represented by a matrix where the rows are individual items and the columns are the unique words (processing tokens) in the items. The values in the matrix represent how strongly that particular word represents concepts in the item. Figure 6.2 provides an example of a database with 5 items and 8 terms.

To determine the relationship between terms, a similarity measure is required. The measure calculates the similarity between two terms. In Chapter 7 a number of similarity measures are presented. The similarity measure is not critical

	Term1	Term2	Term3	Term4	Term5	Term6	Term7	Term8
Item 1	0	4	0	0	0	2	1	3
Item 2	3	1	4	3	1	2	0	1
Item 3	3	0	0	0	3	0	3	0
Item 4	0	1	0	3	0	0	2	0
Item 5	2	2	2	3	1	4	0	2

Figure 6.2 Vector Example

in understanding the methodology so the following simple measure is used:

$$SIM(Term_i, Term_j) = \Sigma \ (Term_{k,i}) \ (Term_{k,j})$$

where "k" is summed across the set of all items. In effect the formula takes the two columns of the two terms being analyzed, multiplying and accumulating the values in each row. The results can be paced in a resultant "m" by "m" matrix, called a Term-Term Matrix (Salton-83), where "m" is the number of columns (terms) in the original matrix. This simple formula is reflexive so that the matrix that is generated is symmetric. Other similarity formulas could produce a non-symmetric matrix. Using the data in Figure 6.2, the Term-Term matrix produced is shown in Figure 6.3. There are no values on the diagonal since that represents the auto-correlation of a word to itself. The next step is to select a threshold that determines if two terms are considered similar enough to each other to be in the same class. In this example, the threshold value of 10 is used. Thus two terms are considered similar if the similarity value between them is 10 or greater. This produces a new binary matrix called the Term Relationship matrix (Figure 6.4) that defines which terms are similar. A one in the matrix indicates that the terms specified by the column and the row are similar enough to be in the same class. Term 7 demonstrates that a term may exist on its own with no other similar terms identified. In any of the clustering processes described below this term will always migrate to a class by itself.

The final step in creating clusters is to determine when two objects (words) are in the same cluster. There are many different algorithms available. The following algorithms are the most common: cliques, single link, stars and connected components.

	Term1	Term2	Term3	Term4	Term5	Term6	Term7	Term8
Term 1		7	16	15	14	14	9	7
Term 2	7		8	12	3	18	6	17
Term 3	16	8		18	6	16	0	8
Term 4	15	12	18		6	18	6	9
Term 5	14	3	6	6		6	9	3
Term 6	14	18	16	18	6		2	16
Term 7	9	6	0	6	9	2		3
Term 8	7	17	8	9	3	16	3	

Figure 6.3 Term-Term Matrix

	Term1	Term2	Term3	Term4	Term5	Term6	Term7	Term8
Term 1		0	1	1	1	1	0	0
Term 2	0		0	1	0	1	0	1
Term 3	1	0		1	0	1	0	0
Term 4	1	1	1		0	1	0	0
Term 5	1	0	0	0		0	0	0
Term 6	1	1	1	1	0		0	1
Term 7	0	0	0	0	0	0		0
Term 8	0	1	0	0	0	1	0	

Figure 6.4 Term Relationship Matrix

Cliques require all items in a cluster to be within the threshold of all other items. The methodology to create the clusters using cliques is:

0. Let i = 1
1. Select term$_i$ and place it in a new class
2. Start with term$_k$ where r = k = i + 1
3. Validate if term$_k$ is within the threshold of all terms within the current class
4. If not, let k = k + 1
5. If k > m (number of words)
   then r = r + 1
      if r = m then go to 6 else
         k = r
         create a new class with term$_i$ in it
         go to 3
   else go to 3

6. If current class only has term$_i$ in it and there are other classes
   with term$_i$ in them
         then delete current class
         else i = i + 1
7. If i = m + 1 then go to 8
      else go to 1
8. Eliminate any classes that duplicate or are subsets of other classes.

Applying the algorithm to Figure 6.4, the following classes are created:

Class 1 (Term 1, Term 3, Term 4, Term 6)
Class 2 (Term 1, Term 5)
Class 3 (Term 2, Term 4, Term 6)
Class 4 (Term 2, Term 6, Term 8)
Class 5 (Term 7)

Notice that Term 1 and Term 6 are in more than one class. A characteristic of this approach is that terms can be found in multiple classes.

In single link clustering the strong constraint that every term in a class is similar to every other term is relaxed. The rule to generate single link clusters is that any term that is similar to any term in the cluster can be added to the cluster. It is impossible for a term to be in two different clusters. This in effect partitions the set of terms into the clusters. The algorithm is:

1. Select a term that is not in a class and place it in a new class
2. Place in that class all other terms that are related to it
3. For each term entered into the class, perform step 2
4. When no new terms can be identified in step 2, go to step 1.

Applying the algorithm for creating clusters using single link to the Term Relationship Matrix, Figure 6.4, the following classes are created:

Class 1 (Term 1, Term 3, Term 4, Term 5, Term 6, Term 2)
Class 2 (Term 7)

There are many other conditions that can be placed on the selection of terms to be clustered. The Star technique selects a term and then places in the class all terms that are related to that term (i.e., in effect a star with the selected term as the core). Terms not yet in classes are selected as new seeds until all terms are assigned to a class. There are many different classes that can be created using the Star technique. If we always choose as the starting point for a class the lowest numbered term not already in a class, using Figure 6.4, the following classes are created:

Class 1 (Term 1, Term 3, Term 4, Term 5, Term 6)
Class 2 (Term 2, Term 4, Term 8)
Class 3 (Term 7)

This technique allows terms to be in multiple clusters (e.g., Term 4). This could be eliminated by expanding the constraints to exclude any term that has already been selected for a previous cluster
    The String technique starts with a term and includes in the class one additional term that is similar to the term selected and not already in a class. The new term is then used as the new node and the process is repeated until no new terms can be added because the term being analyzed does not have another term related to it or the terms related to it are already in the class. A new class is started with any term not currently in any existing class. Using the additional guidelines to select the lowest number term similar to the current term and not to select any term already in an existing class produces the following classes:

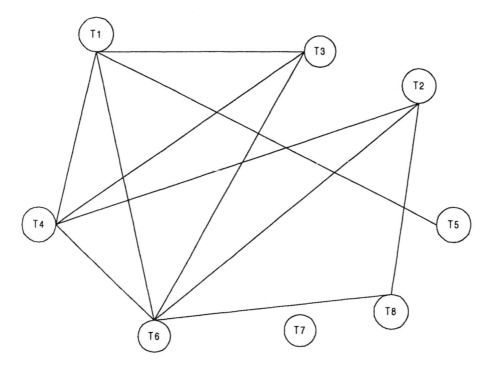

Figure 6.5 Network Diagram of Term Similarities

Class 1 (Term 1, Term 3, Term 4, Term 2, Term 8, Term 6)
Class 2 (Term 5)
Class 3 (Term 7)

A technique to understand these different algorithms for generating classes is based upon a network diagram of the terms. Each term is considered a node and arcs between the nodes indicate terms that are similar. A network diagram for Figure 6.4 is given in Figure 6. 5. To determine cliques, sub-networks are identified where all of the items are connected by arcs. From this diagram it is obvious that Term 7 (T7) is in a class by itself and Term 5 (T5) is in a class with Term 1 (T1). Other common structures to look for are triangles and four sided polygons with diagonals. To find all classes for an item, it is necessary to find all subnetworks, where each subnetwork has the maximum number of nodes, that the term is contained. For Term 1 (T1), it is the subnetwork T1, T3, T4, and T6. Term 2 (T2) has two subnetworks: T2, T4, T6 and the subnetwork T2, T6, T8. The network diagram provides a simple visual tool when there are a small number of nodes to identify classes using any of the other techniques.

The clique technique produces classes that have the strongest relationships between all of the words in the class. This suggests that the class is more likely to be describing a particular concept. The clique algorithm produces more classes than the other techniques because the requirement for all terms to be similar to all other terms will reduce the number of terms in a class. This will require more classes to include all the terms. The single link technique partitions the terms into classes. It produces the fewest number of classes and the weakest relationship between terms (Salton-72, Jones-71, Salton-75). It is possible using the single link algorithm that two terms that have a similarity value of zero will be in the same class. Classes will not be associated with a concept but cover a diversity of concepts. The other techniques lie between these two extremes.

The selection of the technique is also governed by the density of the term relationship matrix and objectives of the thesaurus. When the Term Relationship Matrix is sparse (i.e., contains a few number of ones), then the constraint dependencies between terms need to be relaxed such as in single link to create classes with a reasonable number of items. If the matrix is dense (i.e., lots of ones implying relationships between many terms), then the tighter constraints of the clique are needed so the number of items in a class does not become too large.

Cliques provide the highest precision when the statistical thesaurus is used for query term expansion. The single link algorithm maximizes recall but can cause selection of many non-relevant items. The single link assignment process has the least overhead in assignment of terms to classes, requiring $O(n^2)$ comparisons (Croft-77)

similar weights. The majority of terms in Class 1 have weights in the high 20's/2, thus Term 5 was assigned to Class 3. Term 7 is assigned to Class 1 even though its similarity weights are not in alignment with the other terms in that class. Figure 6.8 shows the new centroids and results of similarity comparisons for the next iteration.

$$Class\ 1 = 8/3,\ 2/3,\ 3/3,\ 3/3,\ 4/3$$
$$Class\ 2 = 2/4,\ 12/4,\ 3/4,\ 3/4,\ 11/4$$
$$Class\ 3 = 0/1,\ 1/1,\ 3/1,\ 0/1,\ 1/1$$

	Term1	Term2	Term3	Term4	Term5	Term6	Term7	Term8
Class 1	23/3	45/3	16/3	27/3	15/3	36/3	23/3	34/3
Class 2	67/4	45/4	70/4	78/4	33/4	72/4	17/4	40/4
Class 3	12/1	3/1	6/1	6/1	11/1	6/1	9/1	3/1
Assign	Class2	Class1	Class2	Class2	Class3	Class2	Class3	Class1

Figure 6.8 New Centroids and Cluster Assignments

In this iteration of the process,, the only change is Term 7 moves from Class 1 to Class 3. This is reasonable, given it was not that strongly related to the other terms in Class 1.

Although the process requires fewer calculations than the complete term relationship method, it has inherent limitations. The primary problem is that the number of classes is defined at the start of the process and can not grow. It is possible for there to be fewer classes at the end of the process. Since all terms must be assigned to a class, it forces terms to be allocated to classes, even if their similarity to the class is very weak compared to other terms assigned.

6.2.2.3 One Pass Assignments

This technique has the minimum overhead in that only one pass of all of the terms is used to assign terms to classes. The first term is assigned to the first class. Each additional term is compared to the centroids of the existing classes. A threshold is chosen. If the item is greater than the threshold, it is assigned to the class with the highest similarity. A new centroid has to be calculated for the modified class. If the similarity to all of the existing centroids is less than the threshold, the term is the first item in a new class. This process continues until all items are assigned to classes. Using the system defined in Figure 6.3, with a threshold of 10 the following classes would be generated:

Class 1 = Term 1, Term 3, Term 4
Class 2 = Term 2, Term 6, Term 8
Class 3 = Term 5
Class 4 = Term 7

NOTE: the centroid values used during the one-pass process:

Class1 (Term1, Term3) = 0, 7/2, 3/2, 0, 4/2
Class1 (Term1, Term2, Term4) = 0, 10/3, 3/3, 3/3, 7/3
Class2 (Term2, Term6) = 6/2, 3/2, 0/2, 1/2, 6/2

Although this process has minimal computation on the order of $O(n)$, it does not produce optimum clustered classes. The different classes can be produced if the order in which the items are analyzed changes. Items that would have been in the same cluster could appear in different clusters due to the averaging nature of centroids.

6.3 Item Clustering

Clustering of items is very similar to term clustering for the generation of thesauri. Manual item clustering is inherent in any library or filing system. In this case someone reads the item and determines the category or categories to which it belongs. When physical clustering occurs, each item is usually assigned to one category. With the advent of indexing, an item is physically stored in a primary category, but it can be found in other categories as defined by the index terms assigned to the item.

With the advent of electronic holdings of items, it is possible to perform automatic clustering of the items. The techniques described for the clustering of terms in Sections 6.2.2.1 through 6.2.2.3 also apply to item clustering. Similarity between documents is based upon two items that have terms in common versus terms with items in common. Thus, the similarity function is performed between rows of the item matrix. Using Figure 6.2 as the set of items and their terms and similarity equation:

$$SIM(Item_i, Item_j) = \Sigma \, (Term_{i,k}) \, (Term_{j,k})$$

as k goes from 1 to 8 for the eight terms, an Item-Item matrix is created (Figure 6.9). Using a threshold of 10 produces the Item Relationship matrix shown in Figure 6.10.

	Item 1	Item 2	Item 3	Item 4	Item 5
Item 1		11	3	6	22
Item 2	11		12	10	36
Item 3	3	12		6	9
Item 4	6	10	6		11
Item 5	22	36	9	11	

Figure 6.9 Item/Item Matrix

	Item1	Item2	Item3	Item4	Item5
Item1		1	0	0	1
Item2	1		1	1	1
Item3	0	1		0	0
Item4	0	1	0		1
Item5	1	1	0	1	

Figure 6.10 Item Relationship Matrix

Using the Clique algorithm for assigning items to classes produces the following classes based upon Figure 6.10:

> Class 1 = Item 1, Item 2, Item 5
> Class 2 = Item 2, Item 3
> Class 3 = Item 2, Item 4

Application of the single link technique produces:

> Class 1 = Item 1, Item 2, Item 5, Item 3, Item 4

All the items are in this one cluster, with Item 3 and Item 4 added because of their similarity to Item 2. The Star technique (i.e., always selecting the lowest non-assigned item) produces:

> Class 1 - Item 1, Item 2, Item 5
> Class 2 - Item 2, Item 3, Item 4, Item 5

Using the String technique and stopping when all items are assigned to classes produces the following:

Class 1 - Item 1, Item 2, Item 3
Class 2 - Item 4, Item 5

In the vocabulary domain homographs introduce ambiguities and erroneous hits. In the item domain multiple topics in an item may cause similar problems. This is especially true when the decision is made to partition the document space. Without precoordination of semantic concepts, an item that discusses "Politics" in "America" and "Economics" in "Mexico" could get clustered with a class that is focused around "Politics" in "Mexico."

Clustering by starting with existing clusters can be performed in a manner similar to the term model. Lets start with item 1 and item 3 in Class 1, and item 2 and item 4 in Class 2. The centroids are:

Class 1 = 3/2, 4/2, 0/2, 0/2, 3/2, 2/2, 4/2, 3/2
Class 2 = 3/2, 2/2, 4/2, 6/2, 1/2, 2/2, 2/2, 1/2

The results of recalculating the similarities of each item to each centroid and reassigning terms is shown in Figure 6.11.

	Class1	Class 2	Assign
Item 1	33/2	17/2	Class 1
Item 2	23/2	51/2	Class 2
Item 3	30/2	18/2	Class 2
Item 4	8/2	24/2	Class 2
Item 5	31/2	47/2	Class 2

Figure 6.11 Item Clustering with Initial Clusters

Finding the centroid for Class 2, which now contains four items, and recalculating the similarities does not result in reassignment for any of the items.

Instead of using words as a basis for clustering items, the Acquaintance system uses n-grams (Damashek-95, Cohen-95). Not only does their algorithm cluster items, but when items can be from more than one language, it will also recognize the different languages.

6.4 Hierarchy of Clusters

Hierarchical clustering in Information Retrieval focuses on the area of hierarchical agglomerative clustering methods (HACM) (Willet-88). The term agglomerative means the clustering process starts with unclustered items and performs pairwise similarity measures to determine the clusters. Divisive is the term applied to starting with a cluster and breaking it down into smaller clusters. The objectives of creating a hierarchy of clusters are to:

>Reduce the overhead of search
>Provide for a visual representation of the information space
>Expand the retrieval of relevant items.

Search overhead is reduced by performing top-down searches of the centroids of the clusters in the hierarchy and trimming those branches that are not relevant (discussed in greater depth in Chapter 7). It is difficult to create a visual display of the total item space. Use of dendograms along with visual cues on the size of clusters (e.g., size of the ellipse) and strengths of the linkages between clusters (e.g., dashed lines indicate reduced similarities) allows a user to determine alternate paths of browsing the database (see Figure 6.12). The dendogram allows the user to determine which clusters to be reviewed are likely to have items of interest. Even without the visual display of the hierarchy, a user can use the

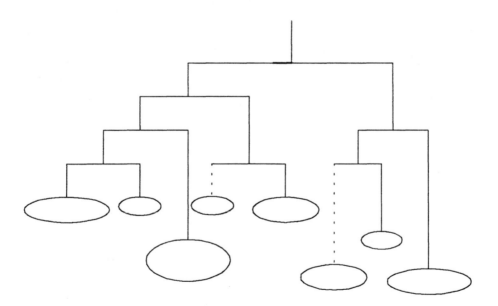

Figure 6.12 Dendogram

logical hierarchy to browse items of interest. A user, once having identified an item of interest, can request to see other items in the cluster. The user can increase the specificity of items by going to children clusters or by increasing the generality of items being reviewed by going to a parent cluster.

Most of the existing HACM approaches can be defined in terms of the Lance-Williams dissimilarity update formula (Lance-66). It defines a general formula for calculating the dissimilarity D between any existing cluster C_k and a new cluster $C_{i,j}$ created by combining clusters C_i and C_j.

$$D(C_{i,j}, C_k) = \alpha_i D(C_i, C_k) + \alpha_j D(C_j, C_k) + \beta D(C_i, C_j) + \gamma | D(C_i, C_k) - D(C_j, C_k)|$$

By proper selection of α, β, and γ, the current techniques for HACM can be represented (Frakes-92). In comparing the various methods of creating hierarchical clusters Voorhees and later El-Hamdouchi and Willet determined that the group average method produced the best results on document collections (Voorhees-86, El-Hamdouchi-89).

The similarity between two clusters can be treated as the similarity between all objects in one cluster and all objects in the other cluster. Voorhees showed that the similarity between a cluster centroid and any item is equal to the mean similarity between the item and all items in the cluster. Since the centroid is the average of all items in the cluster, this means that similarities between centroids can be used to calculate the similarities between clusters.

Ward's Method (Ward-63) chooses the minimum square Euclidean distance between points (e.g., centroids in this case) normalized by the number of objects in each cluster. He uses the formula for the variance I, choosing the minimum variance:

$$I_{i,j} = ((m_i m_j)/(m_i + m_j))d_{i,j}^2$$

$$d_{i,j}^2 = \Sigma_{k=1} (x_{i,k} - x_{j,k})^2$$

where m_i is the number of objects in Class$_i$ and $d_{i,j}^2$ is the squared Euclidean distance. The process of selection of centroids can be improved by using the reciprocal nearest neighbor algorithm (Murtaugh-83, Murtaugh-85).

The techniques discribed in Section 6.2 created independent sets of classes. The automatic clustering techniques can also be used to create a hierarchy of objects (items or terms). The automatic approach has been applied to creating item hierarchies more than in hierarchical statistical thesaurus generation. In the manual creation of thesauri, network relationships are frequently allowed between terms and classes creating an expanded thesaurus called semantic networks (e.g., in TOPIC and RetrievalWare). Hierarchies have also been created going from general categories to more specific classes of terms. The human creator ensures that the generalization or specification as the hierarchy is created makes semantic sense. Automatic creation of a hierarchy for a statistical thesaurus introduces too many errors to be productive.

But for item hierarchies the algorithms can be applied. Centroids were used to reduce computation required for adjustments in term assignments to classes. For both terms and items, the centroid has the same structure as any of the items or terms when viewed as a vector from the Item/Term matrix (see Figure 6.2). A term is a vector composed of a column whereas an item is a vector composed of a row.

When the creation of the classes is complete, a centroid can be calculated for each class. When there are a large number of classes, the next higher level in the hierarchy can be created by using the same algorithms used in the initial clustering to cluster the centroids. The only change required may be in the thresholds used. When this process is complete, if there are still too many of these higher level clusters, an additional iteration of clustering can be applied to their centroids. This process will continue until the desired number of clusters at the highest level is achieved.

6.5 Summary

Thesauri, semantic nets and item clusters are essential tools in Information Retrieval Systems, assisting the user in locating relevant items. They provide more benefit to the recall process than in improving precision. Thesauri, either humanly generated or statistical, and semantic nets are used to expand search statements, providing a mapping between the users vocabulary and that of the authors. The number of false hits on non-relevant items retrieved is determined by how tightly coupled the terms are in the classes. When automatic techniques are used to create a statistical thesaurus, techniques such as cliques produce classes where the items are more likely to be related to the same concept than any of the other approaches. When a manually created thesaurus is used, human intervention is required to eliminate homonyms that produce false hits. A homonym is when a term has multiple, different meanings (e.g., the term field meaning an area of grass or an electromagnetic field). The longer (more terms) in the search statement, the less important the human intervention to eliminate homonyms. This is because items identified by the wrong interpretation of the homonym should have a low weight because the other search terms are not likely to be found in the item. When search statements are short, significant decreases in precision will occur if homonym pruning is not applied.

Item clustering also assists the user in identifying relevant items. It is used in two ways: to directly find additional items that may not have been found by the query and to serve as a basis for visualization of the Hit file. Each item cluster has a common semantic basis containing similar terms and thus similar concepts. To assist the user in understanding the major topics resulting from a search, the items retrieved can be clustered and used to create a visual (e.g., graphical) representation of the clusters and their topics (see Chapter 8 for examples). This allows a user to navigate between topics, potentially showing topics the user had not considered. The topics are not defined by the query but by the text of the items retrieved.

When items in the database have been clustered, it is possible to retrieve all of the items in a cluster, even if they were not identified by the search statement. When the user retrieves a strongly relevant item, the user can look at other items like it without issuing another search. When relevant items are used to create a new query (i.e., relevance feedback discussed in Section 7.3), the retrieved hits are similar to what might be produced by a clustering algorithm. As with the term clustering, item clustering assists in mapping between a user's vocabulary and the vocabulary of the authors.

From another perspective term clustering and item clustering achieve the same objective even though they are the inverse of each other. The objective of both is to determine additional relevant items by a co-ocurrence process. A statistical thesaurus creates a cluster of terms that co-occur in the same set of items. For all of the terms within the same cluster (assuming they are tightly coupled) there will be significant overlap of the set of items they are found in. Item clustering is based upon the same terms being found in the other items in the cluster. Thus the set of items that caused a term clustering has a strong possibility of being in the same item cluster based upon the terms. For example, if a term cluster has 10 terms in it (assuming they are tightly related), then there will be a set of items where each item contains major subsets of the terms. From the item perspective, the set of items that has the commonality of terms, has a strong possibility to be placed in the same item cluster.

Hierarchical clustering of items is of theoretical interest, but has minimal practical application. The major rationale for using hierarchical clustering is to improve performance in search of clusters. The complexity of maintaining the clusters as new items are added to the system and the possibility of reduced recall (discussed in Chapter 7) are examples of why this is not used in commercial systems. Hierarchical thesauri are used in operational systems because there is additional knowledge in the human generated hierarchy. They have been historically used as a means to select index terms when indexing items. It provides a controlled vocabulary and standards between indexers.

EXERCISES

1.   If clustering has been completed on two different domains. Discuss the impact of merging the domains into a single cluster for both term clustering and item clustering. What factors will affect the amount of work that will be required to merge the clusters together? (HINT: consider the steps in clustering)

2. Which of the guidelines and additional decisions can be incorporated in an automatic statistical thesaurus construction program? Describe how they would be implemented and the risks with their implementation. Describe your justification for the guidelines and exercises selected that can not be automated.

3. Prove that a term could not be found in multiple clusters when using the single link technique.

4. Describe what effect increasing and decreasing the threshold value has on the creation of classes and under what condition you would make the change.

5. Given the following Term-Term matrix:

	T1	T2	T3	T4	T5	T6	T7	T8	T9
T1		14	9	0	3	0	12	0	16
T2	14		0	6	4	0	14	0	11
T3	9	0		12	7	4	1	0	14
T4	0	6	12		3	0	14	9	8
T5	3	4	7	3		12	6	16	0
T6	0	0	4	0	12		9	2	9
T7	12	14	1	14	6	9		0	12
T8	0	0	0	9	16	2	0		8
T9	16	11	14	8	0	9	12	8	

a. Determine the Term Relationship matrix using a threshold of 10 or higher

b. Determine the clusters using the clique technique

c. Determine the clusters using the single link technique

d. Determine the clusters using the star technique where the term selected for the new seed for the next star is the smallest number term nor already part of a class.

e. Discuss the differences between the single link, the clique and the star clusters. What are the characteristics of the items that would suggest which technique to use?

6. Given the following set of items:

	Term1	Term2	Term3	Term4	Term5	Term6	Term7	Term8
Item 1	3	0	2	2	0	0	4	3
Item 2	0	0	4	3	2	0	0	2
Item 3	2	2	0	2	2	1	0	0
Item 4	0	1	0	2	2	0	1	0
Item 5	0	0	0	0	0	2	0	0
Item 6	2	1	3	4	2	2	0	2

    a. Starting with Item 1 and Item 2 in Class 1, and with Item 3 and Item 4 in Class 2, determine which items should be assigned to the clusters.

    b. Use the one-pass technique to determine cluster assignment.

    c. What are the differences in the results from the two processes?

7.   Will the clustering process always come to the same final set of clusters no matter what the starting clusters? Explain your answer.

8.   Can statistical thesaurus generation be used to develop a hierarchical cluster representation of a set of items? Discuss the value of creating the hierarchy and how you would use it in a system.

9.   What is the effect of clustering techniques on reducing the user overhead of finding relevant items.

7 User Search Techniques

7.1   Search Statements and Binding
7.2   Similarity Measures for Queries and Ranking
7.3   Relevance Feedback
7.4   Selective Dissemination of Information Search
7.5   Weighted Searches of Boolean Systems
7.6   Searching the INTERNET and Hypertext
7.7   Summary

Previous chapters defined the concept of indexing and the data structures most commonly associated with Information Retrieval Systems. Chapter 5 described different weighting algorithms associated with processing tokens. Applying these algorithms creates a data structure that can be used in search. Chapter 6 describes how clustering can be used to enhance retrieval and reduce the overhead of search. Chapter 7 focuses on how search is performed. To understand the search process, it is first necessary to look at the different binding levels of the search statement entered by the user to the database being searched. The selection and ranking of items is accomplished via similarity measures that calculate the similarity between the user's search statement and the weighted stored representation of the semantics in an item. Relevance feedback can help a user enhance search by making use of results from previous searches. This technique uses information from items judged as relevant and non-relevant to determine an expanded search statement. Chapter 6 introduces the concept of representing multiple items via an single averaged representation called a "centroid." Searching centroids can reduce search computation, but there is an associated risk of missing relevant items because of the averaging nature of a centroid. Hyperlinked items introduce new concepts in search originating from the dynamic nature of the linkages between items.

7.1 Search Statements and Binding

Search statements are the statements of an information need generated by users to specify the concepts they are trying to locate in items. As discussed in Chapter 2, the search statement use traditional Boolean logic and/or Natural Language. In generation of the search statement, the user may have the ability to weight (assign an importance) to different concepts in the statement. At this point the binding is to the vocabulary and past experiences of the user. Binding in this sense is when a more abstract form is redefined into a more specific form. The search statement is the user's attempt to specify the conditions needed to subset logically the total item space to that cluster of items that contains the information needed by the user.

The next level of binding comes when the search statement is parsed for use by a specific search system. The search system translates the query to its own metalanguage. This process is similar to the indexing of item processes described in Chapter 5. For example, statistical systems determine the processing tokens of interest and the weights assigned to each processing token based upon frequency of occurrence from the search statement. Natural language systems determine the syntactical and discourse semantics using algorithms similar to those used in indexing. Concept systems map the search statement to the set of concepts used to index items.

The final level of binding comes as the search is applied to a specific database. This binding is based upon the statistics of the processing tokens in the database and the semantics used in the database. This is especially true in statistical and concept indexing systems. Some of the statistics used in weighting are based upon the current contents of the database. Some examples are Document Frequency and Total Frequency for a specific term. Frequently in a concept indexing system, the concepts that are used as the basis for indexing are determined by applying a statistical algorithm against a representative sample of the database versus being generic across all databases (see Chapter 5). Natural Language indexing techniques tend to use the most corpora-independent algorithms. Figure 7.1 illustrates the three potential different levels of binding. Parenthesis are used in the second binding step to indicate expansion by a thesaurus.

The length of search statements directly affect the ability of Information Retrieval Systems to find relevant items. The longer the search query, the easier it is for the system to find items. Profiles used as search statements for Selective Dissemination of Information systems are usually very long, typically 75 to 100 terms. In large systems used by research specialists and analysts, the typical ad hoc search statement is approximately 7 terms. In a paper to be published in SIGIR-97, Fox et al. at Virginia Tech have noted that the typical search statement on the Internet is one or two words. These extremely short search statements for ad hoc queries significantly reduce the effectiveness of many of the techniques

INPUT	Binding
"Find me information on the impact of the oil spills in Alaska on the price of oil"	User search statement using vocabulary of user
impact, oil (petroleum), spills (accidents), Alaska, price (cost, value)	Statistical system binding extracts processing tokens
impact (.308), oil (.606), petroleum (.65), spills (.12), accidents (.23), Alaska (.45), price (.16), cost (.25), value (.10)	Weights assigned to search terms based upon inverse document frequency algorithm and database

Figure 7.1 Examples of Query Binding

whose performance is discussed in Chapter 10 and are requiring investigation into new automatic search expansion algorithms.

7.2 Similarity Measures and Ranking

Searching in general is concerned with calculating the similarity between a user's search statement and the items in the database. Although many of the older systems are unweighted, the newer classes of Information Retrieval Systems have logically stored weighted values for the indexes to an item. The similarity may be applied to the total item or constrained to logical passages in the item. For example, every paragraph may be defined as a passage or every 100 words. The PIRCS system from Queen's College, CUNY, applies its algorithms to subdocuments defined as 550 word chunks (Kwok-96, Kwok-95). In this case, the similarity will be to the passages versus the total item. The highest similarity for any of the passages is used as the similarity measure for the item. Restricting the similarity measure to passages gains significant precision with minimal impact on recall. In results presented at TREC-4, it was discovered that passage retrieval makes a significant difference when search statements are long (hundreds of terms) but does not make a major difference for short queries. The lack of a large number of terms makes it harder to find shorter passages that contain the search terms expanded from the shorter queries.

Once items are identified as possibly relevant to the user's query, it is best to present the most likely relevant items first. This process is called "ranking." Usually the output of the use of a similarity measure in the search process is a scalar number that represents how similar an item is to the query.

7.2.1 Similarity Measures

A variety of different similarity measures can be used to calculate the similarity between the item and the search statement. A characteristic of a similarity formula is that the results of the formula increase as the items become more similar. The value is zero if the items are totally dissimilar. An example of a simple "sum of the products" similarity measure from the examples in Chapter 6 to determine the similarity between documents for clustering purposes is:

$$\text{SIM}(\text{Item}_i, \text{Item}_j) = \Sigma \, (\text{Term}_{i,k}) \, (\text{Term}_{j,k})$$

This formula uses the summation of the product of the various terms of two items when treating the index as a vector. If Item_j is replaced with Query_j then the same formula generates the similarity between every Item and Query_j. The problem with this simple measure is in the normalization needed to account for variances in the length of items. Additional normalization is also used to have the final results come between zero and +1 (some formulas use the range −1 to +1).

One of the originators of the theory behind statistical indexing and similarity functions was Robertson and Spark Jones (Robertson-76). Their model suggests that knowledge of terms in relevant items retrieved from a query should adjust the weights of those terms in the weighting process. They used the number of relevant documents versus the number of non-relevant documents in the database and the number of relevant documents having a specific query term versus the number of non-relevant documents having that term to devise four formulas for weighting. This assumption of the availability of relevance information in the weighting process was later relaxed by Croft and Harper (Croft-79). Croft expanded this original concept, taking into account the frequency of occurrence of terms within an item producing the following similarity formula (Croft-83):

$$\text{SIM}(\text{DOC}_i, \text{QUERY}_j) = \sum_{i=1}^{Q} (C + IDFi) * fi, j)$$

where C is a constant used in tuning, IDF_i is the inverse document frequency for term "i" in the collection and

$$f_{i,j} = K + (K - 1) \, \text{TF}_{i,j}/\text{maxfreq}_j$$

where K is a tuning constant, $TF_{i,j}$ is the frequency of term i "i" item j and maxfreq$_j$ is the maximum frequency of any term in item "j." The best values for K seemed to range between 0.3 and 0.5.

Another early similarity formula was used by Salton in the SMART system (Salton-83). Salton treated the index and the search query as n-dimensional vectors (see Chapter 5). To determine the "weight" an item has with respect to the search statement, the Cosine formula is used to calculate the distance between the vector for the item and the vector for the query:

$$SIM(DOC_i, QUERY_j) = \frac{\sum_{k=1}^{n} (DOC_{i,k} * QTERM_{j,k})}{\sqrt{\sum_{k=1}^{n}(DOC_i,k)^2 * \sum_{k=1}^{n}(QTERM_j,k)^2}}$$

where $DOC_{i,k}$ is the kth term in the weighted vector for Item "i" and $QTERM_{j,k}$ is the kth term in query "j." The Cosine formula calculates the Cosine of the angle between the two vectors. As the Cosine approaches "1," the two vectors become coincident (i.e., the term and the query represent the same concept). If the two are totally unrelated, then they will be orthogonal and the value of the Cosine is "0." What is not taken into account is the length of the vectors. For example, if the following vectors are in a three dimensional (three term) system:

Item =	(4 , 8, 0)
Query 1 =	(1, 2, 0)
Query 2 =	(3, 6, 0)

then the Cosine value is identical for both queries even though Query 2 has significantly higher weights in the terms in common. To improve the formula, Salton and Buckley (Salton-88) changed the term factors in the query to:

$$QTERM_{i,k} = (0.5 + (0.5\ TF_{i,k}/maxfreq_k)) * IDF_i$$

where $TF_{i,k}$ is the frequency of term "i" in query "k," $maxfreq_k$ is the maximum frequency of any term in query "k" and IDF_i is the inverse document frequency for term "i" (see Chapter 5 for the formula). In the most recent evolution of the formula, the IDF factor has been dropped (Buckley-96).

Two other commonly used measures are the Jaccard and the Dice similarity measures (Rijsbergen-79). Both change the normalizing factor in the denominator to account for different characteristics of the data. The denominator in the Cosine formula is invariant to the number of terms in common and produces very small numbers when the vectors are large and the number of common elements is small. In the Jaccard similarity measure, the denominator becomes dependent upon the number of terms in common.   As the common elements increase, the similarity value quickly decreases, but is always in the range -1 to +1. The Jaccard formula is :

$$SIM(DOC_i, QUERY_j) = \frac{\sum\limits_{k=1}^{n} (DOC_{i,k} * QTERM_{j,k})}{\sum\limits_{k=1}^{n} DOC_{i,k} + \sum\limits_{k=1}^{n} QTERM_{j,k} - \sum\limits_{k=1}^{n} (DOC_{i,k} * QTERM_{j,k})}$$

The Dice measure simplifies the denominator from the Jaccard measure and introduces a factor of 2 in the numerator. The normalization in the Dice formula is also invariant to the number of terms in common.

$$SIM(DOC_i, QUERY_j) = \frac{2 * \sum\limits_{k=1}^{n} (DOC_{i,k} * QTERM_{j,k})}{\sum\limits_{k=1}^{n} DOC_{i,k} + \sum\limits_{k=1}^{n} QTERM_{j,k}}$$

Figure 7.2 shows how the normalizing denominator results vary with the commonality of terms. For the Dice value, the numerator factor of 2 is divided into the denominator. Notice that as long as the vector values are same, independent of their order, the Cosine and Dice normalization factors do not change. Also notice that when there are a number of terms in common between the query and the document, that the Jaccard formula can produce a negative normalization factor.

It might appear that similarity measures only apply to statistical systems where the formulas directly apply to the stored indexes. In the implementation of Natural Language systems, also weighted values come from statistical data in conjunction with the natural language processing stored as indexes. Similarity algorithms are applied to these values in a similar fashion to statistical systems. But in addition to the similarity measures, constructs are used at the discourse level to perform additional filtering of the items.

Use of a similarity algorithm returns the complete data base as search results. Many of the items have a similarity close or equal to zero (or minimum value the similarity measure produces). For this reason, thresholds are usually

QUERY = (2, 2, 0, 0, 4)
DOC1 = (0, 2, 6, 4, 0)
DOC2 = (2, 6, 0, 0, 4)

	Cosine	Jaccard	Dice
DOC1	36.66	16	10
DOC2	36.66	−12	10

Figure 7.2 Normalizing Factors for Similarity Measures

associated with the search process. The threshold defines the items in the resultant Hit file from the query. Thresholds are either a value that the similarity measure must equal or exceed or a number that limits the number of items in the Hit file. A default is always the case where the similarity is greater than zero. Figure 7.3 illustrates the threshold process. The simple "sum of the products" similarity formula is used to calculate similarity between the query and each document. If no threshold is specified, all three documents are considered hits. If a threshold of 4 is selected, then only DOC1 is returned.

One special area of concern arises from search of clusters of terms that are stored in a hierarchical scheme (see Chapter 6). The items are stored in

Vector: American, geography, lake, Mexico, painter, oil,
              reserve, subject

DOC1   geography *of* Mexico *suggests* oil reserves *are available*
              vector (0, 1, 0, 2, 0, 3, 1, 0)

DOC2   American geography *has* lakes *available everywhere*
              vector (1, 3, 2, 0, 0, 0, 0, 0)

DOC3   painters *suggest* Mexico lakes *as* subjects
              vector (0, 0, 1, 3, 3, 0, 0, 2)

QUERY   oil reserves *in* Mexico
              vector (0, 0, 0, 1, 0, 1, 1, 0)

SIM (Q, DOC1) = 6, SIM (Q, DOC2) = 0, SIM(Q, DO3) = 3

Figure 7.3 Query Threshold Process

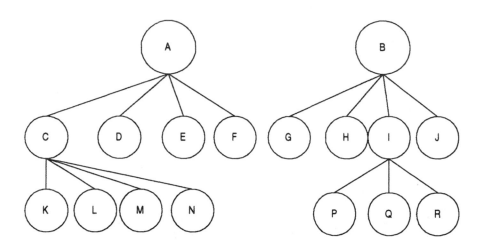

Figure 7.4 Item Cluster Hierarchy

clusters that are represented by the centroid for each cluster. Figure 7.4 shows a cluster representation of an item space. In Figure 7.4, each letter at the leaf (bottom nodes) represent an item (i.e., K, L, M, N, D, E, F, G, H, P, Q, R, J). The letters at the higher nodes (A, C, B, I) represent the centroid of their immediate children nodes. The hierarchy is used in search by performing a top-down process. The query is compared to the centroids "A" and "B." If the results of the similarity measure are above the threshold, the query is then applied to the nodes' children. If not, then that part of the tree is pruned and not searched. This continues until the actual leaf nodes that are not pruned are compared. The problem comes from the nature of a centroid which is an average of a collection of items (in Physics, the center of gravity). The risk is that the average may not be similar enough to the query for continued search, but specific items used to calculate the centroid may be close enough to satisfy the search. The risks of missing items and thus reducing recall increases as the standard deviation increases. Use of centroids reduces the similarity computations but could cause a decrease in recall. It should have no effect on recall since that is based upon the similarity calculations at the leaf (item) level.

In Figure 7.5 the filled circle represents the query and the filled boxes represent the centroids for the three clusters represented by the ovals. In this case, the query may only be similar enough to the end two circles for additional analysis. But there are specific items in the right cluster that are much closer to the query than the cluster centroid and could satisfy the query. These items cannot be returned because when their centroid is eliminated they are no longer considered.

As part of investigating improved techniques to present Hits to users, Hearst and Pedersen from XEROX Palo Alto Research Center (PARC) are

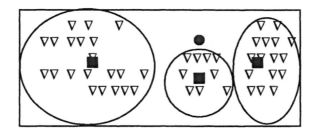

Figure 7.5 Centroid Comparisons

pursuing topical clustering as an alternative to similarity search ranking (Hearst-96).   In their experiments they applied the clustering to the entire corpora. Although the clustering conveyed some of the content and structure of the corpora, it was shown to be less effective in retrieval than a standard similarity query (Pirolli-96).   Constraining the search to the hierarchy retrieved fewer relevant items than a similarity query that focused the results on a indexed logical subset of the corpus.

7.2.2 Ranking Algorithms

A by-product of use of similarity measures for selecting Hit items is a value that can be used in ranking the output. Ranking the output implies ordering the output from most likely items that satisfy the query to least likely items. This reduces the user overhead by allowing the user to display the most likely relevant items first.   The original Boolean systems returned items ordered by date of entry into the system versus by likelihood of relevance to the user's search statement. With the inclusion of statistical similarity techniques into commercial systems and the large number of hits that originate from searching diverse corpora, such as the Internet, ranking has become a common feature of modern systems. A summary of ranking algorithms from the research community is found in an article written by Belden and Croft (Belkin-87).

In most of the commercial systems, heuristic rules are used to assist in the ranking of items.   Generally, systems do not want to use factors that require knowledge across the corpus (e.g., inverse document frequency) as a basis for their similarity or ranking functions because it is too difficult to maintain current values as the database changes and the added complexity has not been shown to significantly improve the overall weighting process. A good example of how a commercial product integrates efficiency with theoretical concepts is the

RetrievalWare system's approach to queries and ranking (RETRIEVALWARE-95).

RetrievalWare first uses indexes (inversion lists) to identify potential relevant items. It then applies coarse grain and fine grain ranking. The coarse grain ranking is based on the presence of query terms within items. In the fine grain ranking, the exact rank of the item is calculated. The coarse grain ranking is a weighted formula that can be adjusted based on completeness, contextual evidence or variety, and semantic distance. Completeness is the proportion of the number of query terms (or related terms if a query term is expanded using the RetrievalWare semantic network/thesaurus) found in the item versus the number in the query. It sets an upper limit on the rank value for the item. If weights are assigned to query terms, the weights are factored into the value. Contextual evidence occurs when related words from the semantic network are also in the item. Thus if the user has indicated that the query term "charge" has the context of "paying for an object" then finding words such as "buy," "purchase," "debt" suggests that the term "charge" in the item has the meaning the user desires and that more weight should be placed in ranking the item. Semantic distance evaluates how close the additional words are to the query term. Synonyms add additional weight; antonyms decrease weight. The coarse grain process provides an initial rank to the item based upon existence of words within the item. Since physical proximity is not considered in coarse grain ranking, the ranking value can be easily calculated.

Fine grain ranking considers the physical location of query terms and related words using factors of proximity in addition to the other three factors in coarse grain evaluation. If the related terms and query terms occur in close proximity (same sentence or paragraph) the item is judged more relevant. A factor is calculated that maximizes at adjacency and decreases as the physical separation increases. If the query terms are widely distributed throughout a long item, it is possible for the item to have a fine grain rank of zero even though it contains the query terms.

Although ranking creates a ranking score, most systems try to use other ways of indicating the rank value to the user as Hit lists are displayed. The scores have a tendency to be misleading and confusing to the user. The differences between the values may be very close or very large. It has been found to be better to indicate the general relevance of items than to be over specific (see Chapter 8).

7.3 Relevance Feedback

As discussed in the early chapters in this text, one of the major problems in finding relevant items lies in the difference in vocabulary between the authors and the user. Thesuari and semantic networks provide utility in generally expanding a user's search statement to include potential related search terms. But this still does not correlate to the vocabulary used by the authors that contributes to a particular database. There is also a significant risk that the thesaurus does not include the latest jargon being used, acronyms or proper nouns. In an interactive system, users can manually modify an inefficient query or have the system automatically expand the query via a thesaurus. The user can also use relevant items that have been found by the system (irrespective of their ranking) to improve future searches, which is the basis behind relevance feedback. Relevant items (or portions of relevant items) are used to reweight the existing query terms and possibly expand the user's search statement with new terms.

The first major work on relevance feedback was published in 1965 by Rocchio (republished in 1971: Rocchio-71).   Rocchio was documenting experiments on reweighting query terms and query expansion based upon a vector representation of queries and items.   The concepts are also found in the probabilistic model presented by Robertson and Sparck Jones (Robertson-76). The relevance feedback concept was that the new query should be based on the old query modified to increase the weight of terms in relevant items and decrease the weight of terms that are in non-relevant items. This technique not only modified the terms in the original query but also allowed expansion of new terms from the relevant items. The formula used is:

$$Q_n = Q_o + \frac{1}{r} \sum_{i=1}^{r} DR_I - \frac{1}{nr} \sum_{j=1}^{nr} DNR_j$$

where

Q_n	= the revised vector for the new query	
Q_o	= the original query	
r	= number of relevant items	
DR_i	= the vectors for the relevant items	
nr	= number of non-relevant items	
DNR_j	= the vectors for the non-relevant items.	

The factors r and nr were later modified to be constants that account for the number of items along with the importance of that particular factor in the equation. Additionally a constant was added to Q_o to allow adjustments to the importance of the weight assigned to the original query. This led to the revised version of the formula:

$$Q_n = \alpha Q_o + \beta \sum_{i=1}^{r} DR_I - \gamma \sum_{j=1}^{nr} DNR_j$$

where α, β, and γ are the constants associated with each factor (usually $1/n$ or $1/nr$ times a constant). The factor $\beta \sum_{i=1}^{r} DR_I$ is referred to as positive feedback because it is using the user judgments on relevant items to increase the values of terms for the next iteration of searching. The factor $\gamma \sum_{j=1}^{rnr} DNR_j$ is referred to as negative feedback since it decreases the values of terms in the query vector. Positive feedback is weighted significantly greater than negative feedback. Many times only positive feedback is used in a relevance feedback environment. Positive feedback is more likely to move a query closer to a user's information needs. Negative feedback may help, but in some cases it actually reduces the effectiveness of a query. Figure 7.6 gives an example of the impacts of positive and negative feedback. The filled circles represent non-relevant items; the other circles represent relevant items. The oval represents the items that are returned from the query. The solid box is logically where the query is initially. The hollow box is the query modified by relevance feedback (positive only or negative only in the Figure).

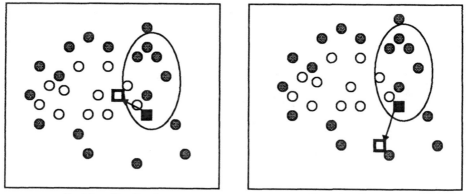

Positive Feedback   Negative Feedback

Figure 7.6 Impact of Relevance Feedback

Positive feedback moves the query to retrieve items similar to the items retrieved and thus in the direction of more relevant items. Negative feedback moves the query away from the non-relevant items retrieved, but not necessarily closer to more relevant items.

Figure 7.7 shows how the formula is applied to three items (two relevant and one non-relevant). If we use the factors $\alpha = 1$, $\beta = \frac{1}{4}$ (½ times a constant ½), γ

= ¼ (1/1 times a constant ¼) in the foregoing formula we get the following revised query (NOTE: negative values are changed to a zero value in the revised Query vector):

$$Q_n = (3, 0, 0, 2, 0) + ¼ (2+1, 4+3, 0+0, 0+0, 2+0) - ¼ (0, 0, 4, 3, 2)$$
$$= (3¾, 1¾, 0 \{-1\}, 1¼, 0)$$

	Term 1	Term 2	Term 3	Term 4	Term 5
Q_o	3	0	0	2	0
$DOC1_r$	2	4	0	0	2
$DOC2_r$	1	3	0	0	0
$DOC3_{nr}$	0	0	4	3	3
Q_n	3¾	1¾	0	1¼	0

Figure 7.7 Query Modification via Relevance Feedback

Using the unnormalized similarity formula $SIM(Q_k, DOC_l) = \sum_{i=n}^{5} TERM_{k,i} *$
$TERM_{l,I}$ produces the results shown in Figure 7.8:

	DOC1	DOC2	DOC3
Q_o	6	3	6
Q_n	11½	7½	3¼

Figure 7.8 Effect of Relevance Feedback

In addition to showing the benefits of relevance feedback, this example illustrates the problems of identifying information. Although DOC3 is not relevant to the user, the initial query produced one of the highest similarity measures for it. This was caused by a query term (Term 4) of interest to the user that has a significant weight in DOC3. The fewer the number of terms in a user query, the more likely a specific term to cause non-relevant items to be returned.   The modification to the query by the relevance feedback process significantly increased the similarity measure values for the two relevant items (DOC1 and DOC2) while decreasing the value of the non-relevant item. It is also of interest to note that the new query added a weight to Term 2 that was not in the original query. One reason that the user might not have initially had a value to Term 2 is that it might not have been in the user's vocabulary. For example, the user may have been searching on "PC" and "word processor" and not been aware that many authors use the specific term "Macintosh" rather than "PC."

Relevance feedback, in particular positive feedback, has been proven to be of significant value in producing better queries. Some of the early experiments on the SMART system (Ide-69, Ide-71, Salton-83) indicated the possible improvements that would be gained by the process. But the small collection sizes and evaluation techniques put into question the actual gains by using relevance feedback. One of the early problems addressed in relevance feedback is how to treat query terms that are not found in any retrieved relevant items. Just applying the algorithm would have the effect of reducing the relative weight of those terms with respect to other query terms. From the user's perspective, this may not be desired because the term may still have significant value to the user if found in the future iterations of the search process. Harper and van Rijisbergen addressed this issue in their proposed EMIM weighting scheme (Harper-78, Harper-80). Relevance feedback has become a common feature in most information systems. When the original query is modified based upon relevance feedback, the systems ensure that the original query terms are in the modified query, even if negative feedback would have eliminated them. In some systems the modified query is presented to the user to allow the user to readjust the weights and review the new terms added.

Recent experiments with relevance feedback during the TREC sessions have shown conclusively the advantages of relevance feedback. Queries using relevance feedback produce significantly better results than those being manually enhanced. When users enter queries with a few number of terms, automatic relevance feedback based upon just the rank values of items has been used. This concept in information systems that does not require human relevance judgments. The highest ranked items from a query are automatically assumed to be relevant and applying relevance feedback (positive only) used to create and execute an expanded query. The system returns to the user a Hit file based upon the expanded query. This technique also showed improved performance over not using the automatic relevance feedback process. In the automatic query processing tests from TREC (see Chapter 10) most systems use the highest ranked hits from the first pass to generate the relevance feedback for the second pass.

7.4 Selective Dissemination of Information Search

Selective Dissemination of Information, frequently called dissemination systems, are becoming more prevalent with the growth of the Internet. A dissemination system is sometimes labeled a "push" system while a search system is called a "pull" system. The differences are that in a search system the user proactively makes a decision that he needs information and directs the query to the information system to search. In a dissemination system, the user defines a profile (similar to a stored query) and as new information is added to the system it is automatically compared to the user's profile. If it is considered a match, it is asynchronously sent to the user's "mail" file (see Chapter 1).

One concept that ties together the two search statements (query and profile) is the introduction of a time parameter associated with a search statement. As long as the time is in the future, the search statement can be considered active and disseminating as items arrive. Once the time parameter is past, the user's need for the information is no longer exists except upon demand (i.e., issuing the search statement as an ad hoc query).

The differences between the two functions lie in the dynamic nature of the profiling process, the size and diversity of the search statements and number of simultaneous searches per item. In the search system, an existing database exists. As such, corpora statistics exist on term frequency within and between terms. These can be used for weighting factors in the indexing process and the similarity comparison (e.g., inverse document frequency algorithms). A dissemination system does not necessarily have a retrospective database associated with it. Thus its algorithms need to avoid dependency upon previous data or develop a technique to estimate terms for their formula. This class of system is also discussed as a binary classification system because there is no possibility for real time feedback from the user to assist in search statement refinement. The system makes a binary decision to reject or file the item (Lewis-95).

Profiles are relatively static search statements that cover a diversity of topics. Rather than specifying a particular information need, they usually generalize all of the potential information needs of a user. They are focused on current information needs of the user. Thus profiles have a tendency to contain significantly more terms than an ad hoc query (hundreds of terms versus a small number). The size tends to make them more complex and discourages users from wanting to change them without expert advice.

One of the first commercial search techniques for dissemination was the Logicon Message Dissemination System (LMDS). The system originated from a system created by Chase, Rosen and Wallace (CRW Inc.). It was designed for speed to support the search of thousands of profiles with items arriving every 20 seconds. It demonstrated one approach to the problem where the profiles were treated as the static database and the new item acted like the query. It uses the terms in the item to search the profile structure to identify those profiles whose logic could be satisfied by the item. The system uses a least frequently occurring trigraph (three character) algorithm that quickly identifies which profiles are not satisfied by the item. The potential profiles are analyzed in detail to confirm if the item is a hit.

Another example of a dissemination approach is the Personal Library Software (PLS) system. It uses the approach of accumulating newly received items into the database and periodically running user's profiles against the database. This makes maximum use of the retrospective search software but loses near real time delivery of items. More recent examples of a similar approach are the

Retrievalware and the InRoute software systems. In these systems the item is processed into the searchable form. Since the Profiles are relatively static, some use is made in identifying all the terms used in all the profiles. Any words in the items that are members of this list can not contribute to the similarity process and thus are eliminated from the search structure. Every profile is then compared to the item. Retrievalware uses a statistical algorithm but it does not include any corpora data. Thus not having a database does not affect its similarity measure. InRoute, like the INQUERY system used against retrospective database, uses inverse document frequency information. It creates this information as it processes items, storing and modifying it for use as future items come arrive. This would suggest that the values would be continually changing as items arrive until sufficient items have arrived to stabilize the inverse document frequency weights.

Relevance feedback has been proven to enhance the search capabilities of ad hoc queries against retrospective databases. Relevance feedback can also be applied to dissemination systems. Unlike an ad hoc query situation, the dissemination process is continuous, and the issue is the practicality of archiving all of the previous relevance judgments to be used in the relevance feedback process. Allen performed experiments on the number of items that have to arrive and be judged before the effects of relevance feedback stabilize (Allen-96). Previous work has been done on the number of documents needed to generate a new query and the amount of training needed (Buckley-94, Aalbersberg-92, Lewis-94). The two major choices are to save relevant items or relevance statistics for words. By saving dissimilar items, Allan demonstrated that the system sees a 2-3 per cent loss in effectiveness by archiving 10 per cent of the relevance judgments. This still requires significant storage space. He was able to achieve high effectiveness by storing information on as few as 250 terms.

Another approach to dissemination uses a statistical classification technique and explicit error minimization to determine the decision criteria for selecting items for a particular profile (Schutze-95). In this case, the classification process is related to assignment for each item into one of two classes: relevant to a user's profile or non-relevant. Error minimization encounters problems in high dimension spaces. The dimensionality of an information space is defined by the number of unique terms where each term is another dimension. This is caused by there being too many dimensions for a realistic training set to establish the error minimization parameters. To reduce the dimensionality, a version of latent semantic indexing (LSI) can be used. The process requires a training data set along with its associated profiles. Relevance feedback is an example of a simple case of a learning algorithm that does not use error minimization. Other examples of algorithms used in linear classifiers that perform explicit error minimization are linear discriminant analysis, logistic regression and linear neural networks.

Schutze et al. used two approaches to reduce the dimensionality: selecting a set of existing features to use or creating a new much smaller set of features that the original features are mapped into. A χ^2 measure was used to determine the most important features. The test was applied to a table that contained the number of relevant (N_r) and non-relevant (N_{nr}) items in which a term occurs plus the number of relevant and non-relevant items in which the term does not occur (N_{r-}, N_{nr-} respectively). The formula used was:

$$\chi^2 = \frac{N(N_r N_{nr-} - N_{r-} N_{nr})^2}{(N_r + N_{r-})(N_{nr} + N_{nr-})(N_r + N_{nr})(N_{r-} + N_{nr-})}$$

To focus the analysis, only items in the local region defined by a profile were analyzed. The chi-squared technique provides a more effective mechanism than frequency of occurrence of terms. A high χ^2 score indicates a feature whose frequency has a significant dependence on occurrence in a relevant or non-relevant item.

An alternative technique to identify the reduced feature (vector) set is to use a modified latent semantic index (LSI) technique to determine a new reduced set of concept vectors. The technique varies from the LSI technique described in Chapter 5 by creating a separate representation of terms and items by each profile to create the "local" space of items likely to be relevant (i.e., Local LSI). The results of the analysis go into a learning algorithm associated with the classification technique (Hull-94). The use of the profile to define a local region is essential when working with large databases. Otherwise the number of LSI factors is in the hundreds and the ability to process them is currently unrealistic. Rather than keeping the LSI factors separate per profile, another approach is to merge the results from all of the queries into a single LSI analysis (Dumais-93). This increases the number of factors with associated increase in computational complexity.

Once the reduced vector set has been identified, then learning algorithms can be used for the classification process. Linear discriminate analysis, logistic regression and neural networks are three possible techniques that were compared by Schutze et al. Other possible techniques are classification trees (Tong-94, Lewis-94a), Bayesian networks (Croft-94), Bayesian classifiers (Lewis-92), rules induction (Apte-94), nearest neighbor techniques (Masand-92, Yang-94), and least square methods (Fuhr-89). Linear discrimination analysis uses the covariance class for each document class to detect feature dependence (Gnanadesikan-79). Assuming a sample of data from two groups with n_1 and n_2 members, mean vectors $\bar{x}_1$ and $\bar{x}_2$ and covariance matrices C_1 and C_2 respectively, the objective is to maximize the separation between the two groups. This can be achieved by maximizing the distance between the vector means, scaling to reflect the structure in the pooled covariance matrix. Thus choose a such that:

$$a^* = \arg_a \max \frac{a^T (\bar{x}_1 - \bar{x}_2)}{\sqrt{a^T C_a}}$$

is maximized where T is the transpose and $(n_1 + n_2 - 2)C = (n_1 - 1)C_1 + (n_2 - 1)C_2$. Since C is positive, the Cholesky decomposition of $C = R^T$. Let $b = Ra$; then the formula becomes;

$$a^* = \arg_b \max \frac{b^T R^{T-1} (\bar{x}_1 - \bar{x}_2)}{\sqrt{b^T b}}$$

which is maximized by choosing $b \propto R^{T-1}(\bar{x}_1 - \bar{x}_2)$. This means:

$$a^* = R^{-1}b = C^{-1} (\bar{x}_1 - \bar{x}_2)$$

The one dimensional space defined by $y = a^{*T}x$ should cause the group means to be well separated. To produce a non-linear classifier, a pair of shrinkage parameters is used to create a very general family of estimators for the group covariance matrix (Freidman-89). This process called Regularized Discriminant Analysis looks at a weighted combination of the pooled and unpooled covariance matrices. The optimal values of the shrinkage parameters are selected based upon the cross validation over the training set. The non-linear classifier produced by this technique has not been shown to make major improvements in the classification process (Hull-95).

A second approach is to use logistic regression (Cooper-94a). It models a binary response variable by a linear combination of one or more predictor variables, using a logit link function:

$$g(\pi) = \log(\pi/(1 - \pi))$$

and modeling variance with a binomial random variable. This is achieved by modeling the dependent variable $\log(\pi/(1 - \pi))$ as a linear combination of independent variables using a form $g(\pi) = x_i\beta$. In this formula π is the estimated response probability (probability of relevance), x_i is the feature vector (reduced vector) for document I, and β is the weight vector which is estimated from the matrix of feature vectors. The optimal value of β can be calculated using the maximum likelihood and the Newton-Raphson method of numerical optimization (McCullagh-89). The major difference from previous experiments using logistic regression is that Schutze et al. do not use information from all the profiles but restrict the analysis for each profile.

        A third technique is to use neural networks for the learning function. A
neural network is a network of input and output cells (based upon neuron functions
in the brain) originating with the work of McCulloch and Pitts (McCulloch-43).
Each input pattern is propagated forward through the network. When an error is
detected it is propagated backward adjusting the cell parameters to reduce the
error, thus achieving learning.   This technique is very flexible and can
accommodate a wide range of distributions. A major risk of neural networks is
that they can overfit by learning the characteristics of the training data set and not
be generalized enough for the normal input of items. In applying training to a
neural network approach, a validation set of items is used in addition to the
training items to ensure that overfitting has not occurred. As each iteration of
parameter adjustment occurs on the training set, the validation set is retested.
Whenever the errors on the validation set increase, it indicates that overfitting is
occurring and establishes the number of iterations on training that improve the
parameter values while not harming generalization.
        The linear and non-linear architectures for an implementation of neural
nets is shown in Figure 7.9.

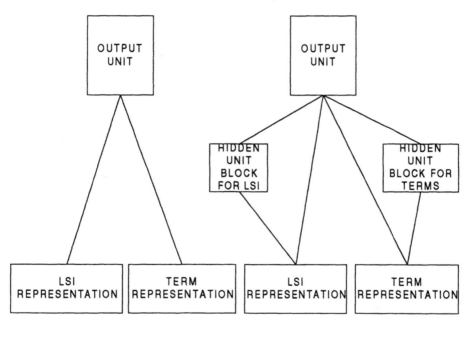

Linear Neural network   Non-linear Neural network

Figure 7.9 Linear and Non-linear networks

In the non-linear network, each of the hidden blocks consists of three hidden
units. A hidden unit can be interpreted as feature detectors that estimate the

probability of a feature being present in the input. Propagating this to the output unit can improve the overall estimation of relevance in the output unit. The networks show input of both terms and the LSI representation (reduced feature set). In both architectures, all input units are directly connected to the output units. Relevance is computed by setting the activations of the input units to the document's representation and propagating the activation through the network to the output unit, then propagating the error back through the network using a gradient descent algorithm (Rumelhart-95). A sigmoid was chosen as:

$$f(x) = \frac{e^x}{1+e^x}$$

as the activation function for the units of the network (Schutze-95). In this case backpropagation minimizes the same error as logistic regression (Rumelhart-95a). The cross-entropy error is:

$$L = -\sum t_i \log \sigma_i + 1 - t_i) \log(1 - \sigma_i)$$

where t_i is the relevance for document I and σ_I is the estimated relevance (or activation of the output unit) for document i. The definition of the sigmoid is equivalent to:

$$x = \log \left(\frac{f(x)}{1 - f(x)}\right)$$

which is the same as the logit link function.

Schutze et al. performed experiments with the Tipster test database to compare the three algorithms. They show that the linear classification schemes perform 10-15 per cent better than the traditional relevance feedback. To use the learning algorithms based upon error minimization and numerical computation one must use some technique of dimensionality reduction. Their experiments show that local latent semantic indexing is best for linear discrimination analysis and logistic regression since they have no mechanism for protecting against overfitting. When there are mechanisms to avoid overfitting such as in neural networks, other less precise techniques of dimension reduction can be used. This work suggests that there are alternatives to the statistical classification scheme associated with profiles and dissemination.

An issue with Mail files is the logical reorganization associated with display of items. In a retrospective query, the search is issued once and the hit list is a static file that does not change in size or order of presentation. The dissemination function is always adding items that satisfy a user's profile to the user's Mail file. If the items are stored sorted by rank, then the relative order of items can always be changing as new items are inserted in their position based upon the rank value. This constant reordering can be confusing to the user who remembers items by spatial relationships as well as naming. Thus the user may remember an item next to another item is of significant interest. But in trying to retrieve it at a later time, the reordering process can make it significantly harder to find.

7.5 Weighted Searches of Boolean Systems

The two major approaches to generating queries are Boolean and natural language. Natural language queries are easily represented within statistical models and are usable by the similarity measures discussed. Issues arise when Boolean queries are associated with weighted index systems. Some of the issues are associated with how the logic (AND, OR, NOT) operators function with weighted values and how weights are associated with the query terms. If the operators are interpreted in their normal interpretation, thay act too restrictive or too general (i.e., AND and OR operators respectively). Salton, Fox and Wu showed that using the strict definition of the operators will suboptimize the retrieval expected by the user (Salton-83a). Closely related to the strict definition problem is the lack of ranking that is missing from a pure Boolean process. Some of the early work addressing this problem recognized the fuzziness associated with mixing Boolean and weighted systems (Brookstein-78, Brookstein-80)

To integrate the Boolean and weighted systems model, Fox and Sharat proposed a fuzzy set approach (Fox-86). Fuzzy sets introduce the concept of degree of membership to a set (Zadeh-65). The degree of membership for AND and OR operations are defined as:

$$DEG_{A \cap B} = min(DEG_A, DEG_B)$$

$$DEG_{A \cup B} = max(DEG_A, DEG_B)$$

where A and B are terms in an item. DEG is the degree of membership. The Mixed Min and Max (MMM) model considers the similarity between query and document to be a linear combination of the minimum and maximum item weights. Fox proposed the following similarity formula:

$$SIM(QUERY_{OR}, DOC) = C_{OR\,1} * \ max(DOC1_1, DOC_2, \ldots, DOC_n) + C_{OR2} * min(DOC_1, DOC_2, \ldots, DOC_n)$$
$$SIM(QUERY_{AND}, DOC) = C_{AND1} * min(DOC_1, DOC_2, \ldots, DOC_n) + C_{AND2} * \ max(DOC1_1, DOC_2, \ldots, DOC_n)$$

where C_{OR1} and C_{OR2} are weighting coefficients for the OR operation and C_{AND1} and C_{AND2} are the weighting coefficients for the AND operation. Lee and Fox found in their experiments that the best performance comes when C_{AND1} is between 0.5 to 0.8 and C_{OR1} is greater than 0.2.

The MMM technique was expanded by Paice (Paice-84) considering all item weights versus the maximum/minimum approach. The similarity measure is calculated as:

$$\text{SIM(QUERY DOC)} = \sum_{i=1}^{n} r^{i-1} d_i \ / \ \sum_{i=1}^{n} r^{i-1}$$

where the d_i's are inspected in ascending order for AND queries and descending order for OR queries. The r terms are weighting coefficients. Lee and Fox showed that the best values for r are 1.0 for AND queries and 0.7 for OR queries (Lee-88). This technique requires more computation since the values need to be stored in ascending or descending order and thus must be sorted.

An alternative approach is using the P-norm model which allows terms within the query to have weights in addition to the terms in the items. Similar to the Cosine similarity technique, it considers the membership values $(d_{A1}, \ldots, d_{An})$ to be coordinates in an "n" dimensional space. For an OR query, the origin (all values equal zero) is the worst possibility. For an AND query the ideal point is the unit vector where all the D_i values equal 1. Thus the best ranked documents will have maximum distance from the origin in an OR query and minimal distance from the unit vector point. The generalized queries are:

$Q_{OR} = (A_1, a_1) \text{ OR } (A_2, a_2) \text{ OR } \ldots \text{ OR } (A_n, a_n)$

$Q_{AND} = (A_1, a_1) \text{ AND } (A_2, a_2) \text{ AND } \ldots \text{ AND } (A_n, a_n)$

The operators (AND and OR) will have a strictness value assigned that varies from 1 to infinity where infinity is the strict definition of the Boolean operator. The a_i values are the query term weights. If we assign the strictness value to a parameter labeled "S" then the similarity formulas between queries and items are:

$$\text{SIM}(Q_{OR}, \text{DOC}) = \sqrt[s]{(a_1^S d_{A1}^S + \bullet\bullet\bullet + a_n^S d_{An}^S)/(a_1^S + a_2^S + \bullet\bullet\bullet + a_n^S)}$$

$$\text{SIM}(Q_{AND}, \text{DOC}) = 1 - \sqrt[s]{(a_1^S(1-d_{A1})^S + \bullet\bullet\bullet + a_n^S(1-d_{An})^S)/(a_1^S + a_2^S + \bullet\bullet\bullet + a_n^S)}$$

$\text{SIM}(Q_{not}, \text{DOC}) = 1 - \text{SIM}(Q, \text{DOC})$

Another approach suggested by Salton provides additional insight into the issues of merging the Boolean queries and weighted query terms under the assumption that there are no weights available in the indexes (Salton-83). The objective is to perform the normal Boolean operations and then refine the results using weighting techniques. The following procedure is a modification to his approach for defining search results. The normal Boolean operations produce the following results:

"A OR B" retrieves those items that contain the term A or the term B or both

"A AND B" retrieves those items that contain both terms A and B

"A NOT B" retrieves those items that contain term A and not contain term B.

If weights are then assigned to the terms between the values 0.0 to 1.0, they may be interpreted as the significance that users are placing on each term. The value 1.0 is assumed to be the strict interpretation of a Boolean query. The value 0.0 is interpreted to mean that the user places little value on the term. Under these assumptions, a term assigned a value of 0.0 should have no effect on the retrieved set. Thus

"A_1 OR B_0" should return the set of items that contain A as a term
"A_1 AND B_0" will also return the set of items that contain term A
"A_1 NOT B_0" also return set A.

This suggests that as the weight for term B goes from 0.0 to 1.0 the resultant set changes from the set of all items that contains term A to the set normally generated from the Boolean operation. The process can be visualized by use of the VENN diagrams shown in Figure 7.10. Under the strict interpretation "A_1 OR B_1" would include all items that are in all the shaded areas in the VENN diagram. "A_1 OR B_0" would be only those items in A (i.e., the horizontally and cross hatched shaded areas) which is everything except items in "B NOT A." Thus as the value of query term B goes from 0.0 to 1.0, items from "B NOT A" are proportionally added until at 1.0 all of the items will be added.

Similarly, under the strict interpretation "A_1 AND B_1" would include all of the items that are in the cross hatched area. "A_1 AND B_0" will be all of the items in A as described above. Thus, as the value of query term B goes from 1.0 to 0.0 items will be proportionally added from "A NOT B" (horizontal only stripped area) until at 0.0 all of the items will be added.

Finally, the strict interpretation of "A_1 NOT B_1" is the horizontally stripped area while "A_1 NOT B_0" is all of A. Thus as the value of B goes from

0.0 to 1.0, items are proportionally added from "A AND B" (the cross hatched area) until at 1.0 all of the items have been added.

The final issue is the determination of which items are to be added or dropped in interpreting the weighted values. Inspecting the items in the totally

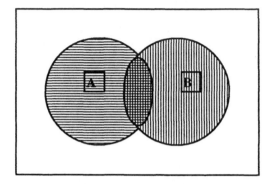

Figure 7.10 VENN Diagram

strict case (both terms having weight 1.0) and the case where the value is 0.0 there is a set of items that are in both solutions (invariant set). In adding items they should be the items most similar to the set of items that does not change in either situation. In dropping items, they should be the items least similar to those that are in both situations.

Thus the algorithm follows the following steps:

1. Determine the items that are satisfied by applying strict interpretation of the Boolean functions

2. Determine the items that are part of the set that is invariant

3. Determine the Centroid of the invariant set

4. Determine the number of items to be added or deleted by multiplying the term weight times the number of items outside of the invariant set and rounding up to the nearest whole number

5. Determine the similarity between items outside of the invariant set and the Centroid

6. Select the items to be included or removed from the final set

Figure 7.11 gives an example of solving a weighted Boolean query.

QUERY$_1$ ends up with a set containing all of the items that contain the term "Computer" and two items from the set "computer" NOT "program." The symbol $\lceil \ \rceil$ stands for rounding up to the next integer. In QUERY$_2$ the final set

	Computer	program	cost	sale
D1	0	4	0	8
D2	0	2	0	0
D3	4	0	2	4
D4	0	6	4	6
D5	0	4	6	4
D6	6	0	4	0
D7	0	0	0	0
D8	4	2	0	2

$$Q1 = QUERY_1 = Computer_{1.0} \ \ OR \ \ program_{.333}$$
$$Q2 = QUERY_2 = cost_{.75} \ \ AND \ \ sale_{1.0}$$

$Q1_{\text{strict interpretation}} = (D1, D2, D3, D4, D5, D6, D8)$
$Q2_{\text{strict interpretation}} = (D3, D4, D5)$

$Q1_{\text{invariant}} = (D3, D6, D8)$
$Q2_{\text{invariant}} = (D3, D4, D5)$

$Q1_{\text{optional}} = (D1, D2, D4, D5)$ which means $\lceil .333$ times 4 items$\rceil = 2$ items
$Q2_{\text{optonal}} = (D1, D8)$ which means $\lceil (1 - .75)$ times 2 items$\rceil = 1$ item

Figure 7.11 Example of Weighted Boolean Query

contains all of set "cost" AND "sale" plus .25 of the set of "sale" NOT "cost." Using the simple similarity measure:

$$SIM(Item_i, Item_j) = \Sigma \ (Term_{i,k}) \ (Term_{j,k})$$

leads to the following set of similarity values based upon the centroids:

CENTROID (Q1) = (D3, D6, D8) = 1/3(4+6+4, 0+0+2, 2+4+0, 4+0+2)
CENTROID (Q2) = (D3, D4, D5) = 1/3(4+0+0, 0+6+4, 2+4+6, 4+6+4)

$SIM(CENTROID_{Q1}, D1) = 1/3(0 + 8 + 0 + 48)$ $= 1/3(56)$
$SIM(CENTROID_{Q1}, D2) = 1/3(0 + 4 + 0 + 0)$ $= 1/3(4)$

$$SIM(CENTROID_{Q1},D4) = 1/3(0 + 12 + 24 + 36) \qquad = 1/3(72)$$
$$SIM(CENTROID_{Q1},D5) = 1/3(0 + 8 + 36 + 24) \qquad = 1/3(68)$$

$$SIM(CENTROID_{Q2},D1) = 1/3(0 + 40 + 0 + 112) \qquad =1/3(152)$$
$$SIM(CENTROID_{Q2},D8) = 1/3(16 + 20 +0 +28) \qquad = 1/3(64)$$

For Q1, two additional items are added to the invariant set (D3, D6, D8) $\cup$ (D4, D5) giving the answer of (D3, D4, D5, D6, D8). For Q2, one additional item is added to the invariant set (D3, D4, D5) $\cup$ (D1) giving the answer (D1, D3, D4, D5).

7.6 Searching the INTERNET and Hypertext

The Internet has multiple different mechanisms that are the basis for search of items. The primary techniques are associated with servers on the Internet that create indexes of items on the Internet and allow search of them. Some of the most commonly used nodes are YAHOO, AltaVista and Lycos. In all of these systems there are active processes that visit a large number of Internet sites and retrieve textual data which they index. The primary design decisions are on the level to which they retrieve data and their general philosophy on user access. LYCOS (http://www.lycos.com) and AltaVista automatically go out to other Internet sites and return the text at the sites for automatic indexing (http://www.altavista.digital.com). Lycos returns home pages from each site for automatic indexing while Altavista indexes all of the text at a site. The retrieved text is then used to create an index to the source items storing the Universal Resource Locator (URL) to provide to the user to retrieve an item. All of the systems use some form of ranking algorithm to assist in display of the retrieved items. The algorithm is kept relatively simple using statistical information on the occurrence of words within the retrieved text.

Closely associated with the creation of the indexes is the technique for accessing nodes on the Internet to locate text to be indexed. This search process is also directly available to users via Intelligent Agents. Intelligent Agents provide the capability for a user to specify an information need which will be used by the Intelligent Agent as it independently moves between Internet sites locating information of interest. There are six key characteristics of intelligent agents (Heilmann-96):

> 1. Autonomy - the search agent must be able to operate without interaction with a human agent. It must have control over its own internal states and make independent decisions. This implies a search capability to traverse information sites based upon pre-established criteria collecting potentially relevant information.

2. Communications Ability - the agent must be able to communicate with the information sites as it traverses them. This implies a universally accepted language defining the external interfaces (e.g., Z39.50).

3. Capacity for Cooperation - this concept suggests that intelligent agents need to cooperate to perform mutually beneficial tasks.

4. Capacity for Reasoning - There are three types of reasoning scenarios (Roseler-94):

> Rule-based - where user has defined a set of conditions and actions to be taken

> Knowledge-based - where the intelligent agents have stored previous conditions and actions taken which are used to deduce future actions

> Artificial evolution based - where intelligent agents spawn new agents with higher logic capability to perform its objectives.

5. Adaptive Behavior - closely tied to 1 and 4 , adaptive behavior permits the intelligent agent to assess its current state and make decisions on the actions it should take

6. Trustworthiness - the user must trust that the intelligent agent will act on the user's behalf to locate information that the user has access to and is relevant to the user.

There are many implementation aspects of Intelligent Agents. They include communications to traverse the Internet, how to wrap the agent in an appropriate interface shell to work within an Internet server, and security and protection for both the agent and the servers. Although these are critical for the implementation of the agents, the major focus for information storage and retrieval is how to optimize the location of relevant items as the agent performs its task. This requires expansion of search capabilities into conditional and learning feedback mechanisms that are becoming major topics in information retrieval.

Automatic relevance feedback is being used in a two-step process to enhance user's queries to include corpora-specific terminology. As an intelligent agent moves from site to site, it is necessary for it to use similar techniques to learn the language of the authors and correlate it to the search need of the user. How much information gained from relevance feedback from one site should be carried to the next site has yet to be resolved. Some basic groundwork is being laid by the work on incremental relevance feedback discussed earlier.   It will also need capabilities to normalize ranking values across multiple systems. The quantity of possible information being returned necessitates a merged ranking to allow the user to focus on the most likely relevant items first.

Finally, there is the process of searching for information on the Internet by following Hyperlinks. A Hyperlink is an embedded link to another item that can be instantiated by clicking on the item reference. Frequently hidden to the user is a URL associated with the text being displayed. As discussed in Chapter 5, inserting hyperlinks in an item is a method of indexing related information. One of the issues of the existing Hyperlink process is the inability for the link to have attributes. In particular, a link may be a pointer to another object that is an integral aspect of the item being displayed (e.g. an embedded image or quoted text in another item). But the reference could also be to another item that generally supports the current text. It could also be to another related topic that the author feels may be of interest to the reader. There are many other interpretations of the rationale behind the link that are author specific.

Understanding the context of the link in the item being viewed determines the utility of following the associated path. Thus the Hyperlinks create a static network of linked items based upon an item being viewed. The user can manually move through this network space by following links. The search in this sense is the ability to start with an item and create the network of associated items (i.e., following the links). The results of the search is a network diagram that defines the interrelated items which can be displayed to the user to assist in identification of where the user is in the network and to facilitate movement to other nodes (items) within the network (Gershon-95, Hasan-95, Mukherjea-95, Munzner-95). The information retrieval aspect of this problem is how to automatically follow the hyperlinks and how the additional information as each link is instantiated impacts the resolution of the user's search need.   One approach is to use the function described in Section 5.5 as a mechanism for assigning weights to the terms in original and linked items to use with the search statement to determine hits.

New search capabilities are continually becoming available on the Internet. Dissemination systems are proliferating to provide individual users with items they are potentially interested in for personal or business reasons. Some examples are the Pointcast system, FishWrap newspaper service at MIT and SFGATE (San Francisco Examiner and San Francisco Chronicle) that allow users to define specific areas of interest. Items will be e-mailed as found or stored in a file for later retrieval. The systems will continually update your screen if you are on the Internet with new items as they are found (http://fishwrap-docs.www.media.mit.edu/docs/, http:/www.sfgate.com, http:/www.pointcast.com). There are also many search sites that collect relevance information from user interaction and use relevance feedback algorithms and proprietary heuristics and provide modifications on information being delivered. Firefly interacts with a user, learning the user's preferences for record albums and movies.   It provides recommendations on potential products of interest. The Firefly system also compares the user's continually changing interest profile with other users and informs users of others with similar interests for possible collaboration (http:/www.ffly.com). Another system that uses feedback across multiple users to categorize and classify interests is the Empirical Media system (http:/www.empiracal.com). Based upon an individual user's relevance ranking of what is being displayed the system learns a user's preference. It also judges from other user's rankings of items the likelihood that an item will be of interest to other users that show the same pattern of interest. Thus it uses this "Collaborative Intelligence" in addition to its internal ranking algorithms to provide a final ranking of items to individual users. Early research attempts at using queries across multiple users to classify document systems did not show much promise (Salton-83). But the orders of magnitude increase (million times greater or more) in user interaction from the Internet provides a basis for realistic clustering and learning.

7.7 Summary

Creating the index to an Information Retrieval System defines the searchable concepts that represent the items received by a system. The user search process is the mechanism that correlates the user's search statement with the index via a similarity function. There are a number of techniques to define the indexes to an item. It is typically more efficient to incur system overhead at index creation time than search time. An item is processed once at index time, but there will be millions of searches against the index. Also, the user is directly affected by the response time of a search but, in general, is not aware of how long it takes from receipt of an item to its being available in the index. The selection and implementation of similarity algorithms for search must be optimized for performance and scaleable to accommodate very large databases.

It is typical during search parsing that the user's initial search statement is expanded via a thesaurus or semantic net to account for vocabulary differences between the user and the authors. But excessive expansion takes significantly more processing and increases the response time due to the number of terms that have to be processed. Most systems have default limits on the number of new terms added to a search statement. Chapter 7 describes some of the basic algorithms that can be used as similarity measures. These algorithms are still in a state of evolution and are continually being modified to improve their performance. The search algorithms in a probabilistic indexing and search system are much more complex than the similarity measures described. For systems based upon natural language processing, once the initial similarity comparisons are completed, there is an additional search processing step to make use of discourse level information, adding additional precision to the final results.

Relevance feedback is an alternative to thesaurus expansion to assist the user in creating a search statement that will return the needed information. Thesaurus and semantic net expansions are dependent upon the user's ability to use the appropriate vocabulary in the search statement that represents the required information. If the user selects poor terms, they will be expanded with many more poor terms. Thesaurus expansion does not introduce new concepts that are relevant to the users information need, it just expands the description of existing concepts. Relevance feedback starts with the text of an item that the user has identified as meeting his information need; incorporating it into a revised search statement. The vocabulary in the relevant item text has the potential for introducing new concepts that better reflect the user's information need along with adding additional terms related to existing search terms and adjusting the weights (importance) of existing terms.

Selective Dissemination of Information search is different from searches against the persistent information database in that it is assumed there is no information from a large corpus available to determine parameters in determining a temporary index for the item to use in the similarity comparison process (e.g., inverse document frequency factors.) An aspect of dissemination systems that helps in the search process is the tendency for the profiles to have significantly more terms than ad hoc queries. The additional information helps to identify relevant items and increase the precision of the search process. Relevance feedback can also be used with profiles with some constraints. Relevance feedback used with ad hoc queries against an existing database tends to move the terminology defining the search concepts towards the information need of the user that is available in the current database. Concepts in the initial search statement will eventually lose importance in the revised queries if they are not in the database. The goal of profiles is to define the coverage of concepts that the user cares about if they are ever found in new items. Relevance feedback applied to profiles aides the user by enhancing the search profile with new terminology about areas of interest. But, even though a concept has not been found in any items received, that area may still be of critical importance to the user if it ever is found in any new items. Thus weighting of original terms takes on added significance over the ad hoc situation.

Searching the Internet for information has brought into focus the deficiencies in the search algorithms developed to date. The ad hoc queries are extremely short (usually less than three terms) and most users do not know how to use the advanced features associated with most search sites. Until recently research had focused on a larger more sophisticated query. With the Internet being the largest most available information system supporting information retrieval search, algorithms are in the process of being modified to account for the lack of information provided by the users in their queries. Intelligent Agents are being proposed as a potential mechanism to assist users in locating the information they require. The requirements for autonomy and the need for reasoning in the agents will lead to the merging of information retrieval algorithms and the learning processes associated with Artificial Intelligence. The use of hyperlinks is adding another level of ambiguity in what should be defined as an item. When similarity measures are being applied to identify the relevance weight, how much of the hyperlinked information should be considered part of the item? The impacts on the definition of information retrieval boundaries are just starting to be analyzed while experimental products are being developed in Web years and immediately being made available.

EXERCISES

1. Discuss the sources of potential errors in the final set of search terms from when a user first identifies a need for information to the creation of the final query. (HINT: you may also want to use information from Chapter 1)

2. Why are there three levels of binding in the creation of a search?

3. Why does the numerator remain basically the same in all of the similarity measures.?   Discuss other possible approaches and their impact on the formulas.

4. Given the following set of retrieved documents with relevance judgments

TERM	T1	T2	T3	T4	T5	T6
QUERY	0	0	4	2	6	0
REL D1	0	4	4	0	2	0
REL D2	0	2	6	0	1	0
NOT REL D3	6	0	0	6	1	0
NOT REL D4	4	0	1	2	0	10

a. Calculate a new query using a factor of 1/2 for positive feedback and 1/4 for negative feedback

b. Determine which documents would be retrieved by the original and by the new query

c. Discuss the differences in documents retrieved by the original versus the new query.

5. Is the use of positive feedback always better than using negative feedback to improve a query?

6. What are some potential ambiguities in use of relevance feedback on hypertext documents.

7. Given the following documents, determine which documents will be returned by the query $(A_{1.0}$ and $B_{0.5})$

TERM	A	B	C	D
D1	2	0	2	1
D2	0	2	0	3
D3	3	2	1	0
D4	2	1	2	0
D5	1	0	3	3
D6	3	0	1	2
D7	1	4	0	4
D8	4	0	0	3
D9	0	4	1	2
D10	0	2	0	0
D11	2	0	6	2
D12	4	0	0	3

8. How would you define an item on the Internet with respect to a search statement and similarity function?

8 Information Visualization

The primary focus on Information Retrieval Systems has been in the areas of indexing, searching and clustering versus information display. This has been due to the inability of technology to provide the technical platforms needed for sophisticated display, academic's focusing on the more interesting algorithmic based search aspects of information retrieval, and the multi-disciplinary nature of the human-computer interface (HCI). The core technologies needed to address sophisticated information visualization have matured, supporting productive research and implementation into commercial products. The commercial demand for these technologies is growing with availability of the "information highway." System designers need to treat the display of data as visual computing instead of treating the monitor as a replica of paper. Functions that are available with electronic display and visualization of data that were not previously provided are (Brown-96):

> modify representations of data and information or the display condition (e.g., changing color scales)

> use the same representation while showing changes in data (e.g., moving between clusters of items showing new linkages)

> animate the display to show changes in space and time

> enable interactive input from the user to allow dynamic movement between information spaces and allow the user to modify data presentation to optimize personal preferences for understanding the data.

Create hyperlinks under user control to establish relationships between data

If information retrieval had achieved development of the perfect search algorithm providing close to one hundred per cent precision and recall, the need for advances in information visualization would not be so great. But reality has demonstrated in TREC and other information fora that advancements are not even close to achieving this goal. Thus, any technique that can reduce the user overhead of finding the needed information will supplement algorithmic achievements in finding potential relevant items. Information Visualization addresses how the results of a search may be optimally displayed to the users to facilitate their understanding of what the search has provided and their selection of most likely items of interest to read. Visual displays can consolidate the search results into a form easily processed by the user's cognitive abilities, but in general they do not answer the specific retrieval needs of the user other than suggesting database coverage of the concept and related concepts.

The theoretical disciplines of cognitive engineering and perception provide a theoretical base for information visualization. Cognitive engineering derives design principles for visualization techniques from what we know about the neural processes involved with attention, memory, imagery and information processing of the human visual system. By 1989 research had determined that mental depiction plays a role in cognition that is different from mental description. Thus, the visual representation of an item plays as important a role as its symbolic definition in cognition.

Cognitive engineering results can be applied to methods of reviewing the concepts contained in items selected by search of an information system. Visualization can be divided into two broad classes: link visualization and attribute (concept) visualization. Link visualization displays relationships among items. Attribute visualization reveals content relationships across large numbers of items. Related to attribute visualization is the capability to provide visual cues on how search terms affected the search results. This assists a user in determining changes required to search statements that will return more relevant items.

8.1 Introduction to Information Visualization

The beginnings of the theory of visualization began over 2400 years ago. The philosopher Plato discerned that we perceive objects through the senses, using the mind. Our perception of the real world is a translation from physical energy from our environment into encoded neural signals. The mind is continually interpreting and categorizing our *perception* of our surroundings. Use of a computer is another source of input to the mind's processing functions. Text-only interfaces reduce the complexity of the interface but also restrict use of the more powerful information processing functions the mind has developed since birth.

Information visualization is a relatively new discipline growing out of the debates in the 1970s on the way the brain processes and uses mental images. It required significant advancements in technology and information retrieval techniques to become a possibility. One of the earliest researchers in information visualization was Doyle, who in 1962 discussed the concept of "semantic road maps" that could provide a user a view of the whole database (Doyle-62). The road maps show the items that are related to a specific semantic theme. The user could use this view to focus his query on a specific semantic portion of the database. The concept was extended in the late 1960s, emphasizing a spatial organization that maps to the information in the database (Miller-68). Sammon implemented a non-linear mapping algorithm that could reveal document associations providing the information required to create a road map or spatial organization (Sammons-69).

In the 1990s technical advancements along with exponential growth of available information moved the discipline into practical research and commercialization. Information visualization techniques have the potential to significantly enhance the user's ability to minimize resources expended to locate needed information. The way users interact with computers changed with the introduction of user interfaces based upon Windows, Icons, Menus, and Pointing devices (WIMPs). Although movement in the right direction to provide a more natural human interface, the technologies still required humans to perform activities optimized for the computer to understand. A better approach was stated by Donald A. Norman (Rose-96):

> ... *people are required to conform to technology. It is time to reverse this trend, time to make technology conform to people*

Norman stresses that to optimize the user's ability to find information, the focus should be on understanding the aspects of the user's interface and processing of information which then can be migrated to a computer interface (Norman-90).

Although using text to present an overview of a significant amount of information makes it difficult for the user to understand the information, it is essential in presenting the details. In information retrieval, the process of getting to the relevant details starts with filtering many items via a search process. The results of this process is still a large number of potentially relevant items. In most systems the results of the search are presented as a textual list of each item perhaps ordered by rank. The user has to read all of the pages of lists of the items to see what is in the Hit list. Understanding the human cognitive process associated with visual data suggests alternative ways of presenting and manipulating information to focus on the likely relevant items. There are many areas that information visualization and presentation can help the user:

a. reduce the amount of time to understand the results of a search and likely clusters of relevant information

b. yield information that comes from the relationships between items versus treating each item as independent

c. perform simple actions that produce sophisticated information search functions

A study was performed by Fox et al. using interviews and user task analysis on professionals in human factors engineering, library science, and computer science to determine the requirements to optimize their work with documents (Fox-93a). Once past the initial requirement for easy access from their office, the researchers' primary objective was the capability to locate and explore patterns in document databases. They wanted visual representations of the patterns and items of interest. There was a consistent theme that the tools should allow the users to view and search documents with the system sensitive to their view of the information space. The users wanted to be able to focus on particular areas of their interest (not generic system interest definitions) and then easily see new topical areas of potential interest to investigate. They sought an interface that permits easy identification of trends, interest in various topics and newly emerging topics. Representing information in a visual mode allows for cognitive parallel processing of multiple facts and data relationships satisfying many of these requirements.

The exponential growth in available information produces large Hit files from most searches. To understand issues with the search statement and retrieved items, the user has to review a significant number of status screens. Even with the review, it is hard to generalize if the search can be improved. Information visualization provides an intuitive interface to the user to aggregate the results of the search into a display that provides a high-level summary and facilitates focusing on likely centers of relevant items. The query logically extracts a virtual workspace (information space) of potential relevant items which can be viewed and manipulated by the user. By representing the aggregate semantics of the workspace, relationships between items become visible. It is impossible for the user to perceive these relationships by viewing the items individually. The aggregate presentation allows the user to manipulate the aggregates to refine the items in the workspace. For example, if the workspace is represented by a set of named clusters (name based upon major semantic content), the user may select a set of clusters that defines the next iteration of the search.

An alternative use of aggregates is to correlate the search terms with items retrieved. Inspecting relevant and non-relevant items in a form that highlights the effect of the expanded search terms provides insights on what terms were the major causes for the results. A user may have thought a particular term was very important. A visual display could show that the term in fact had a minimal effect on the item selection process, suggesting a need to substitute other search terms.

Using a textual display on the results of a search provides no mechanism to display inter-relationships between items. For example, if the user is interested in the development of a polio vaccine, there is no way for a textual listing of found items to show "date" and "researcher" relationships based upon published items. The textual summary list of the Hit file can only be sorted via one attribute, typically relevance rank.

Aspects of human cognition are the technical basis for understanding the details of information visualization systems. Many techniques are being developed heuristically with the correlation to human cognition and perception analyzed after the techniques are in test. The commercial pressures to provide visualization in delivered systems places the creativity under the intuitive concepts of the developer.

8.2 Cognition and Perception

The user-machine interface has primarily focused on a paradigm of a typewriter. As computers displays became ubiquitous, man-machine interfaces focused on treating the display as an extension of paper with the focus on consistency of operations. The advent of WIMP interfaces and simultaneous parallel tasks in the user work environment expanded the complexity of the interface to manipulate the multiple tasks. The evolution of the interface focused on how to represent to the user what is taking place in the computer environment. The advancements in computer technology, information sciences and understanding human information processing are providing the basis for extending the human computer interface to improve the information flow, thus reducing wasted user overhead in locating needed information. Although the major focus is on enhanced visualization of information, other senses are also being looked at for future interfaces. The audio sense has always been part of simple alerts in computers. Illegal inputs are usually associated with a beep, and more recently users have a spectrum of audio sounds to associate with everything from start-up to shut down. The sounds are now being replaced by speech in both input and output interfaces. Still in the research arena is the value of using audio to encapsulate information (e.g., higher pitch as you move through an information space plus increased relevance). The tactile (touch) sense is being addressed in the experiments using Virtual Realty (VR). For example, VR is used as a training environment for areas such as medical procedures where tactile feedback plays an increasing role. Olfactory and taste are two areas where practical use for information processing or computer interfaces in general has yet to be identified. For Information Retrieval Systems, the primary area of interest is in information visualization.

8.2.1 Background

A significant portion of the brain is devoted to vision and supports the maximum information transfer function from the environment to a human being. The center of debates in the 1970s was whether vision should be considered data collection or also has aspects of information processing. In 1969 Arnheim questioned the then current psychological division of cognitive operations of perception and thinking as separate processes (Arnheim-69). Until then perception was considered a data collection task and thinking as a higher level function using the data. He contended that visual perception includes the process of understanding the information, providing an ongoing feedback mechanism between the perception and thinking. He further expanded his views arguing that treating perception and thinking as separate functions treats the mind as a serial automata (Arnheim-86). Under this paradigm, the two mental functions exclude each other, with perception dealing with individual instances versus generalizations. Visualization is the transformation of information into a visual form which enables the user to observe and understand the information. This concept can be extended where the visual images provide a fundamentally different way to understand information that treats the visual input not as discrete facts but as an understanding process. The Gestalt psychologists postulate that the mind follows a set of rules to combine the input stimuli to a mental representation that differs from the sum of the individual inputs (Rock-90):

> Proximity - nearby figures are grouped together

> Similarity - similar figures are grouped together

> Continuity - figures are interpreted as smooth continuous patterns rather than discontinuous concatenations of shapes (e.g., a circle with its diameter drawn is perceived as two continuous shapes, a circle and a line, versus two half circles concatenated together)

> Closure - gaps within a figure are filled in to create a whole (e.g., using dashed lines to represent a square does not prevent understanding it as a square)

> Connectedness - uniform and linked spots, lines or areas are perceived as a single unit

Shifting the information processing load from slower cognitive processes to faster perceptual systems significantly improves the information-carrying interfaces between humans and computers (Card-96). There are many ways to present information in the visual space. An understanding of the way the cognitive processes work provides insights for the decisions on which of the presentations will maximize the information passing and understanding. There is not a single correct answer on the best way to present information.

8.2.2 Aspects of the Visualization Process

One of the first-level cognitive processes is preattention, that is, taking the significant visual information from the photoreceptors and forming primitives. Primitives are part of the preconscious processes that consist of involuntary lower order information processing (Friedhoff-89). An example of this is the ease with which our visual systems detect borders between changes in orientation of the same object. In Figure 8.1 the visual system detects the difference in orientations between the left and middle portion of the figure and determines the logical border between them. An example of using the conscious processing capabilities of the brain is the detection of the different shaped objects and the border between them shown between the left side and middle of the Figure 8.1. The reader can likely detect the differences in the time it takes to visualize the two different boundaries.

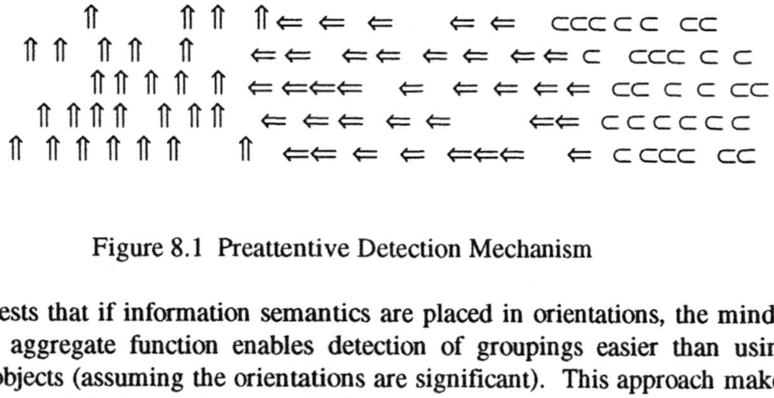

Figure 8.1 Preattentive Detection Mechanism

This suggests that if information semantics are placed in orientations, the mind's clustering aggregate function enables detection of groupings easier than using different objects (assuming the orientations are significant). This approach makes maximum use of the feature detectors in the retina.

The preattentive process can detect the boundaries between orientation groups of the same object. A harder process is to identify the equivalence of rotated objects. For example, a rotated square requires more effort to recognize it as a square. As we migrate into characters, the problem of identification of the character is affected by rotating the character in a direction not normally encountered. It is easier to detect the symmetry when the axis is vertical. Figure 8.2 demonstrates these effects.

Another visual factor is the optical illusion that makes a light object on a dark background to appear larger than if the item is dark and the background is light. Making use of this factor suggests that a visual display of small objects should use bright colors. An even more complex area is the use of colors. Colors have many attributes that can be modified such as hue, saturation and lightness. Hue is the physiological attribute of color sensation. Saturation is the degree to which a hue is different from a gray line with the same lightness, while lightness is the sensation of the amount of white or black. Complementary colors are two colors that form white or gray when combined (red/green, yellow/blue). Color is one of the most frequently used visualization techniques to organize, classify, and enhance features (Thorell-90). Humans have an innate attraction to the primary

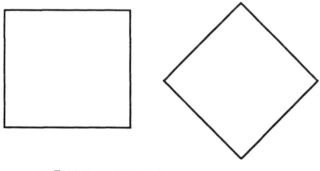

R Ǝ ∀ L   R E A L

Figure 8.2 Rotating a Square and Reversing Letters in "REAL"

colors (red, blue, green and yellow), and their retention of images associated with these colors is longer. But colors also affect emotion, and some people have strong aversion to certain colors. The negative side of use of colors is that some people are color blind to some or many colors. Thus any display that uses colors should have other options available.

Depth, like color, is frequently used for representing visual information. Classified as monocular cues, changes in shading, blurring (proportional to distance), perspective, motion, stereoscopic vision, occlusion and texture depict depth. Most of the cues are affected more by lightness than contrast. Thus, choice of colors that maximizes brightness in contrast to the background can assist in presenting depth as a mechanism for representing information. Depth has the advantage that depth/size recognition are learned early in life and used all of the time. Gibson and Walk showed that six-month-old children already understand depth suggesting that depth may be an innate concept (Gibson-60). The cognitive processes are well developed, and the use of this information in classifying objects is ubiquitous to daily life. The visual information processing system is attuned to processing information using depth and correlating it to real world paradigms.

Another higher level processing technique is the use of configural aspects of a display (Rose-95). A configural effect occurs when arrangements of objects are presented to the user allowing for easy recognition of a high-level abstract condition.   Configural clues substitute a lower level visual process for a higher level one that requires more concentration (see preattentive above). These clues are frequently used to detect changes from a normal operating environment such as in monitoring an operational system. An example is shown in Figure 8.3 where the sides of a regular polygon (e.g., a square in this example) are modified. The visual processing system quickly detects deviations from normally equally sized objects.

Another visual cue that can be used is spatial frequency. The human visual and cognitive system tends towards order and builds an coherent visual image whenever possible. The multiple spatial channel theory proposes that a complex image is constructed from the external inputs, not received as a single image. The final image is constructed from multiple receptors that detect changes

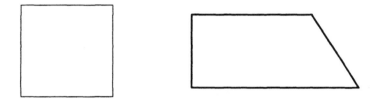

Figure 8.3 Distortions of a Regular Polygon

in spatial frequency, orientation, contrast, and spatial phase. Spatial frequency is an acuity measure relative to regular light-dark changes that are in the visual field or similar channels. A cycle is one complete light-dark change. The spatial frequency is the number of cycles per one degree of visual field. Our visual systems are less sensitive to spatial frequencies of about 5-6 cycles per degree of visual field (NOTE: one degree of visual field is approximately the viewing angle subtended by the width of a finger at arms length). Other animals have significantly more sensitive systems that allow them to detect outlines of camouflaged prey not detected by humans until we focus on the area. Associated with not processing the higher spatial frequencies is a reduction in the cognitive processing time, allowing animals (e.g. cats) to react faster to motion. When looking at a distinct, well defined image versus a blurred image, our visual system will detect motion/changes in the distinct image easier than the blurred image. If motion is being used as a way of aggregating and displaying information, certain spatial frequencies facilitate extraction of patterns of interest. Dr. Mary Kaiser of NASA-AMES is experimenting with perceptually derived displays for aircraft. She is interested in applying the human vision filters such as limits of spatial and temporal resolution, mechanisms of stereopsis, and attentional focus to aircraft (Kaiser-96).

The human sensory systems learn from usage. In deciding upon visual information techniques, parallels need to be made between what is being used to represent information and encountering those techniques in the real world environment. The human system is adept at working with horizontal and vertical references. They are easily detected and processed. Using other orientations requires additional cognitive processes to understand the changes from the expected inputs. The typical color environment is subdued without large areas of bright colors. Thus using an analogous situation, bright colors represent items to be focused on correlating to normal processing (i.e., noticing brightly colored flowers in a garden). Another example of taking advantage of sensory information that the brain is use to processing is terrain and depth information. Using a graphical representation that uses depth of rectangular objects to represent information is an image that the visual system is used to processing. Movement in that space is more easily interpreted and understood by the cognitive processes than if, for example, a three-dimensional image of a sphere represented a visual information space.

In using cognitive engineering in designing information visualization techniques, a hidden risk is that "understanding is in the eye of the beholder." The integration of the visual cues into an interpretation of what is being seen is also based upon the user's background and context of the information. The human mind uses the latest information to assist in interpreting new information. If a particular shape has been representing important information, the mind has a predisposition to interpret new inputs as the same shape. For example, if users have been focusing on clusters of items, they may see clusters in a new presentation that do not exist. This leads to the question of changing visualization presentations to minimize legacy dispositions. Another issue is that our past experiences can affect our interpretation of a graphic. Users may interpret figures according to what is most common in their life experiences rather than what the designer intended.

8-3 Information Visualization Technologies

The theories associated with information visualization are being applied in commercial and experimental systems to determine the best way to improve the user interface, facilitating the localization of information. They have been applied to many different situations and environments (e.g., weather forecasting to architectural design). The ones focused on Information Retrieval Systems are investigating how best to display the results of searches, structured data from DBMSs and the results of link analysis correlating data. The goals for displaying the result from searches fall into two major classes: document clustering and search statement analysis. The goal of document clustering is to present the user with a visual representation of the document space constrained by the search criteria. Within this constrained space there exist clusters of documents defined by the document content. Visualization tools in this area attempt to display the clusters, with an indication of their size and topic, as a basis for users to navigate to items of interest. This is equivalent to searching the index at a library and then pursuing all the books on the different shelf locations that are retrieved by the search. The second goal is to assist the user in understanding why items were retrieved, thereby providing information needed to refine the query. Unlike the traditional Boolean systems where the user can easily correlate the query to the retrieved set of items, modern search algorithms and their associated ranking techniques make it difficult to understand the impacts of the expanded words in the search statement. Visualization techniques approach this problem by displaying the total set of terms, including additional terms from relevance feedback or thesaurus expansion, along with documents retrieved and indicate the importance of the term to the retrieval and ranking process.

Structured databases are important to information retrieval because structured files are the best implementation to hold certain citation and semantic data that describe documents. Link analysis is also important because it provides aggregate-level information within an information system. Rather than treating each item as independent, link analysis considers information flowing between documents with value in the correlation between multiple documents. For example, a time/event link analysis correlates multiple documents discussing a oil spill caused by a tanker. Even if all of the items retrieved on the topic are relevant, displaying the documents correlated by time may show dependencies of events that are of information importance and are not described in any specific document. This section summarizes some of the major techniques being applied. This can assist in correlating the theory of visual perception to the practice of implementing systems.

One way of organizing information is hierarchical. A tree structure is useful in representing information that ranges over time (e.g., genealogical lineage), constituents of a larger unit (e.g., organization structures, mechanical device definitions) and aggregates from the higher to lower level (e.g., hierarchical clustering of documents). A two-dimensional representation becomes difficult for a user to understand as the hierarchy becomes large. One of the earliest experiments in information visualization was the Information Visualizer developed by XEROX PARC. It incorporates various visualization formats such as DataMap, InfoGrid, ConeTree, and the Perspective wall. The Cone-Tree is a 3-Dimensional representation of data, where one node of the tree is represented at the apex and all the information subordinate to it is arranged in a circular structure at its base. Any child node may also be the parent of another cone. Selecting a particular node, rotates it to the front of the display. Compared to other hierarchical representations (e.g., node and link trees) the cone makes the maximum information available to the user providing a perspective on size of each of the subtrees (Gershon-95a, Robertson-93). An example of a Cone-Tree is shown in

Figure 8.4. The squares at the leaf nodes in tree are the actual documents. Higher level nodes can be considered centroids representing the semantic of the child nodes. Where the database is large, the boxes may represent a cluster of related items versus a single item. These clusters could be expanded to lower levels of the tree. The perspective wall divides the information into three visual areas with the area being focused on in the front and other areas out of focus to each side (see Figure 8.5). This allows the user to keep all of the information in perspective while focusing on a perticular area.

Another technique used in display of hierarchical information is tree maps (Johnson-91). This technique makes maximum use of the display screen space by using rectangular boxes that are recursively subdivided based upon parent-child relationships between the data. A particular information work space focused on articles on computers may appear as shown in Figure 8.6. The size of the boxes can represent the number of items on a particular topic. The location of the boxes can indicate a relationship between the topics. In Figure 8.6, the CPU, OS, Memory, and Network management articles are all related to a general category of computer operating systems versus computer applications which are shown in the rest of the figure.

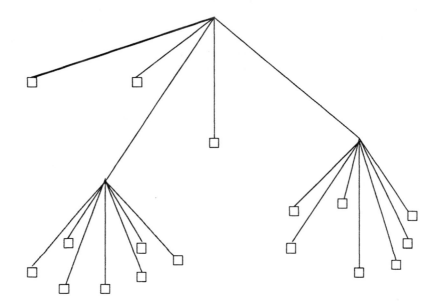

Figure 8.4   Cone Tree

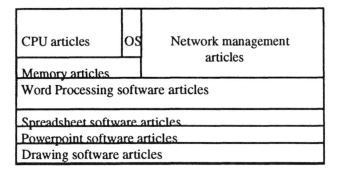

Figure 8.5 Perspective Wall
From inXight web site - www.inxight.com

CPU articles	OS	Network management articles
Memory articles		
Word Processing software articles		
Spreadsheet software articles		
Powerpoint software articles		
Drawing software articles		

Figure 8.6   Tree Map

When the information has network-type relationships, an approach using clusters can be shown via a semantic scatterplot. Both the Vineta and Bead systems display clustering patterns using a three-dimensional scatterplot (Krohn-95, Chalmers-92 respectively). Battelle Pacific Northwest National Laboratory correlates documents and performs multidimensional scaling to plot each as a point in Euclidean vector space. The difficulty of representing all of the axis is overcome by projecting the space onto a plane and using elevation to indicate the frequency of occurrence and importance of a theme (concept) creating a semantic landscape (Wise-95 Card-96). The detailed relationships between items and their composite themes can be seen by the valleys, cliffs and ranges shown on the terrain map. One way of overcoming the multidimensional space representation in a hierarchical environment is to create embedded coordinate spaces. In this technique the larger coordinate space is redefined with coordinates inside of other coordinates. Thus a six-dimensional coordinate space may have three of the coordinates defined as a subspace within the other three coordinate spaces. This has been called Feiner's "worlds within worlds" approach (Feiner-90). Other techniques suggested to solve this representation problem can be found in semantic regions suggested by Kohonen, linked trees or graphs in the Narcissus system, or a non-Euclidean landscape suggested by Lamping and Rao (Munzner-95, Lin-91 and Lin-92, Hendley-95, Lamping-95 respectively). When searches are used to define the user's infospace of interest and provide additional focusing of semantic interest, the "information crystal" (similar to a VENN diagram) assists the user in detecting patterns of term relationships in the constrained Hit file (Spoerri-93). The CyberWorld system constrains its clustering visualization to a three-dimensional sphere (Hemmje-94). Another clustering system that uses statistical information for a small number of items (50 - 120) to show term relationships via spatial positioning is the VIBE system (Olsen-93). The VIBE system allows users to associate query terms with different locations in the visual display. Documents are distributed to show their relevance to the different terms. Lin has taken the self-organization concept further by using Kohonen's algorithm to automatically determine a table of contents (TOC) and display the results in a map display (Lin-96).

The goal of many visualization techniques is to show the semantic relationships between individual items to assist the user in locating those groups of items of interest. Another objective of visualization is in assisting the users in refining their search statements. It is difficult for users in systems using similarity measures to determine what are the primary causes for the selection and ranking of items in a Hit file. The automatic expansion of terms and intricacies of the similarity algorithms can make it difficult to determine the effects that the various words in the search statement are having on creating the Hit file. Visualization tools need to assist the user in understanding the effects of his search statement even to the level of identifying important terms that are not contributing to the

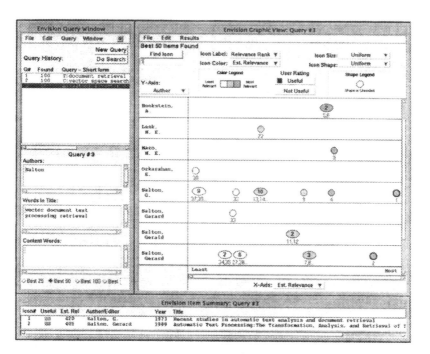

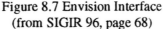

Figure 8.7 Envision Interface
(from SIGIR 96, page 68)

search process.   One solution is a graphical display of the characteristics of the
retrieved items which contributed to their selection.   This is effected in the
Envision system when index terms are selected as an axis.

The Envision system not only displays the relevance rank and estimated
relevance of each item found by a query, but also simultaneously presents other
query information.   The design is intentionally graphical and simple using two-
dimensional visualization.   This allows a larger variety of user computer platforms
to have access to their system (Nowell-96). Figure 8.7 shows Envision's three
interactive windows to display search results: Query window, Graphic View
window, and Item Summary window.   The Query window provides an editable
version of the query.   The Item Summary window provides bibliographic citation
information on items selected in the Graphic View window.   The Graphic View
window is similar to scatterplot graphs.   Each item in the Hit file is represented by
an icon in the window.   Selecting an item in the window provides bibliographic
information on the same display.   Circles represent single items with the relevance
weights displayed below them.   Ellipses represent clusters of multiple items that
are located at the same point in the scatterplot with the number of items in the

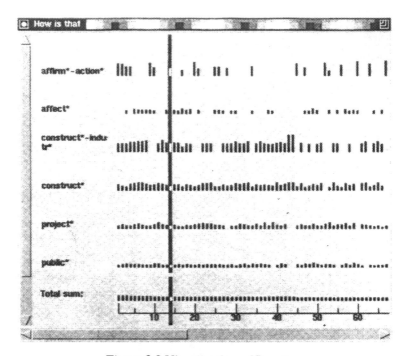

Figure 8.8 Visualization of Results
(from SIGIR 96, page 88)

ellipse and their weights below the ellipse. In this example, estimated relevance is on the X-axis and author's name is on the Y-axis. This type of interface provides a very user friendly environment but encounters problems when the number of relevant items and entries for an axis becomes very large. Envision plans to address this issue by a "zoom" feature that will allow seeing larger areas of the scatterplot at lesser detail.

A similar technique is used by Veerasamy and Belkin (Veerasamy-96). They use a series of vertical columns of bars. The columns of bars represent documents, and the rows represent index terms. The height of the bar corresponds to the weight of the corresponding term (row) in the corresponding item (column). In addition to the query terms, the system shows the additional words added to the system by relevance feedback. Figure 8.8 provides an example for a search statement of "How affirmative action affected the construction industry." This approach quickly allows a user to determine which terms had the most effect on retrieving a specific item (i.e. by scanning down the column). It also allows the user to determine how the various terms contributed to the retrieval process (i.e. by scanning a row). This latter process is very important because it allows a user to

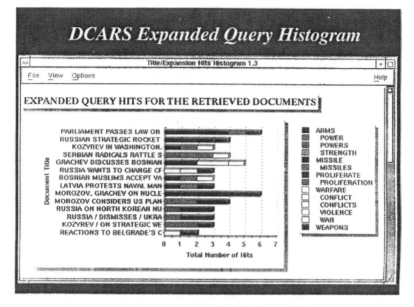

Figure 8.9 Example of DCARS Query Histogram
(from briefing by CALSPAN)

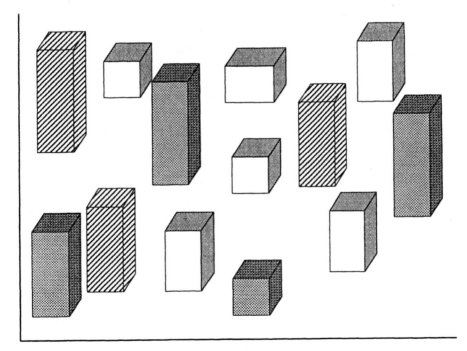

Figure 8.10 CityScape Example

determine if what he considers to be an important search term is not contributing strongly or not found at all in the items being retrieved. It also shows search terms that are causing items to be retrieved allowing their removal or reduction in query weight if they are causing false hits. In the Boolean environment this function was accomplished by vocabulary browsing (see Chapter 2) that allows for a user to see the number of items a particular term is in prior to including it in a search.

A slightly different commercial version having properties similar to the systems above is the Document Content Analysis and Retrieval System (DCARS) being developed by Calspan Advanced Technology Center. Their system is designed to augment the RetrievalWare search product. They display the query results as a histogram with the items as rows and each term's contribution to the selection indicated by the width of a tile bar on the row (see Figure 8.9). DCARS provides a friendly user interface that indicates why a particular item was found, but it is much harder to use the information in determining how to modify search statements to improve them.

Another representation that is widely used for both hierarchical and network related information is the "cityscape" which uses the metaphor of movement within a city. In lieu of using hills, as in the terrain approach, skyscrapers represent the theme (concept) area as shown in Figure 8.10. This is similar to extending bar charts to three dimensions. Buildings can be connected by lines which can vary in representation to describe interrelationships between themes. Colors or fill designs can be used for the visualization presenting another layer of information (e.g., the building having the same color may be members of a higher concept). Movement within the cityscape (or terrain) of the viewer perspective allows zooming in on specific information areas that will bring into view additional structures that might have been hidden by the previous viewpoint.

An easily understood metaphor for users is that of a library. Information content can be represented as areas within a library that the user can navigate through. Once in a particular "information room" the user can view the virtual "books" available within that space as if they are sitting on a bookshelf. Once the book is accessed, the user can scan a group of related items with each item represented as a page within the book. The user can fan the pages out. This is exemplified by the WebBook (Card-96a).

Correlating items or words within items was described in detail in Chapter 6 to cluster items or create statistical thesauri. When the complete term relationship method is used, a very large matrix is created. Each cell in the matrix defines the similarity between two terms (or items). Meaningful display of the table is not possible in table form. Mitre Corporation has developed an interface that displays the complete matrix using clusters of dots to represent correlation's. Once the user zooms in on a particular area of correlation, the specific words become visible along with clusters showing their correlation to other words (Gershon-96). Anther approach to representing thesaurus and contents is being tested by Zizi and Pediotakis (Zizi-96). They build a thesaurus automatically from the abstracts of the items extracting both single and two-word expressions. They create a presentation view and a document view. They divide the display space, based upon thesaurus classes, into regions. Each area is sized proportionally to the importance of the class for the collection. Once the presentation view is defined, the document view is created. The documents are placed on ellipses corresponding to the presentation view, and the weight of the document is reflected by the radius of the ellipse.

Another task in information systems is the visualization of specific text within an item versus between items. In some situations, items are allowed to change over time via editing. Thus, there is both the static representation and a time varying representation. Text changing representations are very important when the text being represented is a software program of millions of lines of code. AT&T Bell laboratories created the SeeSoft system which uses columns and color codes to show when different lines of code have been changed. This technique was used as a basis for a similar code visualization tool, DEC FUSE/SoftVis (Zaremba-95). They created small pictures of files that represent the code in the file with the size of the picture scaled to the number of lines of code in the file. Color coding indicates different characteristics of the code (e.g., green is comments). A user can quickly see the relative structure of all of the code files composing a system along with the complexity of each of the modules. The TileBars tool from Xerox PARC provides the user with a visualization of the distribution of query terms within each item in a Hit file. Using this tool, the user can quickly locate the section of the item that is most likely to be of interest.

Although information retrieval focuses on the unstructured text, another aspect of informational items is the citation data and structured aspects of indexing items. This data structure can be manipulated via structured databases as well as traditional information systems. Visualization tools have also been constructed for databases. The first visualization tool was the Query By Example user interface developed by IBM (Zloof-75). The interface presented the user with two-dimensional tables on the display screen and based upon the user is defining values of interest on the tables, the system would complete the search. Current visual query languages use visual representations of the database structure and contents (Catarci-96). The Information Visualization and Exploration Environment (IVEE) makes use of the three dimensional representation of the structured database as constrained by the user's search statement (Ahlberg-95). In one representation a three-dimensional box represents a larger space and smaller boxes within the space represent realizations of specific values (e.g., the box represents a department and the smaller boxes represent employees in the department). It has additional visualizations of data as maps and starfields. The user is provided with sliders and toggles to manipulate the search. Another specialized tool for displaying homes for sale in a database is the HomeFinder system. It presents a starfield display of homes for sale and overlays it with a city map showing the geographic location for each icon that represents a home (Ahlberg-94).

When hyperlinks are used as the information retrieval basis for locating relevant items, the user encounters orientation problems associated with the path the user followed to get to the current location. This is effect getting "lost in cyberspace." One solution is providing the user with a view of the information space. The user can user a pointing device to indicate the item the user would like to navigate to. MITRE Corporation has developed a tool used with web browsers that enables a user to see a tree structure visual representation of the information space they have navigated through (Gershon-96).

Another area in information visualization is the representation of pattern and linkage analysis. A system that incorporates many information visualization techniques including those used to represent linkage analysis is the Pathfinder Project sponsored by the Army (Rose-96). It contains the Document Browser, CAMEO, Counts, CrossField Matrix, OILSTOCK and SPIRE tools. The Document Browser uses different colors and their density for words in the text of items to indicate the relative importance of the item to their profile of interest. CAMEO models an analytic process by creating nodes and links to represent a problem. Queries are associated with the nodes. The color of the nodes change based on how well the found items satisfy the query. Counts uses statistical information on words and phrases and plots them over time. Time is used as a parameter to show trends in development of events. The display uses a three-dimensional cityscape representation of the data. The Cross Field Matrix creates a two-dimensional matrix of two fields in a dataset. Selected values in each of the datasets will be in each row and column for the two fields. Colors are used to represent time span. For example, countries could be on one axis and products on the other axis. The colors would indicate how long the country has been producing a particular product. InterSection can be used to access all the items that supported the particular product in a particular country. OILSTOCK allows the placement of data on a geographic mapping tool. The relationship of data to maps is a different use of information visualization. Discussion of this area is left to the many sources on Geographic Information Systems (GIS). The SPIRE tool is a type of scattergraph of information. Items are clustered and displayed in a star chart configuration. Distance between two points is indicative of their similarity based upon concurrence of terms.

8.4 Summary

Information visualization is not a new concept. The well known saying that "a picture is worth a thousand words" is part of our daily life. Everything from advertisements to briefings make use of visual aides to significantly increase the amount of information presented and provide maximum impact on the audience. The significant amount of "noise" (non-relevant items) in interactions with information systems requires use of user interface aides to maximize the information being presented to the user. Pure textual interfaces provide no capabilities for aggregation of data, allowing a user to see an overview of the results of a search. Viewing the results of a search using a hierarchical paradigm allows higher levels of abstraction showing overall results of searches before the details consume the display.

Visualization techniques attempt to represent aggregate information using a metaphor (e.g., peaks, valleys, cityscapes) to highlight the major concepts of the aggregation and relationships between them. This allows the user to put into perspective the total information before pursuing the details. It also allows major pruning of areas of non-relevant information. A close analogy is when searching on "fields" in the index at a library, the book shelves on horticulture would be ignored if magnetic fields was the information need. By having the data visualized constrained by the users search, the display is focused on the user's areas of interest. Relationships between data and effectiveness of the search become obvious to the user before the details of individual items hide the higher level relationships.

Cognitive engineering suggests that alternative representations are needed to take maximum advantage of different physilogical and cultural experiences of the user. Colors are useless to a color blind user. A person who grew up on a farm living in the country may have more trouble understanding a "city-scape" than a New York city resident. Using visual cues that a person has developed over his life-experience can facilitate the mapping of the visual metphor to the information it is representing.

As the algorthms and automatic search expansion techniques become more complex, use of visualization will take on additional responsibilities in clarifying to the user, not only what information is being retrieved, but the relationship between the search statement and the items. Showng relationships between items has had limited use in systems and been focused on data mining type efforts. The growth of hypertext linkages will require new visualization tools to present the network relationships between linked items and assist the user in navigating this new structure.

The technical limiter to the use of information visualization is no longer the understanding of useful visual techniques nor the ability of computers to display the techniques. The issue is the computational overhead in calculating the relationships between items based upon a dynamically created subset of an information space. To collect the information to display a "city-scape" display from the results of a search requires:

identifying the sbset of items that is relevant to the search statement

applying a threshold to determine the subset to process for visualization

calculating the pairwise similarity between all of the indicated items and clustering the results

determining the theme or subject of the clusters

determining the strength of the relationships between the clusters

creating the information visualization for the results.

Not only does the user expect to see the aggregate level clustered, but the user expects to be able to expand upon any particular cluster and see the results also displayed using a visualization technique. Thus at each level, the precision of the clustering process increases. The user expects to interact with the system and see the results of the search in near real time processing (e.g., anthing more than 20 seconds is delayed response).

There are two major processing issues in developing the information visualization display. The first is in the third step of calculating the pairwise similarities of all of the items. The second major issue is in the increased precision expected as the user moves from the higher to lower levels of information visualization. This requires an additional level of precision that will likely need natural language processing to achieve. The indexes for items and the algorithms proposed to determine similarity between a query and the items may need adjustments to optimize their performance in locating and organizing the results from a search for the information visualization process.

EXERCISES

1. Describe the need for information visualization. Under what circumstances is information visualization not useful. (HINT: consider SDI functions and also consider possible characteristics of the results of a search)

2. Describe how other senses could be used in displaying results form searches.

3. Discuss the limits associated with use of preattentive processes, configural aspects, and spatial frequency as a basis for information visualization.

4. Access the Internet and locate three informaion visualization techniques that are available. Describe what cognitive engineering principles are beingused in the techniques.

5. Discuss the difficulties of a user being able to correlate his search to the Hit file. What approach would you use to overcome these problems.

9 Text Search Algorithms

Three classical techniques for text retrieval techniques have been defined for organizing items in a textual database, for rapidly identifying the relevant items and for eliminating items that do not satisfy the search. The techniques are full text scanning (streaming), word inversion and multi-attribute retrieval (Faloutsos-85, Salton-83). In addition to using the indexes as a mechanism for searching text in information systems, streaming of text was frequently found in the systems as an additional search mechanism. Streaming of text is a sequential search of the text. This technique is used to complete a query by searching for query terms that could not be satisfied by the index (e.g., imbedded search terms). It is also frequently used to locate the search terms for highlighting in the retrieved item prior to display.

Today most text search is performed by software. But in the earlier history of information systems, where the limited capabilities of hardware (CPU power, memory and disk systems) restricted search applications, specialized hardware text search systems were created. The hardware systems were used to offload the search process from the main computer leaving the user interface, access and display. The need for hardware text search streamers has been declining with the increases in CPU power, disk access and memory. But there is still a market for them in the areas of genetic research, and many existing legacy systems are still in use.

9.1 Introduction to Text Search Techniques

The basic concept of a text scanning system is the ability for one or more users to enter queries with the text of the items to be searched sequentially accessed and compared to the query terms. When all of the text has been accessed, the query is complete. One advantage of this type architecture is that as soon as an item is identified as satisfying a query, the results can be presented to the user for retrieval. Figure 9.1 provides a general diagram of a text streaming search system. The database contains the full text of the items. The term detector is the special

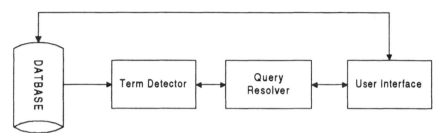

Figure 9.1 Text Streaming Architecture

hardware/software that contains all of the search terms and in some systems the logic between the terms. It inputs the text and detects the existence of the search terms. It outputs to the query resolver the detected terms, allowing for final logical processing of a query against an item. The query resolver performs two major functions: accepting search statements from the users and extracting the logic and search terms to pass to the detector. It also accepts results from the detector and determines which queries are satisfied by the item and possibly the relevance weight associated with hit. The query resolver passes information to the user interface, allowing it to continually update the search status and, on request, retrieve any items that satisfy the user search statement. The text streaming process is focused on finding at least one or all occurrences of a pattern of text (query term) in a text stream. It is assumed that the same alphabet is used in both search terms and text being streamed. In foreign language streamers, different encodings may have to be available for items from the same language (e.g., in Cyrillic there are over six encodings that can be used). The worst case search for a pattern of m characters in a string of n characters is at least $n - m + 1$ or a magnitude of $O(n)$ (Rivest-77). Some of the original brute force methods could require $O(n*m)$ symbol comparisons (Sedgewick-88). More recent improvements have reduced the time to $O(n + m)$.

     In the case of hardware text search machines, multiple parallel search machines (term detectors) may work against the same data stream. This permits more queries or the same queries against different data streams thereby reducing the time to access the complete database. In software systems, multiple detectors may execute at the same time.

     There are two approaches to the data stream. In the first approach the complete database is being sent to the detector(s) which function as a search of the database. In the second approach, random retrieved items are being passed to the detectors. In this second case, an index search is performed that constrains the items from the database requiring additional processing, while the text streamer performs the additional search logic that is not satisfied by the index search (Bird-78, Hollar-79). Examples where index searches may not be able to satisfy the complete search statement are:

> search for stop words

> search for exact matches when stemming is performed

> search for terms that contain both leading and trailing "don't cares"

> search for symbols that are on the interword symbol list (e.g., ," ;)

> search for "fuzzy" search terms (m of n characters - see Chapter 2)

For the last three cases, it is difficult to locate all the possible index values short of searching the complete dictionary of possible terms.

The major disadvantage of basing the search on streaming the text is the dependency of the search on the slowest module in the computer (the I/O module). Inversions/indexes gain their speed by minimizing the amount of data to be retrieved and provide the best ratio between the total number of items delivered to the user versus the total number of items retrieved in response to a query. But unlike inversion systems that can require storage overheads of 50 per cent to 300 per cent of the original databases (BIRD-78), the full text search function does not require any additional storage overhead. There is also the advantage that items that satisfy the query may be returned to the user as soon as found. Typically in an index system, the complete query must be processed before any hits are determined or available. Streaming systems also provide a very accurate estimate of current search status and time to complete the query. Most streaming algorithms locate imbedded query terms, and some algorithms and hardware search units will also perform fuzzy searches. Use of special hardware text search units ensures a scaleable environment where performance bottlenecks can be overcome by adding additional search units to work in parallel on the data being streamed.

Many of the hardware and software text searchers use finite state automata as a basis for their search algorithms. A finite state automata is a logical machine that is composed of five elements:

> **I** - a set of input symbols from the alphabet supported by the automata
> **S** - a set of possible states
> **P** - a set of productions that define the next state based upon the current
>   state and input symbol
> **S_0** - a special state called the initial state
> **S_F** - a set of one or more final states from the set **S**

A finite state automata can be represented by a directed graph consisting of a series of nodes (states) and edges between nodes representing transitions defined by the set of productions. Direction is indicated on the edges from the old state to the new state. The symbol(s) associated with each edge defines the inputs that allow a transition from one node S_i to another node S_j. Figure 9.2a shows a finite state automata that will identify the character string CPU in any input stream. The automata is defined by the automata definition in Figure 9.2b. The automata remains in the initial state until it has an input symbol of "C" which moves it to state S_1. It will remain in that state as long as it receives "C"s as input. If it receives a "P" it will move to S_2. If it receives anything else it falls back to the initial state. Once in state S_2 it will either go to the final state if "U" is the next symbol, go to S_1 if a "C" is received or go back to the initial state S_0 if anything else is received.

I = set of all alphabetic characters
S = set $\{S_0, S_1 S_2 S_3)$
P = set $\{S_0 \rightarrow S_1$ if $I = C$
$\qquad S_0 \rightarrow S_0$ if $I \neq C$
$\qquad S_1 \rightarrow S_2$ if $I = P$
$\qquad S_1 \rightarrow S_0$ if $I \neq \{P, C\}$
$\qquad S_1 \rightarrow S_1$ if $I = C$
$\qquad S_2 \rightarrow S_3$ if $I = U$
$\qquad S_2 \rightarrow S_1$ if $I = C$
$\qquad S_2 \rightarrow S_0$ if $I \neq \{C, U \} \}$
$S_0 = \{ S_0 \}$
$S_F = \{ S_3 \}$

Figure 9.2b Automata Definition

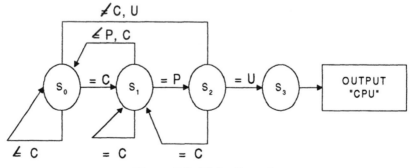

Figure 9.2a Finite State Automata

It is possible to represent the productions by a table with the states as the rows and the input symbols that cause state transitions as each column. The states are representing the current state and the values in the table are the next state given the particular input symbol.

9.2 Software Text Search Algorithms

In software streaming techniques, the item to be searched is read into memory, and then the algorithm is applied. Although nothing in the described architecture prohibits software streaming from being applied to many simultaneous searches against the same item, it is more frequently used to resolve a particular search against a particular item. There are four major algorithms associated with software text search: the brute force approach, Knuth-Morris-Pratt, Boyer-Moore, Shift-OR algorithm, and Rabin-Karp. Of all of the algorithms, Boyer-Moore has been the fastest, requiring at most $O(n + m)$ comparisons (Smit-82) where n is the number of characters being searched and m is the size of the search string. Knuth-Pratt-Morris and Boyer-Moore both require $O(n)$ preprocessing of search strings in addition to the search comparisons (Knuth-77, Boyer-77, Rytter-80).

The brute force approach is the simplest string matching algorithm. The idea is to match the search string against the input text. Whenever a mis-match is detected in the comparison process, the input text is shifted one position, and the comparison process is initialized and restarted. The expected number of comparisons when searching an input text string of n characters for a pattern of m characters is (Baeza-Yates-89):

$$N_c = \frac{c}{c-1}(1 - \frac{1}{c^m})(n - m + 1) + O(1)$$

where N_c is the expected number of comparisons and c is the size of the alphabet for the text.

Applying the formula to an example where the alphabet is c=25 characters, the search pattern is m=7 characters, and the search stream is an item with n=30,000 characters has the number of comparisons is:

$$N_c = 25/(25 - 1)(1 - 1/25^7)(30000 - 7 + 1) = (1.04)(1-0)(29996) \approx n$$

For search of any large streams the number of comparisons can be estimated by the number of characters being searched. For smaller items the length of the text pattern (m) can have an effect on the number of comparisons.

The Knuth-Pratt-Morris algorithm made a major improvement in previous algorithms in that even in the worst case it does not depend upon the length of the search term and does not require comparisons for every character in the input stream. The basic concept behind the algorithm is that whenever a mismatch is detected, the previous matched characters define the number of characters that can be skipped in the input stream prior to starting the comparison process again. For example consider:

           Position   1 2 3 4 5 6 7 8
           Input Stream   = a b d a d e f g
           Search Pattern   = a b d f

When the mismatch occurs in position 4 with a "f" in the pattern and a "c" in the input stream, a brute force approach may shift just one position in the input text and restart the comparison. But since the first three positions of the pattern matched (a b d), then shifting one position can not find an "a" because it has already been identified as a "b." The algorithm allows the comparison to jump at least the three positions associated with the recognized "a b d". Since the mismatch on the position could be the beginning of the search string, four positions can not be skipped. To know the number of positions to jump based upon a mismatch in the search pattern, the search pattern is pre-processed to define a number of character to be jumped for each position. The Shift Table that specifies the number of places to jump given a mismatch is shown in Figure 9.3 for a search pattern = abcabcacab. In the table it should be noted that the alignment is primarily based on aligning over the repeats of the letters "a" and "ab." Figure 9.4 provides an example application of the algorithm (Salton-89) where S is the search pattern and I is the input text stream.

Boyer-Moore recognized that the string algorithm could be significantly enhanced if the comparison process starts at the end of the search pattern, processing right to left versus the start of the search pattern. The advantage is that

Position in pattern	pattern character	length previous repeating substring	number of input characters to jump
1	a	0	1
2	b	0	1
3	c	0	2
4	a	0	3
5	b	1	3
6	c	2	3
7	a	3	3
8	c	4	3
9	a	0	8
10	b	1	8

Figure 9.3   Shift Characters Table

P	1	2	3	4	5	6	7	8	9	10	11	12	13	14	15	16
S	a	b	c	a	b	c	a	c	a	b						
I	b	a	b	c	b	a	b	c	a	b	c	a	a	b	c	a
	↑															

mismatch in position 1 shift one position

P	1	2	3	4	5	6	7	8	9	10	11	12	13	14	15	16
S		a	b	c	a	b	c	a	c	a	b					
I	b	a	b	c	b	a	b	c	a	b	c	a	a	b	c	a
					↑											

mismatch in position 5, no repeat pattern, skip 3 places

P	1	2	3	4	5	6	7	8	9	10	11	12	13	14	15	16
S					a	b	c	a	b	c	a	c	a	b		
I	b	a	b	c	b	a	b	c	a	b	c	a	a	b	c	a
					↑											

mismatch in position 5, shift one position

P	1	2	3	4	5	6	7	8	9	10	11	12	13	14	15	16
S						a	b	c	a	b	c	a	c	a	b	
I	b	a	b	c	b	a	b	c	a	b	c	a	a	b	c	a
													↑			

mismatch in position 13, longest repeating pattern is "a b c a" thus skip 3

P	1	2	3	4	5	6	7	8	9	10	11	12	13	14	15	16
S									a	b	c	a	b	c	a	b
I	b	a	b	c	b	a	b	c	a	b	c	a	a	b	c	a

alignment after last shift

Figure 9.4 Example of Knuth-Morris-Pratt Algorithm

large jumps are possible when the mismatched character in the input stream does not exist in the search pattern which occurs frequently. This leads to two possible sources of determining how many input characters to be jumped. As in the Knuth-Morris-Pratt technique, any characters that have been matched in the search pattern require an alignment with that substring. Additionally, the character in the input stream that was mismatched also requires alignment with its next occurrence in the search pattern or the complete pattern can be moved. This can be defined as:

ALGO$_1$ - on a mismatch, the character in the input stream is compared to the search pattern to determine the shifting of the search pattern (number of characters in input stream to be skipped) to align the input character to a character in the search pattern. If the character does not exist in the search pattern then it is possible to shift the length of the search pattern matched to that position.

ALGO$_2$ - on a mismatch occuring with a previous matching on a substring in the input text, the matching process can jump to the repeating occurrence in the pattern of the initially matched subpattern - thus aligning that portion of the search pattern that is in the input text.

Upon a mismatch, the comparison process can skip the MAXIMUM (ALGO$_1$, ALGO$_2$). Figure 9.5 gives an example of this process. In this example the search pattern is (a b b a b d d) and the alphabet is (a, b, c, d, e, f) with $m = 7$ and $c = 6$.

The comparison starts at the right end of the search pattern and works towards the start of the search pattern. In the first comparison (Figure 9.5 a.), the mismatch occurs in position 4 after matching on positions 7, 6, and 5. ALGO$_1$ wants to align the next occurrence of the input text stream mismatch character "f" which does not exist in the search pattern, thus allowing for a skip of three positions. ALGO$_2$ recognizes that the mismatch occurs after 3 previous search pattern characters had matched. Based upon the pattern stream it knows that the subpattern consisting of the first three characters (a b) repeats in the first two positions of the search pattern. If there is a mismatch in position 4, the search pattern can be moved four places to align the subpattern consisting of the first two characters (a b) over their known occurrence in positions 6, and 7 in the input text. In the next comparison (Figure 9.5 b.) there is a mismatch in position 9. The input character that mismatched is a "d" and the fewest positions to shift to align the next occurrence of a "d" in the search pattern over it is one position. The analysis for ALGO$_2$ is the same as before. With the next jump of four positions, the two patterns match.

The original Boyer-Moore algorithm has been the basis for additional text search techniques. It was originally designed to support scanning for a single search string. It was expanded to handle multiple search strings on a single pass (Kowalski-83). Enhanced and simplified versions of the Boyer-Moore algorithm have been developed by many researchers (Mollier-Nielsen-84, Iyengar-80, Commentz-Walter-79, Baeza-Yates-90, Galil-79, Horspol-80).

A different approach that has similarity to n-grams and signature files defined in Chapter 4 is to divide the text into m-character substrings and calculate a hash function (signature) value for each of the strings (Harrison-71). A hash value is then calculated for the search pattern and compared to that of the text. Karp and Rabin discovered an efficient signature function to calculate these values: $h(k) = k \bmod q$, where q is a large prime number (Karp-87). The signature value

Position	1	2	3	4	5	6	7	8	9	10	11	12	13
Input Stream	f	a	b	f	a	a	b	b	d	a	b	a	b
Search Pattern		a	b	d	a	a	b						

↑

   a.   mismatch in position 4: $ALGO_1 = 3$, $ALGO_2 = 4$, thus skip 4 places

Position	1	2	3	4	5	6	7	8	9	10	11	12	13
Input Stream	f	a	b	f	a	a	b	b	d	a	b	a	b
Search Pattern					a	b	d	a	a	b			

↑

   b.   mismatch in position 8: $ALGO_1 = 1$, $ALGO_2 = 4$ thus skip four places

Position	1	2	3	4	5	6	7	8	9	10	11	12	13	14	15
Input Stream	f	a	b	f	a	a	b	b	d	a	b	d	a	a	b
Search Pattern										a	b	d	a	a	b

   c.   new aligned search continues with a match

Figure 9.5 Boyer-Moore Algorithm

for each location in the text is based upon the value calculated for the previous location. Hashing functions do not guarantee uniqueness. This algorithm finds those positions in the text of an item that have the same hash value as the search pattern. But the actual text must then be compared to ensure there is a match. Detailed implementation of the Karp-Rabin algorithm is presented by Baeza-Yates (Baeza-Yates-92). In his comparison of all of the algorithms on a search of 1000 random patterns in random text, the Horspool simplification of the Boyer-Moore algorithm showed the best execution time for patterns of any length. The major drawback of the Boyer-Moore class of algorithms is the significant preprocessing time to set up the tables. Many of these algorithms are also implemented with hardware.

Another approach based upon Knuth-Pratt-Morris uses a finite state machine to process multiple query terms (Aho-75). The pattern matching machine consists of a set of states. The machine processes the input text by successively reading in the next symbol and, based upon the current state, makes the state transitions while indicating matches when they occur. The machine's operation is based upon three functions: GOTO (i.e., state transition), a failure function and a output function. Figure 9.6 shows the functions for the set of words HE, SHE, HIS, and HER. The initial state is labeled state 0. The GOTO function is a directed

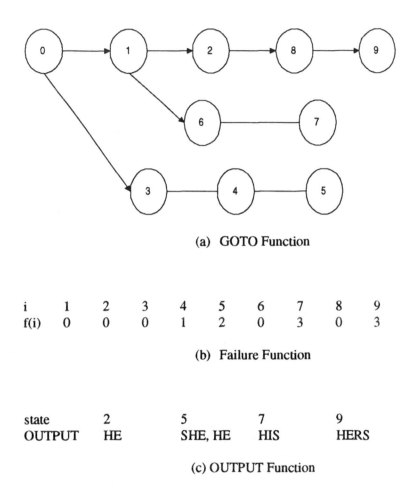

(a) GOTO Function

i	1	2	3	4	5	6	7	8	9
f(i)	0	0	0	1	2	0	3	0	3

(b) Failure Function

state	2	5	7	9
OUTPUT	HE	SHE, HE	HIS	HERS

(c) OUTPUT Function

Figure 9.6 Tables for Aho-Corasick Algorithm

graph where the letter(s) on the connecting line between states (circles) specify the transition for that input given the current state. For example in Figure 9.6, if the current state is 1 and a E or I are received, then the machine will go to states 2 and 6 respectively. The absence of an arrow or current input character that is not on a line leading from the current node represents a failure condition. When a failure occurs, the failure function maps a state into another state (it could be to itself) to continue the search process. Certain states are defined as output states. Whenever they are reached it means one or more query terms have been matched. For example, assume an H has been received and the system is in state 1. If the next input symbol is an E the system moves to state 2; if an I is received then it moves to state 6; if any other letter is received, it will be an error and Failure Function (the third column in 9.6(b)) specifies the system should move to state 0 and the same input character is applied to this state.

The number of characters compared is the same for both the Aho-Corasick and the KMP algorithms. In the new algorithm the number of state transitions required to process a string is independent of the number of search terms and the operation to perform the search is linear with respect to the number of characters in the input stream. The order of magnitude of the number of characters compared is equal to $w \bullet O(T)$ where w is a constant greater than 1 and T is the number of characters in the input string. This is a major enhancement over both Knuth-Morris-Pratt which is proportional to the number of characters in the query, and Boyer-Moore, which can only handle one query term.

These concepts were expanded by Baeza-Yates and Gonnet and can handle "don't care" symbols and complement symbols (Baeza-Yates-92a). The search also handles the cases of up to k mismatches. Their approach uses a vector of m different states, where m is the length of the search pattern, and state i gives the state of the search between the positions $1, \ldots, i$ of the pattern and positions $(j - i + 1), \ldots, j$ of the text where j is the current position in the text. This in effect expands the process to act like it has m simultaneous comparators working. If $s_{i,j}$ is the set of states $(1 \le i \le m)$ after reading the jth character of the text, the vector represents the number of characters that are different in the corresponding positions between $pat_1, \ldots, pat_i$ and $text_{j-i+1}, \ldots, text_j$ where pat is the search pattern and $text$ is the text being searched. If $s_{i,j} = 0$, then there is a perfect match. Otherwise it provides a fuzzy search capability where the search term length and the found term length are the same and the value is for the number of mismatches. For example, let the search pattern be $ababc$ ($m = 5$) and a segment of input text to be $cbbabababcaba$, then Figure 9.7 shows the value for $s_{i,j-1}$ vector. For example, the vector value for vector position 3 is 0 because the three pat characters aba have no matches with the corresponding three characters bab from the input text stream.

When one position in the text is advanced, the new vector is shown in Figure 9.8. If $T(x)$ is a table such that $T_i(x) = 0$ if $x = pat_i$, otherwise $T_i(x) = 1$. Thus everywhere that the current vector value is zero (i.e., the pattern matches), the $T(x)$ value is zero. Every other location has a $T(x)$ value of one. For example in Figure 9.7 the $T_i(x)$ will appear $(1,0,1,0,1)$ and for Figure 9.8 it will be $(0,1,0,1,1)$ which is called $T(new)$. It is then possible to define:

$$s(i,j) = s(i, j-1) + T_i(text_j)$$

	Vector value	Vector Position
a| b a b c	1	1
a b| a b c	0	2
a b a| b c	3	3
a b a b| c	0	4
a b a b c|	5	5
... c b b a b a b a b| c a b a ...	Input Text Stream ...	

Figure 9.7 Vector for Position j - 1

	Vector value	Vector Position
a| b a b c	0	1
a b| a b c	2	2
a b a| b c	0	3
a b a b| c	4	4
a b a b c|	1	5
... c b b a b a b| a b c a b a ...	Input Text Stream ...	

Figure 9.8 Vector for Position j

If $s(0, j) = 0$, then the following shows the effect of moving the one position from Figure 9.7 (call old) to Figure 8 (call new):

$$s(1, \text{new}) = s(0, \text{old}) + T_1(\text{new}) = 0 + 0 = 0$$
$$s(2, \text{new}) = s(1, \text{old}) + T_2(\text{new}) = 1 + 1 = 2$$
$$s(3, \text{new}) = s(2, \text{old}) + T_3(\text{new}) = 0 + 0 = 0$$
$$s(4, \text{new}) = s(3, \text{old}) + T_4(\text{new}) = 3 + 1 = 4$$
$$s(5, \text{new}) = s(4, \text{old}) + T_5(\text{new}) = 0 + 1 = 1$$

Because of these operations, they called the algorithm the Shift-add algorithm. To extend the technique to allow for "don't care" symbols, complements of a character or class (i.e., matches an character that does not belong to the class), or any finite set of symbols, three possibilities exist for any position in the pattern:

a character from the alphabet

a "don't care" character (*)

a complement of a character or class of characters ($\bar{C}$)

Letting m' be the total of the number of elements in each class with * assigned a value of 1 and complements not considered. Let m be the size of the pattern. The pattern:

$$[\text{Pp}]a[\overline{\text{aeiou}}]^* \, \bar{a} \, [p \ldots \text{tx} \ldots z]$$

values each class   2 1   5   1 1   5 + 3

has $m = 6$ and $m' = 18$. The Shift-add algorithm is extended by modifying the table T, such that, for each position every character in the class is processed. Thus if the alphabet equals (a, b, c, d) and the pattern is:

$$a\bar{b} \, [ab]b[\overline{abc}]$$

with $m = 5$ and $m' = 8$. If b=1 (as for string matching), the entries for the table T are:

T(a) = 11000
T(b) = 10011
T(c) = 11101
T(d) = 01101

Baeza-Yates and Gonnet describe the details of the implementation of this algorithm in the referenced paper. One advantage to this algorithm is that it can easily be implemented in a hardware solution. The shift-add algorithm is extended by Wu and Manber to handle insertions and deletions as well as positional mismatches (Wu-92).

9.3 Hardware Text Search Systems

Software text search is applicable to many circumstances but has encountered restrictions on the ability to handle many search terms simultaneously against the same text and limits due to I/O speeds. One approach that off loaded the resource intensive searching from the main processors was to have a specialized hardware machine to perform the searches and pass the results to the main computer which supported the user interface and retrieval of hits. Since the searcher is hardware based, scalability is achieved by increasing the number hardware search devices. The only limit on speed is the time it takes to flow the text off secondary storage (i.e., disk drives) to the searchers. By having one search machine per disk, the maximum time it takes to search a database of any size is the time to search one disk. In some systems, the disks were formatted to optimize the data flow off of the drives. Another major advantage of using a hardware text search unit is in the elimination of the index that represents the document database. Typically the indexes are 70 per cent the size of the actual items. Other advantages are that new items can be searched as soon as received by the system rather than waiting for the index to be created and the search speed is deterministic. Even though it may be slower than using an index, the predictability of how long it will take to stream the data provides the user with an exact search time. As hits as discovered they can immediately be made available to the user versus waiting for the total search to complete as in index searches.

Figure 9.1 represents an architecture for hardware as well as software text search solutions. The algorithmic part of the system is focused on the term detector. There have been three approaches to implementing term detectors: parallel comparators or associative memory, a cellular structure, and a universal finite state automata (Hollar-79).

When the term comparator is implemented with parallel comparators, each term in the query is assigned to an individual comparison element and input data are serially streamed into the detector. When a match occurs, the term comparator informs the external query resolver (usually in the main computer) by setting status flags. In some systems, some of the Boolean logic between terms is resolved in the term detector hardware (e.g., in the GESCAN machine and Fast Data Finder) instead of using specially designed comparators.

Specialized hardware that interfaces with computers and is used to search secondary storage devices was developed from the early 1970s with the most recent product being the Parasel Searcher (previously the Fast Data Finder). The need for this hardware was driven by the limits in computer resources. The typical hardware configuration is shown in Figure 9.9 in the dashed box. The speed of search is then based on the speed of the I/O.

One of the earliest hardware text string search units was the Rapid Search Machine developed by General Electric (Roberts-78). The machine consisted of a special purpose search unit in which a single query was passed against a magnetic tape containing the documents. A more sophisticated search unit was developed by Operating Systems Inc. called the Associative File Processor (AFP) (Bird-77). It is capable of searching against multiple queries at the same time. Following that

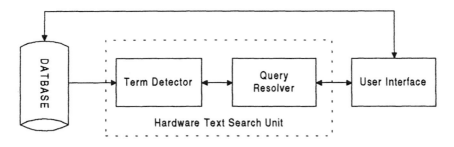

Figure 9.9 Hardware Text Search Unit

initial development, OSI, using a different approach, developed the High Speed Text Search (HSTS) machine. It uses an algorithm similar to the Aho-Corasick software finite state machine algorithm except that it runs three parallel state machines. One state machine is dedicated to contiguous word phrases (see Chapter 2), another for imbedded term match and the final for exact word match.   In parallel with that development effort, GE redesigned their Rapid Search Machine into the GESCAN unit.   TRW, based upon analysis of the HSTS, decided to develop its own text search unit.   This became the Fast Data Finder, now being marketed by Parasal. All of these machines were based upon state machines that input the text string and compared them to the query terms.

The GESCAN system uses a text array processor (TAP) that simultaneously matches many terms and conditions against a given text stream. The TAP receives the query information from the user's computer and directly accesses the textual data from secondary storage. The TAP consists of a large cache memory and an array of four to 128 query processors. The text is loaded into the cache and searched by the query processors (Figure 9.10).   Each query processor is independent and can be loaded at any time. A complete query is handled by each query processor. Queries support exact term matches, fixed length don't cares, variable length "don't cares," terms restricted to specified zones, Boolean logic, and proximity.

A query processor works two operations in parallel: matching query terms to input text and Boolean logic resolution. Term matching is performed by a series of character cells, each containing one character of the query. A string of character cells is implemented on the same LSI chip and the chips can be connected in series for longer strings. When a word or phrase of the query is matched, a signal is sent to the resolution sub-process on the LSI chip. The resolution chip is responsible for resolving the Boolean logic between terms and proximity requirements. If the item satisfies the query, the information is transmitted to the user's computer. The text array processor uses these chips in a matrix arrangement as shown in Figure 9.10. Each row of the matrix is a query processor in which the first chip performs the query resolution while the remaining chips match query terms. The maximum

number of characters in a query is restricted by the length of a row while the
number of rows limit the number of simultaneous queries that can be processed.

Another approach for hardware searchers is to augment disc storage. The
augmentation is a generalized associative search element placed between the read
and write heads on the disk. The content addressable segment sequential memory
(CASSM) system (Roberts-78) uses these search elements in parallel to obtain
structured data from a database. The CASSM system was developed at the
University of Florida as a general purpose search device (Copeland-73). It can be
used to perform string searching across the database. Another special search
machine is the relational associative processor (RAP) developed at the University

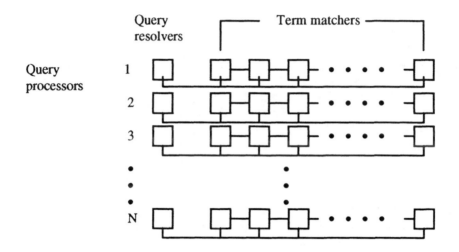

Figure 9.10 GESCAN Text Array Processor

of Toronto (Schuster-79). Like CASSM performs search across a secondary
storage device using a series of cells comparing data in parallel.

The Fast Data Finder (FDF) is the most recent specialized hardware text
search unit still in use in many organizations. It was developed to search text and
has been used to search English and foreign languages. The early Fast Data
Finders consisted of an array of programmable text processing cells connected in
series forming a pipeline hardware search processor (Mettler-93). The cells are
implemented using a VSLI chip. In the TREC tests each chip contained 24
processor cells with a typical system containing 3600 cells (the FDF-3 has a rack
mount configuration with 10,800 cells). Each cell is a comparator for a single
character, limiting the total number of characters in a query to the number of cells.
The cells are interconnected with an 8-bit data path and approximately 20-bit
control path. The text to be searched passes through each cell in a pipeline fashion

until the complete database has been searched. As data are analyzed at each cell, the 20 control lines states are modified depending upon their current state and the results from the comparator. An example of a Fast Data Finder system is shown in Figure 9.11. A cell is composed of both a register cell (Rs) and a comparator (Cs). The input from the Document database is controlled and buffered by the microprocessor/memory and feed through the comparators. The search characters are stored in the registers. The connection between the registers reflects the control lines that are also passing state information.

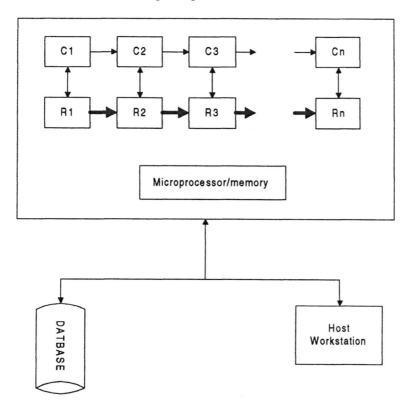

Figure 9.11 Fast Data Finder Architecture

Groups of cells are used to detect query terms, along with logic between the terms, by appropriate programming of the control lines. When a pattern match is detected, a hit is passed to the internal microprocessor that passes it back to the host processor, allowing immediate access by the user to the Hit item. The functions supported by the Fast Data Finder are

Boolean Logic including negation
Proximity on an arbitrary pattern

Variable length "don't cares"
Term counting and thresholds
fuzzy matching
term weights
numeric ranges.

The expense and requirement that the complete database be streamed to complete a search has discouraged general use of hardware text search units. Paracel, who now markets the Fast Data Finder, is modifying its application to the area of genetic analysis. Comparing sequence homology (linear sequence of genes as another chromosone) to known families of proteins can provide insights about functions of newly sequenced genes. Paracel has combined the search capability of the FDF with their Biology Tool Kit (BTK). The major function that is applied is the fuzzy match capability that can be applied to chromosones. Searches can be applied to DNA against DNA, protein against protein, or DNA against protein searches. The FDF is configured to implement linear Smith-Waterman (S-W) and sequence-profile algorithms. The Smith-Waterman dynamic programming algorithm is optimal for finding local sequence similarities. The General Profile algorithm allows search for regions of nucleic acids or proteins that have been conserved during evolution (Paracel-96). The Fast Data Finder is loaded with a sequence and will report back those sequences in the database whose local similarity scores exceed a threshold that most closely resemble the query sequence. The BTK software then completes the analysis process in software.

9.4 Summary

Text search techniques using text scanning have played an important role in the development of Information Retrieval Systems. In the 1970s and 1980s they were essential tools for compensating for the insufficient computer power and for handling some of the more difficult search capabilities such as imbedded character strings and fuzzy searches. They currently play an important role in word processor systems (e.g., the Find function) and in Information Retrieval Systems for locating offensive terms (e.g., imbedded character strings) in the dictionary. The need for specialized hardware text search units to directly search the data on secondary storage has diminished with the growth of processing power of computers.

EXERCISES

1. Trade off the use of hardware versus software text search algorithms citing advantages and disadvantages of each in comparison to the other.

2. Construct finite state automata for each of the following set of terms:

    a. BIT, FIT, HIT, MIT, PIT, SIT

    b. CAN, CAR, CARPET, CASE, CASK, CAKE

    c. HE, SHE, HER, HERE, THERE, SHEAR

    Be sure to define the three sets I, S, and P along with providing the state drawing (e.g., see Figure 9.2).

3. Use the Boyer-Moore text search algorithm to search for the term FANCY in the text string FANCIFUL FANNY FRUIT FILLED MY FANCY.

    a. Show all of the steps and explain each of the required character shifts.
    b. How many character comparisons are required to obtain a match?
    c. Compare this to what it would take using the Knuth-Pratt-Morris algorithm (you do not have to show the work for the KMP algorithm).

4. a. Use the problem defined in question three and create the GOTO, Failure and OUTPUT functions for the Aho-Corasick algorithm (see Figure 9.6).
    b. Trace through the steps in searching for the term FANCY.
    c. What are the trade offs between using the Aho-Corasick versus Boyer-Moore algorithms?

5. What algorithmetic basis is used for the GE-SCAN and Fast Data Finder hardware text search machines? Why was this approach used over others?

10 Information System Evaluation

10.1 Introduction to Information System Evaluation
10.2 Measures Used in System Evaluations
10.3 Measurement Example -TREC-Results
10.4 Summary

Interest in the evaluation techniques for Information Retrieval Systems has significantly increased with the commercial use of information retrieval technologies in the everyday life of the millions of users of the Internet. Until 1993 the evaluations were done primarily by academicians using a few small, well known corpora of test documents or even smaller test databases created within academia. The evaluations focused primarily on the effectiveness of search algorithms. The creation of the annual Text Retrieval Evaluation Conference (TREC) sponsored by the Defense Advanced Research Projects Agency (DARPA) and the National Institute of Standards and Technology (NIST) changed the standard process of evaluating information systems. Conferences have been held every year, starting from 1992, usually in the Fall months. The conference provides a standard database consisting of gigabytes of test data, search statements and the expected results from the searches to academic researchers and commercial companies for testing of their systems. This has placed a standard baseline into comparisons of algorithms. Although there is now a standard database, there is still debate on the accuracy and utility of the results from use of the test corpus. Section 10.2 introduces the measures that are available for evaluating information systems. The techniques are compared stressing their utility from an academic as well as a commercial perspective. Section 10.3 gives examples of results from major comparisons of information systems and algorithms.

10.1 Introduction to Information System Evaluation

In recent years the evaluation of Information Retrieval Systems and techniques for indexing, sorting, searching and retrieving information have become increasingly important (Saracevic-95). This growth in interest is due to two major reasons: the growing number of retrieval systems being used and additional focus on evaluation methods themselves. The Internet is an example of an information space (infospace) whose text content is growing exponentially along with products to find information for value. Information retrieval technologies are the basis behind the search of information on the Internet. In parallel with the commercial interest, the introduction of a large standardized test database and a forum for yearly analysis via TREC has provided a methodology for evaluating the performance of algorithms and systems. There are many reasons to evaluate the effectiveness of an Information Retrieval System (Belkin-93, Callan-93):

> To aid in the selection of a system to procure
> To monitor and evaluate system effectiveness
> To evaluate query generation process for improvements
> To provide inputs to cost-benefit analysis of an information system
> To determine the effects of changes made to an existing information system.

From an academic perspective, measurements are focused on the specific effectiveness of a system and usually are applied to determining the effects of changing a system's algorithms or comparing algorithms among systems. From a commercial perspective, measurements are also focused on availability and reliability. In an operational system there is less concern over 55 per cent versus 65 per cent precision than 90 per cent versus 80 per cent availability. For academic purposes, controlled environments can be created that minimize errors in data. In operational systems, there is no control over the users and care must be taken to ensure the data collected are meaningful.

The most important evaluation metrics of information systems will always be biased by human subjectivity. This problem arises from the specific data collected to measure the user resources in locating relevant information. Metrics to accurately measure user resources expended in information retrieval are inherently inaccurate. A factor in most metrics in determining how well a system is working is the relevancy of items. Relevancy of an item, however, is not a binary evaluation, but a continuous function between an item's being exactly what is being looked for and its being totally unrelated. To discuss relevancy, it is necessary to define the context under which the concept is used. From a human judgment standpoint, relevancy can be considered:

> Subjective   - depends upon a specific user's judgment
> Situational   - relates to a user's requirements
> Cognitive   - depends on human perception and behavior

Temporal   - changes over time
Measurable   - observable at a points in time

The subjective nature of relevance judgments has been documented by Saracevic and was shown in TREC-experiments (Harman-95, Saracevic-91). In TREC-2 and TREC-3, two or three different users were given the same search statement and the same set of possible hits to judge as relevant or not. In general, there was a unanimous agreement on 70-80 per cent of the items judged by the human. Even in this environment (i.e., where the judges are not the creators of the query and are making every effort to be unbiased) there is still significant subjective disagreement on the relevancy of items. In a dynamic environment, each user has his own understanding of the requirement and the threshold on what is acceptable (see Chapter 1). Based upon his cognitive model of the information space and the problem, the user judges a particular item. Some users consider information they already know to be non-relevant to their information need. For example, a user being presented with an article that the user wrote does not provide "new" relevant information to answer the user's query, although the article may be very relevant to the search statement. Also the judgment of relevance can vary over time. Retrieving information on an "XT" class of PCs is not of significant relevance to personal computers in 1996, but would have been valuable in 1992. Thus, relevance judgment is measurable at a point in time constrained by the particular users and their thresholds on acceptability of information.

Another way of specifying relevance is from information, system and situational views. The information view is subjective in nature and pertains to human judgment of the conceptual relatedness between an item and the search. It involves the user's personal judgment of the relevancy (aboutness) of the item to the user's information need. When reference experts (librarians, researchers, subject specialists, indexers) assist the user, it is assumed they can reasonably predict whether certain information will satisfy the user's needs. Ingwersen categorizes the information view into four types of "aboutness" (Ingwersen-92):

Author Aboutness - determined by the author's language as matched by
                   the system in natural language retrieval

Indexer Aboutness - determined by the indexer's transformation of the
                    author's natural language into a controlled vocabulary

Request Aboutness - determined by the user's or intermediary's
                    processing of a search statement into a query

User Aboutness - determined by the indexer's attempt to represent the
                 document according to presupposition about what the
                 user will want to know

In this context, the system view relates to a match between query terms and terms within an item. It can be objectively observed, manipulated and tested without relying on human judgment because it uses metrics associated with the matching of the query to the item (Barry-94, Schamber-90). The semantic relatedness between queries and items is assumed to be inherited via the index terms that represent the semantic content of the item in a consistent and accurate fashion. Other aspects of the system view are presented in Section 10.2.

The situation view pertains to the relationship between information and the user's information problem situation. It assumes that only users can make valid judgments regarding the suitability of information to solve their information need. Lancaster and Warner refer to information and situation views as relevance and pertinence respectively (Lancaster-93). Pertinence can be defined as those items that satisfy the user's information need at the time of retrieval. The TREC-evaluation process uses relevance versus pertinence as its criteria for judging items because pertinence is too variable to attempt to measure in meaningful items (i.e., it depends on each situation).

10.2 Measures Used in System Evaluations

To define the measures that can be used in evaluating Information Retrieval Systems, it is useful to define the major functions associated with identifying relevant items in an information system (see Figure 10.1). Items arrive

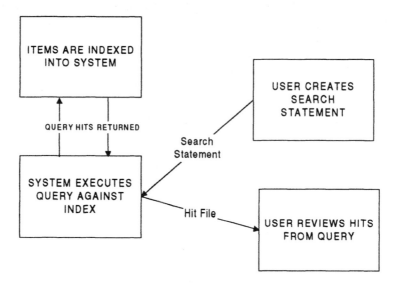

Figure 10.1 Identifying Relevant Items

in the system and are automatically or manually transformed by "indexing" into searchable data structures. The user determines what his information need is and creates a search statement. The system processes the search statement, returning potential hits. The user selects those hits to review and accesses them.

Measurements can be made from two perspectives: user perspective and system perspective. The user perspective was described in Section 10.1. The Author's Aboutness occurs as part of the system executing the query against the index. The Indexer Aboutness and User Aboutness occur when the items are indexed into items are indexed into the system. The Request Aboutness occurs when the user creates the search statement. The ambiguities in the definition of what is relevant occurs when the user is reviewing the hits from the query.

Typically, the system perspective is based upon aggregate functions, whereas the user takes a more personal view. If a user's PC is not connecting to the system, then, from that user's view the system is not operational. From the system operations perspective, one user not having access out of 100 users still results in a 99 per cent availability rate. Another example of how averaging distorts communications between the system and user perspective is the case where there are 150 students taking six courses. Assume there are 5 students in three of the courses and 45 students in the other three courses. From the system perspective there is an average of 25 students per instructor/course. For 10 per cent of the students (15 students) there is a great ratio of 10 students per instructor. But, 90 per cent of the users (students) have a ratio of 45 students to one instructor. Thus most of the users may complain of the poor ratio (45 to one) to a system person who claims it is really good (25 to one). Techniques for collecting measurements can also be objective or subjective. An objective measure is one that is well-defined and based upon numeric values derived from the system operation. A subjective measure can produce a number, but is based upon an individual users judgments.

Measurements with automatic indexing of items arriving at a system are derived from standard performance monitoring associated with any program in a computer (e.g., resources used such as memory and processing cycles) and time to process an item from arrival to availability to a search process. When manual indexing is required, the measures are then associated with the indexing process. The focus of the metrics is on the resources required to perform the indexing function since this is the major system overhead cost. The measure is usually defined in terms of time to index an item. The value is normalized by the exhaustivity and specificity (see Chapter 3) requirements. Another measure in both the automatic and manual indexing process is the completeness and accuracy of the indexes created. These are evaluated by random sampling of indexes by quality assurance personnel.

A more complex area of measurements is associated with the search process. This is associated with a user creating a new search or modifying an existing query. In creating a search, an example of an objective measure is the time required to create the query, measured from when the user enters into a function allowing query input to when the query is complete. Completeness is defined as when the query is executed. Although of value, the possibilities for erroneous data (except in controlled environments) are so great that data of this nature are not collected in this area in operational systems. The erroneous data comes from the user performing other activities in the middle of creating the search such as going to get a cup of coffee.

Response time is a metric frequently collected to determine the efficiency of the search execution. Response time is defined as the time it takes to execute the search. The ambiguity in response time originates from the possible definitions of the end time. The beginning is always correlated to when the user tells the system to begin searching. The end time is affected by the difference between the user's view and a system view. From a user's perspective, a search could be considered complete when the first result is available for the user to review, especially if the system has new items available whenever a user needs to see the next item. From a system perspective, system resources are being used until the search has determined all hits. To ensure consistency, response time is usually associated with the completion of the search. This is one of the most important measurements in a production system. Determining how well a system is working answers the typical concern of a user: "the system is working slow today."

It is difficult to define objective measures on the process of a user selecting hits for review and reviewing them. The problems associated with search creation apply to this operation. Using time as a metric does not account for reading and cognitive skills of the user along with the user performing other activities during the review process. Data are usually gathered on the search creation and Hit file review process by subjective techniques, such as questionnaires to evaluate system effectiveness.

In addition to efficiency of the search process, the quality of the search results are also measured by precision and recall. Precision is a measure of the accuracy of the search process. It directly evaluates the correlation of the query to the database and indirectly is a measure of the completeness of the indexing algorithm. If the indexing algorithm tends to generalize by having a high threshold on the index term selection process or by using concept indexing, then precision is lower, no matter how accurate the similarity algorithm between query and index. Recall is a measure of the ability of the search to find all of the relevant items that are in the database. The following are the formulas for precision and recall:

$$\text{Precision} = \frac{Number\_Retrieved\_Relevant}{Number\_Total\_Retrieved}$$

$$Recall = \frac{Number\_Re\,trieved\_Re\,levant}{Number\_Possible\_Re\,levant}$$

where *Number_Possible_Relevant* is the number of relevant items in the database, *Number_Retrieved_Relevant* is the number of relevant items in the Hit file, and *Number_Total_Retrieved* is the total number of items in the Hit File. In controlled environments it is possible to get values for both of these measures and relate them to each other. Two of the values in the formulas, *Number_Retrieved_Relevant* and *Number_Total_Retrieved,* are always available. *Number_Possible-Relevant* poses a problem in uncontrolled environments because it suggests that all relevant items in the database are known. This was possible with very small databases in some of the early experiments in information systems. To gain the insights associated with testing a search against a large database makes collection of this data almost impossible. Two approaches have been suggested. The first is to use a sampling technique across the database, performing relevance judgments on the returned items. This would form the basis for an estimate of the total relevant items in the database (Gilbert-79). The other technique is to apply different search strategies to the same database for the same query. An assumption is then made that all relevant items in the database will be found in the aggregate from all of the searches (Sparck Jones-75). This later technique is what is applied in the TREC-experiments. In this controlled environment it is possible to create Precision/Recall graphs by reviewing the Hit file in ranked order and recording the changes in precision and recall as each item is judged.

In an operational system it is unrealistic to calculate recall because there is no reasonable approach to determine *Number_Possible_Relevant.* It is possible, however, to calculate precision values associated with queries, assuming the user provides relevance judgments. There is a pragmatic modification that is required to the denominator factor of *Number_Total_Retrieved.* The user can not be forced to review all of the items in the Hit file. Thus, there is a likely possibility that there will be items found by the query that are not retrieved for review. The adjustment to account for this operational scenario is to redefine the denominator to *Number_Total_Reviewed* versus *Nnumber_Total_Retrieved.* Under this condition the Precision factor becomes the precision associated with satisfying the user's information need versus the precision of the query. If reviewing three relevant items satisfies the user's objective in the search, additional relevant items in a Hit file do not contribute to the objective of the information system. The other factor that needs to be accounted for is the user not reviewing items in the Hit file because the summary information in the status display is sufficient to judge the item is not likely to be relevant. Under this definition, precision is a more accurate measure of the use of the user's time.

Although precision and recall formed the initial basis for measuring the effectiveness of information systems, they encounter mathematical ambiguities and a lack of parallelism between their properties (Salton-83). In particular, what is the value of recall if there are no relevant items in the database or recall if no items are retrieved (Fairthorne-64, Robertson-69)? In both cases the mathematical formula becomes 0/0. The lack of parallelism comes from the intuitiveness that finding more relevant items should increase retrieval effectiveness measures and decrease with retrieval of non-relevant items. Recall is unaffected when non-relevant items are retrieved. Another measure that is directly related to retrieving non-relevant items can be used in defining how effective an information system is operating. This measure is called Fallout and defined as (Salton-83):

$$\text{Fallout} = \frac{Number\_Retrieved\_Nonrelevant}{Number\_Total\_Nonrelevant}$$

where *Number_Total_Nonrelevant* is the total number of non-relevant items in the database. Fallout can be viewed as the inverse of recall and will never encounter the situation of 0/0 unless all the items in the database are relevant to the search. It can be viewed as the probability that a retrieved item is non-relevant. Recall can be viewed as the probability that a retrieved item is relevant. From a system perspective, the ideal system demonstrates maximum recall and minimum fallout. This combination implicitly has maximum precision. Of the three measures (precision, recall and fallout), fallout is least sensitive to the accuracy of the search process. The large value for the denominator requires significant changes in the number of retrieved items to affect the current value. Examples of precision, fallout and recall values for systems tested in TREC-4 are given in Section 10.3.

There are other measures of search capabilities that have been proposed. A new measure that provides additional insight in comparing systems or algorithms is the "Unique Relevance Recall" (URR) metric. URR is used to compare more two or more algorithms or systems. It measures the number of relevant items that are retrieved by one algorithm that are not retrieved by the others:

$$\text{Unique\_Relevance\_Recall} = \frac{Number\_unique\_relevant}{Number\_relevant}$$

Number_unique_relevant is the number of relevant items retrieved that were not retrieved by other algorithms. When many algorithms are being compared, the definition of *uniquely* found items for a particular system can be modified, allowing a small number of other systems to also find the same item and still be considered unique. This is accomplished by defining a percentage (P_u) of the total number of systems that can find an item and still consider it unique. *Number_relevant* can take on two different values based upon the objective of the evaluation:

VALUE	INTERPRETATION
Total Number Retrieved Relevant (TNRR)	the total number of relevant items found by all algorithms
Total Unique Relevant Retrieved (TURR)	the total number of unique items found by all the algorithms

A	B	C	D	E	F	G	H	I	J	K	L	M
3	4	2	22	1	100	200	22	100	10	500	6	15

Figure 10.2a Number Relevant Items

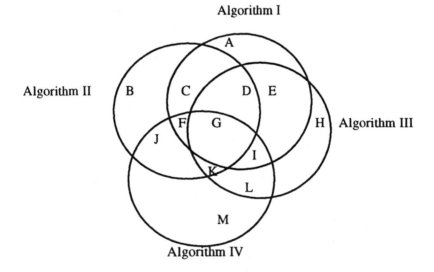

Figure 10.2b Four Algorithms With Overlap of Relevant Retrieved

Using TNRR as the denominator provides a measure for an algorithm of the percent of the total items that were found that are unique and found by that algorithm. It is a measure of the contribution of uniqueness to the total relevant items that the algorithm provides. Using the second measure, TURR, as the denominator, provides a measure of the percent of total unique items that could be found that are actually found by the algorithm. Figure 10.2a and 10.2b provide an example of the overlap of relevant items assuming there are four different algorithms. Figure 10.2a gives the number of items in each area of the overlap diagram in Figure 10.2b. If a relevant item is found by only one or two techniques as a "unique item," then from the diagram the following values URR values can be produced:

Algorithm I   - 6 unique items (areas A, C, E)
Algorithm II   - 16 unique items (areas B, C, J)
Algorithm III   - 29 unique items (areas E, H, L)
Algorithm IV   - 31 unique items (areas J, L, M)

$TNRR = A + B + C + \bullet \; \bullet \; \bullet + M = 985$
$TURR = A + B + C + E + H + J + L + M = 61$

Algorithm	URR_{TNRR}	URR_{TURR}
Algorithm I	$6/985 = .0061$	$6/61 = .098$
Algorithm II	$16/985 = .0162$	$16/61 = .262$
Algorithm III	$29/985 = .0294$	$29/61 = .475$
Algorithm IV	$31/985 = .0315$	$31/61 = .508$

The URR value is used in conjunction with Precision, Recall and Fallout to determine the total effectiveness of an algorithm compared to other algorithms. The URR_{TNRR} value indicates what portion of all unique items retrieved by all of the algorithms was retrieved by a specific algorithm. The URR_{TURR} value indicates the portion of possible unique items that a particular algorithm found. In the example, Algorithm IV found 50 per cent of all unique items found across all the algorithms. The results indicate that if I wanted to increase my recall by running two algorithms, I would choose algorithm III or IV in addition to the algorithm with the highest recall value. Like Precision, URR can be calculated since it is based upon the results of retrieval versus results based upon the complete database. It assists in determining the utility of using multiple search algorithm to improve overall system performance (see Chapter 7).

        Other measures have been proposed for judging the results of searches (Keen-71, Salton-83):

Novelty Ratio: ratio of relevant and not known to the user to total
        relevant retrieved

Coverage Ratio: ratio of relevant items retrieved to total relevant
        by the user before the search

Sought Recall: ratio of the total relevant reviewed by the user after the
        search to the total relevant the user would have liked to examine

In some systems, programs filter text streams, software categorizes data or intelligent agents alert users if important items are found. In these systems, the Information Retrieval System makes decisions without any human input and their decisions are binary in nature (an item is acted upon or ignored). These systems are called binary classification systems for which effectiveness measurements are created to determine how algorithms are working (Lewis-95). One measure is the utility measure that can be defined as (Cooper-73):

$$U = \alpha*(\text{Relevant\_Retrieved}) + \beta*(\text{Non-Relevant\_Not Retrieved}) -$$
$$\delta*(\text{Non-Relevant\_Retrieved}) - \gamma*(\text{Relevant\_Not Retrieved})$$

where α and β are positive weighting factors the user places on retrieving relevant items and not retrieving non-relevant items while δ and γ are factors associated with the negative weight of not retrieving relevant items or retrieving non-relevant items. This formula can be simplified to account only for retrieved items with β and γ equal to zero (Lewis-96). Another family of effectiveness measures called the E-measure that combines recall and precision into a single score was proposed by Van Rijsbergen (Rijsbergen-79).

10.3 Measurement Example -TREC-Results

Until the creation of the Text Retrieval Conferences (TREC) by the Defense Advance Research Projects Agency (DARPA) and the National Institute of Standards and Technology (NIST), experimentation in the area of information retrieval was constrained by the researcher's ability to manually create a test database. One of the first test databases was associated with the Cranfield I and II tests (Cleverdon-62, Cleverdon-66). It contained 1400 documents and 225 queries. It became one of the standard test sets and has been used by a large number of researchers. Other test collections have been created by Fox and Sparck Jones (Fox-83, Sparck Jones-79). Although there has been some standard usage of the same test data, in those cases the evaluation techniques varied sufficiently so that it has been almost impossible to compare results and derive generalizations. This lack of a common base for experimentation constrained the ability of researchers to explain relationships between different experiments and thus did not provide a basis to determine system improvements (Sparck Jones-81). Even if there had been a better attempt at uniformity in use of the standard collections, all of the standard test sets suffered from a lack of size that prevented realistic measurements for operational environments.

The goal of the Text Retrieval Conference was to overcome these problems by making a very large, diverse test data set available to anyone interested in using it as a basis for their testing and to provide a yearly conference to share the results. There have been five TREC-conferences since 1992, usually held in the Fall. Two types of retrieval are examined at TREC: "adhoc" query, and "routing" (dissemination). In TREC-the normal two word "ad hoc" is concatenated into a single word. As experience has been gained from TREC-1 to TREC-5, the details and focus of the experiments have evolved. TREC-provides a set of training documents and a set of test documents, each over 1 Gigabyte in size. It also provides a set of training search topics (along with relevance judgments from the database) and a set of test topics. The researchers send to the TREC-sponsor the list of the top 200 items in ranked order that satisfy the search statements. These lists are used in determining the items to be manually reviewed for relevance and for calculating the results from each system. The search topics are "user need" statements rather than specific queries. This allows maximum flexibility for each researcher to translate the search statement to a query appropriate for their system and assists in the determination of whether an item is relevant.

Figure 10.3 describes the sources and the number and size of items in the test database (Harman-95). Figure 10.3 also includes statistics on the number of terms in an item and number of unique terms in the test databases. The database was initially composed of disks 1 and 2. In later TRECs, disk 3 of data was added to focus on the routing tests. Figure 10.3b includes in the final column the statistics for the Cranfield test collection. Comparing the Cranfield collection to the contents of disk 1 shows that the TREC-test database is approximately 200 times larger and the average length of the items is doubled. Also the dictionary size of unique words is 20 times larger. All of the documents are formatted in Standard Generalized Markup Language (SGML) with a Document Type Definition (DTD) included for each collection allowing easy parsing. SGML is a superset of HTML and is one of the major standards used by the publishing industry. The following describes the source contents of each of the disks shown in Figure 10.3 available for TREC analysis:

Disk 1
    WSJ - Wall street journal (1987, 1988, 1989)
    AP   - AP Newswire (1989)
    ZIFF - Articles from Computer Select disks (ZIFF-Davis Publishing)
    FR   - Federal Register (1989)
    DOE - Short Abstracts from DOE Publications

Disk 2
    WSJ - Wall Street Journal (1990, 1991, 1992)
    AP   - AP Newswire (1988)
    ZIFF - Articles from Computer Select disks (ZIFF-Davis Publishing)
    FR   - Federal register (1988)

Disk 3
   SJMN - San Jose Mercury News (1991)
   AP   - AP Newswire (1990)
   ZIFF - Articles from Computer Select disks (ZIFF-Davis Publishing)
   PAT - U.S. Patents (1993)

It was impossible to perform relevance judgments on all of the items in the test databases (over 700,000 items) to be used in recall and fallout formulas. The option of performing a random sample that would find the estimated 200 or

Subset of collection	WSJ (disks 1&2) SJMN (disk 3)	AP	ZIFF	FR (disks 1&2) PAT (disk 3)	DOE	Cranfield test database
Size of Collection (Mbytes)						
(disk 1)	270	259	245	262	186	1.5
(disk 2)	247	241	178	211		
(disk 3)	290	242	349	245		
Number of Records						
(disk 1)	98,732	84,678	75,180	25,960	226,087	1400
(disk 2)	74,520	79,919	56,920	19,860		
(disk 3)	90,257	78,321	161,021	6,711		
Median Number Terms per record						
(disk 1)	182	353	181	313	82	79
(disk 2)	218	346	167	315		
(disk 3)	279	358	119	2896		
Average Number of Terms per record						
(disk 1)	329	375	412	1017	89	88
(disk 2)	377	370	394	1073		
(disk 3)	337	379	263	3543		
Total Number of Unique Terms						
(disk 1)	156,298	197,608	173,501	126,258		8226

Figure 10.3b TREC-Training and Adhoc Test Collection

Collection Source	Size in MBytes	Mean Terms per record	Median Terms per record	Total Records
ZIFF (disk 3)	249	263	119	161,021
FR (1994)	283	456	390	55,554
IR Digest	7	2,383	2,225	455
News Groups	237	340	235	102,598
Virtual Worlds	28	416	225	10,152

Figure 10.3a Routing Test Database
(from TREC-5 Conference Proceedings to be published, Harmon-96)

more relevant items for each test search would require a very large sample size to be manually analyzed. Instead, the pooling method proposed by Sparck Jones was used. The top 200 documents based upon the relevance rank from each of the researchers was pooled, redundant items were eliminated and the resultant set was manually reviewed for relevance. In general one-third of the possible items retrieved were unique (e.g., out of 3300 items 1278 were unique in TREC-1) (Harman-93). This ratio also been shown to be true in other experiments (Katzer-82). In TREC, each test topic was judged by one person across all of the possible documents to ensure consistency of relevance judgment.

The search Topics in the initial TREC-consisted of a Number, Domain (e.g., Science and Technology), Title, Description of what constituted a relevant item, Narrative natural language text for the search, and Concepts which were specific search terms.

Precision and recall were calculated in the initial TREC. To experiment with a measure called Relative Operating Characteristic (ROC) curves, calculation of Probability of Detection (same as Recall formula) and calculation of Probability of False Alarm (same as Fallout) was also tried. This use of a set of common evaluation formulas between systems allows for consistent comparison between different executions of the same algorithm and between different algorithms. The results are represented on Recall-Precision and Recall-Fallout graphs (ROC curves). Figure 10.4 shows how the two graphs appear. The x-axis plots the recall from zero to 1.0 based upon the assumption that the relevant items judged in the pooling technique account for all relevant items. The precision or fallout value at each of the discrete recall values is calculated based upon reviewing the items, in relevance rank score order, that it requires to reach that recall value. For example, assume there are 200 relevant items. A particular system, to achieve a recall of 40 per cent (.4) requiring retrieval of 80 of the relevant items, requires retrieving the top 160 items with the highest relevance scores. Associated with the Precision/Recall graph, for the x-axis value of .4, the y-axis value would be 80/160 or .5. There are sufficient sources of potential errors in generating the graphs, that they should only be used as relative comparisons between algorithms rather than absolute performance indicators. It has been proven they do provide useul comparative information.

In addition to the search measurements, other standard information on system performance such as system timing, storage, and specific descriptions on the tests are collected on each system. This data is useful because the TREC-objective is to support the migration of techniques developed in a research environment into operational systems.

TREC-5 was held in November 1996. The results from each conference have varied based upon understanding from previous conferences and new objectives. A general trend has been followed to make the tests in each TREC-closer to realistic operational uses of information systems (Harman-96).

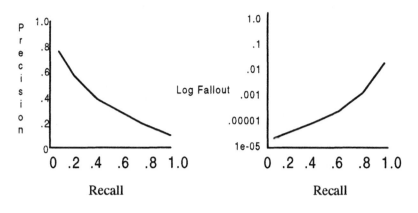

Figure 10.4 Examples of TREC-Result Charts

TREC-1 (1992) was constrained by researchers trying to get their systems to work with the very large test databases. TREC-2 in August 1993 was the first real test of the algorithms which provided insights for the researchers into areas in which their systems needed work. The search statements (user need statements) were very large and complex. They reflect long-standing information needs versus adhoc requests. By TREC-3, the participants were experimenting with techniques for query expansion and the importance of constraining searches to passages within items versus the total item. There were trade offs available between manual and automatic query expansion and the benefits from combining results from multiple retrieval techniques. Some of the experiments were driven by the introduction of shorter and less complex search statements. The "concept" field, which contained terms related to the query that a user might be expected to be aware of, was eliminated from the search statements. This change was a major source for the interest into query expansion techniques. TREC-4 introduced significantly shorter queries (average reduction from 119 terms in TREC-3 to 16 terms in TREC-4) and introduced five new areas of testing called "tracks" (Harman-96). The queries were shortened by dropping the title and a narrative field, which provided additional description of a relevant item.

The multilingual track expanded TREC-4 to test a search in a Spanish test set of 200 Mbytes of articles from the "El Norte" newspaper. The interactive track modified the previous adhoc search testing from a batch to an interactive environment. Since there are no standardized tools for evaluating this environment, the TREC-5 goals included development of evaluation methodologies as well as investigating the search aspects. The database merging task investigated methods for merging results from multiple subcollections into a single Hit file. The confusion track dealt with corrupted data. Data of this type are found in Optical Character Reader (OCR) conversion of hardcopy to characters or speech input. The database for TREC-had random errors created in the text. Usually in real world situations, the errors in these systems tend not to be totally random but bursty or oriented towards particular characters. Finally, additional tests were performed on the routing (dissemination) function that focused on three different objectives: high precision, high recall and balanced precision and recall. Rather than ranking all items, a binary text classification system approach was pursued where each item is either accepted or rejected (Lewis-96, Lewis-95).

Insights into the advancements in information retrieval can be gained by looking at changes in results between TRECs mitigated by the changes in the test search statements. Adhoc query results from TREC-1 were calculated for automatic and manual query construction. Automatic query construction is based upon automatic generation of the query from the Topic fields. Manual construction is also generated from the Topic field manually with some machine assistance if desired. Figures 10.5 shows the Precision/Recall results top two systems for each method. The precision values were very low compared to later TRECs. It also shows that there was very little difference between manual construction of a query and automatic construction.

Routing (dissemination) also allowed for both an automatic and a manual query construction process. The generation of the query followed the same guidelines as the generation of the queries for the adhoc process. Figure 10.6

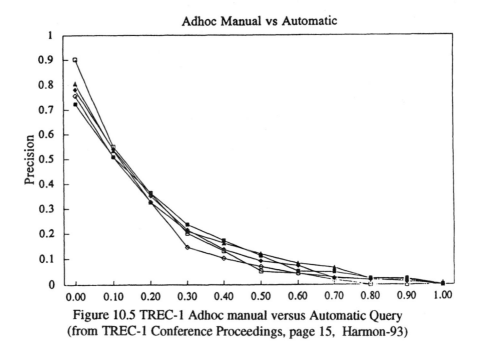

Figure 10.5 TREC-1 Adhoc manual versus Automatic Query
(from TREC-1 Conference Proceedings, page 15, Harmon-93)

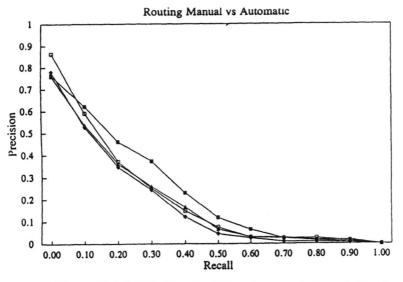

Figure 10.6 TREC-1Routing Manual versus Automatic Results
(from TREC-1 Conference Proceedings, page 18, Harmon-93)

shows the results from the top two manual and automatic routing systems. In this case, unlike the adhoc query process, the automatic query building process is better as shown by the results from the "fuhr1" system.

By TREC-3 and TREC-4 the systems were focusing on how to accommodate the shorter queries. It is clear that if the shorter queries had been executed for TREC-1, the results would have been worse than those described. Figures 10.7 and 10.8 show the precision recall results for Automatic and Manual adhoc searches for TREC-3 and TREC-4 (Harman-96). The significant reduction in query size caused even the best algorithms shown in the figures to perform worse in TREC-4 than in TREC-3. The systems that historically perform best at TRECs (e.g., City University, London - cityal, INQUERY - INQ201, Cornell University - CrnlEA) all experienced 14 per cent to 36 per cent drops in retrieval performance. The manual experiments also suffered from a similar significant decrease in performance. The following is the legend to the Figures:

CrnlEA - Cornell University - SMART system - vector based weighted system
pircs1   - Queens College - PIRCS system - spreading activation on 550
                       word subdocuments from documents
cityal   - City University, London - Okapi system - probabilistic term weighting
INQ201 - University of Massachusetts - INQUERY system - probabilistic
                       weighting using inference nets

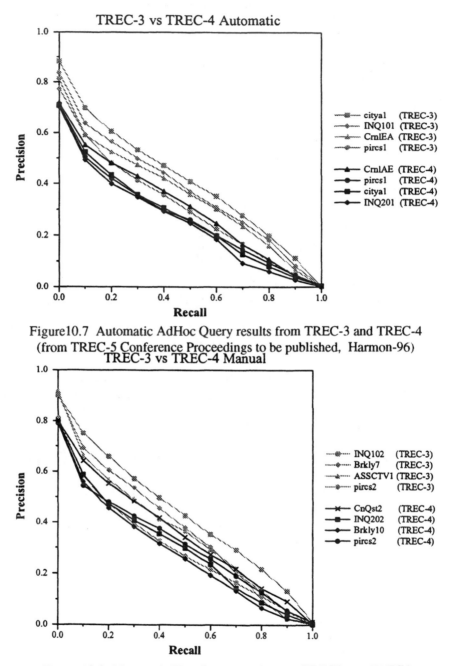

Figure10.7 Automatic AdHoc Query results from TREC-3 and TREC-4
(from TREC-5 Conference Proceedings to be published, Harmon-96)

Figure 10.8 Manual AdHoc Query results fromTREC3 and TREC4
(from TREC-5 Conference Proceedings to be published, Harmon-96)

citri2   - RMIT, Australia - standard cosine with OKAPI measure
CnQst2   - Excalibur Corporation - Retrievalware - two pass weights
brkly-10 - University of California, Berkley - logistic regression model based on
                   6 measures of document relevance
ASSCTV1 - Mead Data Central, Inc. - query expansion via thesaurus

Even though all systems experienced significant problems when the size of the
queries was reduced, a comparison between Figure 10.5 and Figures 10.7 and 10.8
shows a significant improvement   in the Precision/Recall capabilities of the
systems. A significant portion of this improvement occurred between TREC-1 and
TREC-2.

By participating on a yearly basis, systems can determine the effects of
changes they make and compare them with how other approaches are doing. Many
of the systems change their weighting and similarity measures between TRECs.
INQUERY determined they needed better weighting formulas for long documents
so they used the City University algorithms for longer items and their own version
of a probabilistic weighting scheme for shorter items. Another example of the
learning from previous TRECs is the Cornell "SMART" system that made major
modifications to their cosine weighting formula introducing a non-cosine length
normalization technique that performs well for all lengths of documents.   They
also changed their expansion of a query by using the top 20 highest ranked items
from a first pass to generate additional query terms for a second pass. They used 50
terms in TREC-4 versus the 300 terms used in TREC-3. These changes produced
significant improvements and made their technique the best in the Automatic
Adhoc for TREC-4 versus being lower in TREC-3.

In the manual query method, most systems used the same search
algorithms. The difference was in how they manually generated the query. The
major techniques are the automatic generation of a query that is edited, total
manual generation of the query using reference information (e.g., online dictionary
or thesaurus) and a more complex interaction using both automatic generation and
manual expansion.

When TREC-introduced the more realistic short search statements, the
value of previously discovered techniques had to be reevaluated. Passage retrieval
(limiting the similarity measurement to a logical subsets of the item) had a major
impact in TREC-3 but minimal utility in TREC-4. Also more systems began
making use of multiple algorithms and selecting the best combination based upon
characteristics of the items being searched. A lot more effort was spent on testing
better ways of expanding queries (due to their short length) while limiting the
expanded terms to reduce impacts on precision. The automatic techniques showed
a consistent degradation from TREC-3 to TREC-4. For the Manual Adhoc results,
starting at about a level of .6, there was minimal difference between the TRECs.

The Routing systems are very similar to the Adhoc systems. The

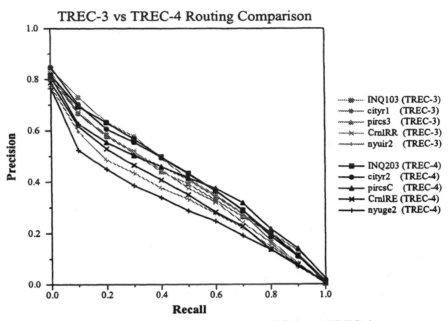

Figure 10.9 Routing results from TREC-3 and TREC-4
(from TREC-5 Conference Proceedings to be published, Harmon-96)

researchers tended to use the same algorithms with minor modifications to adjust
for the lack of a permanent database in dissemination systems. Not surprisingly,
the same systems that do well in the Adhoc tests do well in the Routing tests. There
was significant diversity on how the search statements were expanded (see TREC-4
proceedings). Unlike the Adhoc results, the comparison of TREC-3 and TREC-4
Routing shown in Figure 10.9 has minimal changes with a slight increase in
precision. The following is the legend for the Routing comparison for systems not
defined in the adhoc legend:

nyuge2 - GE Corporate Research and New York University - use of
          natural language processing to identify syntactic phrases
nyuir2 - New York University - use of natural language processing to
           identify syntactic phrases
cityr   - City University, London

As with the adhoc results, comparing Figure 10.6 with Figure 10.8 shows
the significant improvement in Routing capability between TREC-1 and the later

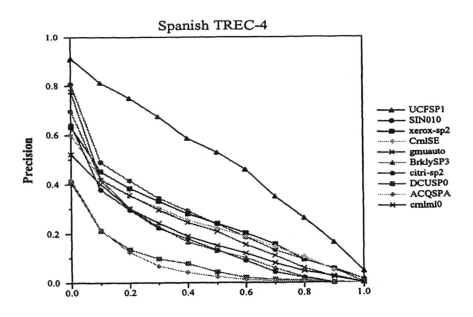

Figure 10.10 Results of TREC-4 Spanish Track
(from TREC-5 Conference Proceedings to be published, Harmon-96)

TRECs. TREC-5 results were very close to those from TREC-4 but the queries had
become more difficult so actual improvements came from not seeing a degradation
in the Precision/Recall and Routing graphs.

The multilingual track expanded between TREC-4 and TREC-5 by the
introduction of Chinese in addition to the previous Spanish tests. The concept in
TREC-5 is that the algorithms being developed should be language independent
(with the exception of stemming and stopwords). In TREC-4, the researchers who
spent extra time in linguistic work in a foreign language showed better results
(e.g., INQUERY enhanced their noun-phrase identifier in their statistical thesaurus
generator). The best results in came from the University of Central Florida, which
built an extensive synonym list. Figure 10.10 shows the results of the Spanish
adhoc search in TREC-4.   In TREC-5 significant improvements in precision were
made in the systems participating from TREC-4. In Spanish, the Precision-Recall
charts are better than those for the Adhoc tests, but the search statements were not
as constrained as in the ad hoc. In Chinese, the results varied significantly between
the participants with some results worse than the adhoc and some better. This
being the first time for Chinese, it is too early to judge the overall types of
performance to be expected. But for Spanish, the results indicate the applicability

to the developed algorithms to other languages. Experiments with Chinese demonstrates the applicability to a language based upon pictographs that represent words versus an alphabet based language.

The confusion track was preliminary in TREC-4. By TREC-5 the test database had expanded by taking the Federal Register (250Mbytes), creating dvi image files and then running NIST OCR programs against it. This produced approximately 5 per cent corruption typical of OCR operations. A second dataset with closer to 20 per cent corruption was produced by down-sampling the images and redoing the OCR (Voorhees-96). A set of known item topics was created by selecting items that seemed to be unique and creating a description of them. These were used and the evaluation metric was the rank of the item in the Hit file. Most of the search systems used some version of n-gram indexing (see Chapter 4). The results are too preliminary to draw any major conclusions from them.

The TREC-series of conferences have achieved their goal of defining a standard test forum for evaluating information retrieval search techniques. It provides a realistic environment with known results. It has been evolving to equate closer to a real world operational environment that allows transition of the test results to inclusion of commercial products with known benefits. By being an open forum, it has encouraged participation by most of the major organizations developing algorithms for information retrieval search.

10.4 Summary

Evaluation of Information Retrieval Systems is essential to understand the source of weaknesses in existing systems and trade offs between using different algorithms. The standard measures of Precision, Recall, and Fallout have been used for the last twenty-five years as the major measures of algorithmic effectiveness. With the insertion of information retrieval technologies into the commercial market and ever growing use on the Internet, other measures will be needed for real time monitoring the operations of systems. One example was given in the modifications to the definition of Precision when a user ends his retrieval activity as soon as sufficient information is found to satisfy the reason for the search.

The measures to date are optimal from a system perspective, and very useful in evaluating the effect of changes to search algorithms. What are missing are the evaluation metrics that consider the total information retrieval system, attempting to estimate the system's support for satisfying a search versus how well an algorithm performs. This would require additional estimates of the effectiveness of techniques to generate queries and techniques to review the results of searches. Being able to take a system perspective may change the evaluation for a particular aspect of the system. For example, assume information visualization techniques are needed to improve the user's effectiveness in locating needed information.

Two levels of search algorithms, one optimized for concept clustering the other optimized for precision, may be more effective than a single algorithm optimized against a standard Precision/Recall measure.

In all cases, evaluation of Information Retrieval Systems will suffer from the subjective nature of information. There is no deterministic methodology for understanding what is relevant to a user's search. The problems with information discussed in Chapter 1 directly affect system evaluation techniques in Chapter 10. Users have trouble in translating their mental perception of information being sought into the written language of a search statement. When facts are needed, users are able to provide a specific relevance judgment on an item. But when general information is needed, relevancy goes from a classification process to a continuous function. The current evaluation metrics require a classification of items into relevant or non-relevant. When forced to make this decision, users have a different threshold. These leads to the suggestion that the existing evaluation formulas could benefit from extension to accommodate a spectrum of values for relevancy of an item versus a binary classification. But the innate issue of the subjective nature of relevant judgments will still exist, just at a different level.

Research on information retrieval suffered for many years from a lack of a large, meaningful test corpora. The Text REtrieval Conferences (TRECs), sponsored on a yearly basis, provide a source of a large "ground truth" database of documents, search statements and expected results from searches essential to evaluate algorithms. It also provides a yearly forum where developers of algorithms can share their techniques with their peers. More recently, developers are starting to combine the best parts of their algorithms with other developers algorithms to produce an improved system.

EXERCISES

1. What are the problems associated with generalizing the results from controlled tests on information systems to their applicability to operational systems? Does this invalidate the utility of the controlled tests?

2. What are the main issues associated with the definition of relevance? How would you overcome these issues in a controlled test environment?

3. What techniques could be applied to evaluate each step in Figure 10.1?

4. Consider the following table of relevant items in ranked order from four algorithms along with the actual relevance of each item. Assume all algorithms have highest to lowest relevance is from left to right (Document 1 to last item). A value of zero implies the document was non-relevant).

Document	1	2	3	4	5	6	7	8	9	10	11	12	13	14
Algo1	1	0	0	1	1	1	0	0	1	1	0	0	1	1
Algo2	0	1	1	0	1	1	1	0	0	1	1	0	1	1
Algo3	0	1	0	0	1	1	1	1	1	0	1	1	1	1
Actual	1	1	1	1	0	0	1	1	1	0	0	1	1	1

Document	15	16	17	18	19	20	21	22	23	24	25	26	27
Algo1	1	0	0	1	1	1	0	0	1	1	0	0	1
Algo2	0	1	1	0	1	1	1	0	0	1	1	0	1
Algo3	0	1	0	0	1	1	1	1	1	0	1	1	1
Actual	1	1	1	1	0	0	1	1	1	0	0	1	1

a. Calculate and graph precision/recall for all the algorithms on one graph.
b. Calculate and graph fallout/recall for all the algorithms on one graph
c. Calculate the TNRR and TURR for each algorithm (assume uniquely
    found is only when one algorithm found a relevant item)
d. Identify which algorithm is best and why.

5.   What is the relationship between precision and TURR.

6.   What problems in information system evaluation does TREC solve? What
    are the problems with TREC as a source of algorithm evaluation?

REFERENCES

Aalbersberg-92 – Aalbersberg, I., Incremental Relevance Feedback", In Proceedings of the Fifteenth Annual ACM SIGIR Conference on Research and Development in Information Retrieval, 1992, pages 11-22.

Adams-92 – Adams, Elizabeth Shaw, A Study of Trigrama and Their Feasibility as Index Terms in a Full Text Information Retrieval System, D.Sc. dissertation, The George Washington University, 1992.

Adamson-74 – Adamson, G. and J. Boreham, "The use of an Association Measure Based on Character Structure to Identify Semantically Related Pairs of Words and Document Titles", Information Storage and Retrieval, #10, 1974, pp. 253-60.

Ahlber-94 – Ahlberg, C. and B. Shneiderman, "Visual information seeking: tightly coupling of dynamic query filters with starfield displays", Proceedings of CHI'94, Boston, Ma., April 1994, pages 313-317 and 479-480.

Ahlberg-95 – Ahlberg, C., and E. Wistrand, "IVEE: An Information Visualization and Exploration Environment", Proc. Information Visualization Symposium, N. Gersho and G Eick, eds., IEEE CS Press, Los Alamitos, Ca., 1995, pages 66-73. (also URL http://www.cs.chalmers.se/SSKKII/software.html , current November 21, 1996).

Aho-75 – Aho, A.V. and M. Corasick, "Efficient String Matching: An Aid to Bibliographic Search", Communications of the ACM, Vol. 18, No. 6, June 1975, pages 333-340.

Aitchison-72 – Aitchison, J. and A. Gilchrist, Thesaurus Construction - A Practical Manual, London : ASLIB, 1972.

Allan-95 – Allan, J., Automatic Hypertext construction, Technical Report TR95-1414, Department of Computer Science, Cornell University, New York February 1995.

Allan-96 – Allan, J., "Incremental Relevance Feedback for Information Filtering", In Proceedings of the Nineteenth Annual ACM SIGIR Conference on Research and Development in Information Retrieval, ACM, New York, N. Y., 1996, pages 270-278.

Angell-83 – Angell, Richard, Freund, George and Peter Willett, "Automatic Spelling Correction Using a Trigram Similarity Measure", Information Processing and Management, Vol. 19, No. 4. 1983, pp. 255-261.

Apte-94 – Apte, C., Damerau, F., and S. Weiss, "Towards Language independent Automated Learning of Text Categorization Models", in Proceedings of the Seventeenth Annual ACM SIGIR Conference on Research and Development in Information Retrieval, ACM, New York, N. Y., 1994, pages 23-30.

Amheim-69 – Arnheim, R., Visual Thinking, University of California Press, 1969.

Amheim-86 – Arnheim, R., New Essays on the Psychology of Art, California Press, 1986.

Avram-75 – Avram, Henriette D. , MARC: Its History and Implications , Washington: Library of Congress, 1975

Baeza-Yates-89 – Baeza-Yates, R., "String Searching Algorithms Revisited", in Workshop in Algorithms and Data Structures, F. Dehne, J. Sack and N. Santoro,eds., Springer Verlag Lecture Notes on Computer Science, Ottawa, Canada, 1989, pages 332-347.

Baeza-Yates-90 – Baeza-Yates, R. and M. Regnier, "Fast Algorithms for Two Dimensional and Multiple Pattern Matching", in 2nd Scandinavian Workshop in Algorithmic Theory, SAT'90, R. Karlsson and J. Gilbert eds. Lecture Notes in Computer Science 447, 1990, pages 332-47.

Baeza-Yates-92 – Baeza-Yates, R., "String Searching Algorithms", in Information Retrieval Data Structures & Algorithms, Prentice Hall, New Jersey, 1992, pages 219-237.

Baeza-Yates-92a – Baeza-Yates, R. and G. Gonnet, "A New Approach to Text Searching", Communications of the ACM, Vol. 35, No. 10, October 1992, pages 74-82.

Barry-94 – Barry, C., "User Defined Relevance Criteria: An Exploratory Study", Journal of the American Society for Information Science, 45 (3), April 1994 pages 149-159.

Belkin-87 – Belkin, N.J. and W.B. Croft, "Retrieval Techniques.", in Williams, M (ed.), Annual Review of Information Science and Technology, Elsevier Science Publishers, New York, New York, 1987, pages 109-45.

Belkin-89 – Belkin, N. and W. Croft, "Retrieval Techniques", in Annual Review of Information Science and Technology, Elsevier Science publishers, New York, 1989, pages 109-145.

Bernstein-84 – The Careful Writer by Theodore M. Bernstein, N.Y., Atheneum, 1984, pages 366-367.

Berra-89 – Berra, P., Ghafoor, A., Mitkas, P., Marcinkowski, S. and . Guizani, "Optical Searching", IEEE Transactions on Knowledge and Data Engineering, (1), 1989, pages 111-132.

Bird-77 – Bird, R., Tu, J. and R. Worthy, "Associative Parallel Processors for Searching Very Large Textual Databases", Proc. Third Non-Numeric Workshop, Syracuse, N.Y., May 1977, pages 8-16.

Bird-78 – Bird, R., Newsbaum, J. and Trefftzs, J.,"Text Files Inversion: An Evaluation", Proceedings of the Fourth Workshop on Computer Architecture for Non-Numeric Processing, Syracuse, N.Y., August 1-4, 1978, pages 42-50.

Bird-79 – Bird, R.M. and J. Tu, "Associative Crosspoint Processor System", U.S. Patent, 4, 152, 762, May 1, 1979.

Boyer-77 – Boyer R. S. and S. Moore, "A Fast String Matchinf: An Aid to Bibliographic Search", Communications of the ACM, Vol. 20, No. 10, Octobler 1977, pages 762-772.

Brookstein-78 – Brookstein, A., "On the Perils of Merging Boolean and Weighted Retrieval Systems", Journal of the ASIS, Vol. 29, No. 3., May 1978, pages 156-158.

Brookstein-80 – Brookstein, A., Fuzzy Requests: An Approach to Weighted Boolean Searches", Journal of the ASIS, Vol. 31, No. 4., July 1980, pages 240-247.

Brookstein-95 – Brookstein, A., Klein, S.T. and T. Raita, "Detecting Content Bearing Words by Serial Clustering - Extended Abstract", SIGIR '95, Proc. of the 18th Annual International ACM SIGIR Conference on Research and Development in Information Retrieval, Seattle Washington, July 1995, pp. 319-327.

Brown-96 – Brown, J.R. and Nahum Gershon, "The Role of Computer Graphics and Visualization in the GII", Computer Graphics and Applications, Vol. 16, No. 2, March 1996, pages 61-63

Buckley-94 – Buckley, C., Salton, G. and J. Allan, "The effect of adding relevance information in a relevance feedback environment", In Proceedings of the Seventeenth Annual ACM SIGIR Conference on Research and Development in Information Retrieval, ACM, New York, N. Y., 1994, pages 293-300.

Buckley-95 – Chris Buckley, Gerald Salton, James Allan, Amit Singhal. Automatic Query Expansion Using SMART: TREC 3. In D.K. Harman, editor,

Overview of the Third Text Retrieval Conference (TREC-3), pages 69-79, NIST Special Publication 500-225, April 1995.

Buckley-96 – Buckley, Chris, Singhal, A., Mitra, M. and Gerald Salton, "New Retrieval Approaches Using SMART : TREC 4", in publishing of the Fourth Text Retrieval Conference (TREC-4), NIST Special Publication, 1996.

Bush-45 – Bush, V., "As we may think", Atlantic Monthly, 176, July 1945, pages 101-108.

Bush-67 – Bush, V. (Ed.) (1967), Science is not Enough, William Morrow and Co. Reprinted in Nyce, J.M. and Kahn, P. (Eds.) From Memex to Hypertex:Vannevar Bush and the Mind's Machine, Academic Press, 1991, pp. 197-216.

Caid-93 – Caid, William, Stephen Gallant, Robert Hecht-Nielsen, Joel Carlton, Kent Pu Qing, and David Sudbeck, "HNC's MatchPlus System", The First Text Retrieval Conference (TREC-1), NIST Special Publication 500-207, NIST, Gaithersburg, Md., March 1993, pages 107-111.

Callan-94 – J.P. Callan. Passage-level evidence in document retrieval. In Proceedings of the Seventeenth Annual International ACM SIGIR Conference on Research and Development in Information Retrieval, pages 302-310, Dublin, Ireland, 1994. Association for Computing Machinery.

Can-95 – Can, F., Fox, E., Snaverly, C. and R. France, "Incremental Clustering for Very Large Document Databases: Initial MARIAN Experience", Information Systems, 84, 1995, pages 101-114.

Card-96 – Card, . K., "Visualizing Retrieved Information: A Survey", IEEE Computer Graphics and Applications, Vol. 16, No. 2, March 1996, pages 63-67.

Card-96a – Card, K., G. G. Robertson and W. York, "The WebBook and the Web Forager: An Information Workspace for the World Wide Web", CHI 96, ACM Conference on Human Factors in Software, ACM Press, New York, 1996.

Catarci-96 – Catarci, Tiziana, "Interaction With Databases", Computer Graphics and Applications, Vol. 16, No. 2, March 1996, pages 67-69.

Chalmers-92 – Chalmers, M. and P. Chitson, "Bead: Explorations in information retrieval", Proceedings of SIGIR 92, Copenhagen, Denmark, June 1992, pages 330-337.

Cleverdon-62 – Cleverdon, C.W., Report on the Testing and Analysis of an Investigation into the Comparative Efficiency of Indexing Systems, College of Aeronautics, Cranfield, England, 1962.

Cleverdon-66 – Cleverdon, C.W., Mills, J. and E. Keen, Factors Determining the Performance of Indexing Systems", Vol. 1:Design, Vol. 2: Test Results, slib Cranfield Research Project, Cranfield, England, 1966.

CNRI-97 – http://www.andle.net/docs/overview.html (current Jan 7, 1997)

Cohen-95 – Cohen, J.,"Highlights: Language and Domain Independent Automatic Indexing Terms for Abstracting", Journal of the American Society for Information Science, 46(3), 1995, pages 162-174.

Commentz-Walter-79 – Commentz-Walter, B., "A String Matching Algorithm Fast on the Average", in ICALP, Lecture Notes in Computer Science 71, 1979, pages 118-32.

Cooper-73 – Cooper, William, "On Selecting a Measure of Retrieval Effectiveness", Journal of the American Society for Information Science, 24, 1973, pages 87-100.

Cooper-78 – Cooper, William and M. Maron, "Foundations of probabilistic and utility-theoretic indexing", Journals of the Association for Computing Machinery, No. 25, 1978, pages 67-80.

Cooper-94 – Cooper, William, "The Formalism of Probability Theory in IR: A foundation or an Encumbrance", Proceedings of the Seventeenth Annual ACM-SIGIR Conference, edited by W. Bruce Croft and C. J. van Rijsbergen, Springer-Verlag, London, 1994, pages 242-247.

Cooper-94a – Cooper, W., Chen, A. and F. Gey, "Full Text Retrieval Based on Probabilistic Equations with Coefficients Fitted by logistic Regression", Proceedings of the Second Text Retrieval Conference (TREC-2), NIST publication, 1994, pages 57-66.

Copeland-73 – Copeland, G., Lipovski, C. and S.Y. Su,"The Architecture of CASSM: A Cellular System for Non-Numeric Processing", Proceedings of the First Annul Symposium on Computer Architecture, ACM, New York, December 1973, pages 121-125.

Crew-67 – Crew, B. and M. Gunzburg, "Information Storage and Retrieval", U.S. Patent 3, 358, 270, December 12, 1967.

Croft-77 – Croft, W.B., "Clustering Large Files of Documents Using the Single Link Method", Journal of the ASIS, Vol 28, No. 6, November 1977, pp. 341-344.

Croft-79 – Croft, W.B. and D. J. Harper, "Using Probabilistic Models of Document retrieval without Relevance Information", Documentation, 35(4), 1979, pages 285-295.

Croft-83 – Croft, W.B., "Experiments with Representation in a Document Retrieval System", Information Technology: Research and Development, 2(1), 1983, pages 1-21.

Croft-94 –, W., Callan, J. and J. Broglio, "Trec-2 Routing and Ad Hoc Retrieval Evaluation using the INQUERY System", in The Second Text Retrieval Conference (TREC-2) Proceedings, NIST publications, 1993.

Cullum-85 – Cullum, J. K. and R. Willoughby, Lanczos, Algorithms for Large Symmetric Eigenvalue Computations - Vol. I Theory, (Chapter 5), Birkhauser, Boston, Mass., 1985.

Cutting-90 – Cutting D., J. Pedersen, "optimization for Dynamic Inverted Index Maintenance." Paper presented at 13th International Conference on Research and Development in Information Retrieval, Brussels, Belgium.

Damashek-95 – Damashek, Marc, "Gauging Similarity with n-grams: Language Independent Categorization of Text", Science, Vol 267, 10 February, 1995, pp. 843-848.

Damerau-64 – Damerau, Fred J., "A Technique for Computer Detection and Correction of Spelling Errors", Communications of the ACM, Vol. 7, No. 3, March 1964, pp. 171-176.

Dawson-74 – Dawson J., "Suffix Removal and Word Conflation." ALLC Bulletin, Michelmas, 1974, 33-46.

Deerwester-90 – Deerwester, S., Dumais, S., Furnas, G., Landauer, T. and R. Harshman, "Indexing by Latent Semantic Analysis", Journal for the American Society for Information Science, 41(6), 1990, pages 391-407.

Dennis-68 – Dennis, S.F., "The Design and Testing of a Fully Automated Indexing-Searching System for Documents Consisting of Expository Text", in Informational Retrieval: A Critical review, g. Schecter, editor, Thompson Book Company, Washington D.C., 1967, pages 67-94.

Deppisch-86 – Deppisch, U., "S-Tree: A Dynamic Balanced Signature Index for Office Retrieval", Proc. of ACM "Research and Development in Information Retrieval", Pisa, Italy, September 1986, pp. 77-87.

Dumais-93 – Dumais, S., "Latent Semantic Indexing and TREC-2", in The Second Text Retrieval Conference (TREC-2) Proceedings, NIST publications, 1993, pages 105-115.

Dumais-95 – Dumais, S.,"Latent Semantic Indexing: TREC-3 Report", In D.K. Harman, editor, Overview of the Third Text Retrieval Conference (TREC-3), NIST Special Publication 500-225, April 1995, pages 219-230.

Edmundson-69 – Edmundson, H., "New Methods in Automatic Abstracting", Journal of the ACM, 16(2), April 1969, pages 264-285.

El-Hamdouchi-89 – El-Hamdouchi, A. and P. Willet, "Comparison of Hierarchic Agglomerative Clustering Methods for Document Retrieval", Computer Journal, 32, 1989, pages 220-227.

Fairthorne-64 – Fairthorne, R. A,"Basic Parameters of Retrieval Tests," Proceedings of 1964 Annual Meeting of the American Documentation Institute, Spartan Books, Washington, 1964, pages 343-347.

Fairthorne-69 – Fairthorne, R. A., "Empirical hyperbolic distributions for bibliometric description and prediction", International ACM SIGIR Conference: Research and Development in Information Retrieval, June5-7, 1985.

Faloutsos-85 – Faloutsos, C.,"Access Methods for Text", ACM Computing Surveys, Vol. 17, No.1, March 1985, pages 49-74.

Faloutsos-87 – Faloutsos, C. and S. Christodoulakis, "Description and Performance Analysis of Signature File Methods", ACM TOOIS, 5 (3), 1987, pp. 237-57

Faloutsos-88 – Faloutsos, C. and R. Chan, "Fast Text Access Methods for Optical and Large Magnetic Disks: Designs and Performance Comparison", Proc. 14th International Conference on VLDB, Long Beach, Ca., August 1988, pp. 280-293.

Faloutsos-92 – Faloutsos, C., Signature Files, in Frakes, W. B., Ricardo Baeza-Yates (Eds), Information Retrieval Data Structures & Algorithms, Prentice Hall, New Jersey, 1992, pp. 44-65.

Feiner-90 – Feiner, S. and C. Beshers, "World Within Worlds: Metaphors for Exploring N-dimensional Virtual Worlds", UIST 94, ACM Symposium on User Interface Software, ACM Press, New York, 1990, pages 76-83

Foster-80 – Foster, M. and H. Kung, "Design of Special Purpose VLSI Chips: Examples and Opinions", Proceedings of the 7th Annual Symposium on Computer Architecture, May 1980, (published as SIGARCH Newsletter, Vol.. 8, no. 3), pages 300-307.

Fox-83 – Fox, E.A., Characteristics of Two New Experimental Collections in Computer and Information Science Containing Textual and Bibliographic Concepts, Technical Reports TR 83-561, Cornell University: Computing Science Department, 1983.

Fox-86 – Fox, E.A. and S. Sharat, "A comparison of Two Models for Soft Boolean Interpretation in Information Retrieval", Technical Report TR-86-1, Virginia Tech, Department of Computer Science, 1986.

Fox-93 – Fox, E.A, Sourcebook on digital libraries: Report for the National Science Foundation, Tech. Rep. TR-93-95, Computer Science Department, VPI&SU, Blacksburg, Va., 1993 (http://fox.cs.vt.edu/DLSB.html).

Fox-93a – Fox, E., Hix, D., Nowell, L., Brueni, D., Wake, W., Heath, L. and D. Rao, "Users, user interfaces and objects:Envision, a digital library", Journal of the American Society for Information Science, Vol.44, No. 5, 1993, pages 480-49.

Fox-96 – Fox, E.A. and G. Marchionini (eds.), Proceedings of the 1ST ACM International Conference on Digital Libraries, ACM, New York, N.Y., 1996.

Frakes-92 – Frakes, W. B., Ricardo Baeza-Yates, Information Retrieval Data Structures & Algorithms, Prentice Hall, New Jersey, 1992.

Friedman-89 – Friedman, J., "Regularized Discriminant Analysis", Journal of the American Statistical Association, 84(405), 1989, pages 165-175.

Freidhoff-89 – Friedhoff, R.M. and W. Benzon, The Second Computer Revolution: Visualization, Harry N. Adams, Inc., New York, 1989.

Fuhr-89 – Fuhr, N., "Optimum Polynominal Retrieval Functions Based on the Probability Ranking Principle", ACM Transactions on Information Systems, 7(3), 1989, pages 183-204.

Fung-95 – Fung, Robert and Brendan Del Favero, "Applying Baysian Networks to information Retrieval", Communications of the ACM, Vol. 58, No. 3., March 1995.

Furuta-89 – Furuta, R., Plaisant, C. and B. Shneiderman, "Automatically transforming regularly structured text into hypertext", Electronic Publishing, 2(4), December 1989, pages 211-229.

Galil-79 – Galil, Z., "On Improving the Worst Case Running Time of the Boyer-Moore String Matching Algorithm", CACM, 22, 1979, pages 505-608.

Gnanadesikan-79 – Gnanadesikan, R., Methods for Statistical Data Analysis of Multivariate Observations, John Wiley and Sons, New York, 1979.

Gershon-95 – Gershon, N. D.,"Moving Happily Through the World Wide Web", Computer Graphics and Applications, Vol. 16, No. 2, March 1996, pages 72-75.

Gershon-95a – Gershon, N.D. and S.G. Eick, "Visualization's New Tack: making sense of information", IEEE Spectrum, Vol. 32, No. 11, November 1995, pages 38-56.

Gey-94 – Gey, Fredric, "Inferring Probability of Relevance Using the Method of Logistic Regression", Proceedings of the Seventeenth Annual ACM-SIGIR Conference, edited by W. Bruce Croft and C. J. van Rijsbergen, Springer-Verlag, London, 1994, pages 222-241.

Gibson-60 –Gibson, E. and R. Walk, "The Visual Cliff", Scientific American, April 1960, pages 140-148,

Gilbert-79 – Gilbert, H. and K. Sparck Jones, Statistical Bases of Relevance Assessments for the Ideal Information Retrieval Test Collection, Computer Laboratory, University of Cambridge, BL R and D Report 5481, Cambridge, England, March 1979.

Gonnet-92 – Gonnet, Gaston, Baeza-Yates, Ricardo, and Tim Snider, New Indices for Text: Pat Trees and Pat Arrays, , in Frakes, W. B., Ricardo Baeza-Yates (Eds), Information Retrieval Data Structures & Algorithms, Prentice Hall, New Jersey, 1992, pp. 66-81.

Gordon-92 – Gordon, M. D. and P. Lenk, "When is the probability ranking principle suboptimal", Journal of the American Society for Information Science, No. 43,1992, pages 1-14.

Gordon-91 – Gordon, M. D. and P. Lenk, "A utility theoretic examination of the probability ranking principle in information retrieval", Journal of the American Society for Information Science, No. 42., 1991, pages 703-714.

Gustafson-71 – Gustafson, R.A., "Elements of the Randomized Combinatorial File Structure", ACM SIGIR, Proc. of the Symposium on Information Storage and Retrieval, University of Maryland, April 1971, pp. 163-74.

Hagler-91 – Hagler, Ronald. The Bibliographic Record and Technology, American Library Association, Chicago, Illinois, 1991.

Hahn-94 – Hahn, Harley and Rick Stout, The INTERNET Complete Reference, McGraw-Hill, Berkley, Ca., 1994, pp. 476-477.

Hafer-74 – Hafer, M., S. Weiss. "Word Segmentation by Letter Successor Varieties," Information Storage and retrieval, 10, 1974, pages 371-385

Halasz-87 – Halasz, F., Moran, T. P. and R.H. Trigg, "Notecards in a Nutshell", Proc. ACM CHI+GI'87, Toronto, Canada, 5-9 April 1987, pp. 45-52.

Harrison-71 – Harrison, M., "Implementation of the Substring Test by Hashing", CACM, 14, 1971, pages 777-79.

Harman-86 – Harman, D., "An Experimental Study of Factors Important in Document Ranking", ACM Conference on Research and development in Information Retrieval, Pisa, Italy, 1986.

Harman-91 – Harman, D. "How Effective is Suffixing?" Journal of the American Society for Information Science, 42(1), 1991, pages 7-15.

Harman-93 – Harman, Donna, "Overview of the First Text Retrieval Conference (TREC-1)", The First Text Retrieval Conference (TREC-1), NIST Special Publication 500-207, NIST, Gaithersburg, Md., March 1993, pages 1-20.

Harman-95 – Donna Harman, "Overview of the Third Text Retrieval Conference (TREC-3)", In D.K. Harman, editor, Overview of the Third Text Retrieval Conference (TREC-3), pages 1-19, NIST Special Publication 500-225, April 1995.

Harman-96 – Donna Harman, "Overview of the Fourth Text Retrieval Conference (TREC-4)", paper to be included in the Overview of the Fifth Text Retrieval Conference (TREC-5), NIST Special Publications.

Harper-78 – Harper, D.J. and C.J. van Rijsbergen, "An Evaluation of Feedback in Document Retrieval Using Co-Occurrence Data", Journal of Documentation, 34(3), 1978, pages 189-216.

Harper-80 – Harper, D.J., Relevance Feedback in Automatic Document Retrieval Systems: An Evaluation of Probabilistic Strategies, Doctoral Dissertation, Jesus College, Cambridge, England.

Hasan-95 – Hasan, M. Z., A.O. Mendelzon and D. Vista, "Visual Web Surfing withHy+", Proceedings of CASCON'95, Toronto, 1995, pages 218-227.

Haskin-83 – Haskin, R. and L. Hollaar, "Operational Characteristics of a Hardware-based Pattern Matcher", ACM Transactions Database, 8 (1), 1983.

Hearst-96 – Hearst, M. and J. Pedersen, "Reexamining the Cluster Hypothesis: Scatter/Gather on Retrieval Results", In Proceedings of the Nineteenth Annual ACM SIGIR Conference on Research and Development in Information Retrieval, ACM, New York, N. Y., 1996, pages 76-83.

Heilmann-96 – Heilmann, K., Kihanya, D., Light, A. and P. Musembwa, "Intelligent Agents: A Technology and Business Application Analysis", http://www.mines.u-ancy.fr/~gueniffe/CoursEMN/131/heilmann/heilmann.html#I, (as of Jan 2, 1997).

Hemmje-94 -- Hemmje, M., Kunkel, C. and A. Willett, "CyberWorld - A visualization user interface supporting full text retrieval", In Proceedings of the Seventeenth Annual ACM SIGIR Conference on Research and Development in Information Retrieval, ACM, New York, N. Y., 1994, pages249-259.

Hendley-95 – Hendley, R.J. et.al.,"Narcissus: Visualizing information", in Proc. Information Visualization Symposium 95, N. Gershon and S.G. Eick eds., IEEE CS Press, Los Alamitos, Ca., 1995, pages 90-96.

Hinton-84 – Hinton, G.E., Distributed Representations, Technical Report CMU-CS-84-157, Carnegie-Mellon University, Department of Computer Science.

Hollaar-79 – Hollaar,L.,"Text Retrieval Computers", IEEE Computer, Vol.12, No. 3, March 1979, pages 40-50.

Holaar-84 – Hollaar, L. and R. Haskin, "Method and System for Matching Encoded Characters", U. S. Patent, 4, 450, 520, May 22, 1984.

Hollaar-92 – Hollaar, L., "Special Purpose Hardware for Information Retrieval", in Information Retrieval Data Structures & Algorithms, Prentice Hall, New Jersey, 1992, pages 443- 458.

Horspool-80 – Horspool, R., "Practical Fast Searching in Strings", Software-Practice and Experience, 10, 1980, pages 501-506.

Hosmer-89 – Hosmer, D and S. Lemeshow, Applied logistic Regression, John Wiley & Sons, New York, 1989.

Howard-81 – Howard, R.A., and J.E. Matheson, Influence Diagrams, in Readings on the Principles and Applications of Decision Analysis, R.A. Howard and J.E. Matheson, Eds., Strategic Decision Group, Menlo Park, Ca., 1981, pages 721-762.

Hull-94 – Hull, D., "Improving Text Retrieval for the Routing Problem Using Latent Semantic Indexing", In Proceedings of the Seventeenth Annual ACM SIGIR Conference on Research and Development in Information Retrieval, ACM, New York, N. Y., 1994, pages 282-289.

Hull-95 - Hull, D., Information Retrieval using Statistical Classification, Ph.D. Thesis, Stanford University, 1995.

Hull-96 – Hull, D., Pedersen, J. and H. Schutze, "Method Combination for Document Filtering", In Proceedings of the Nineteenth Annual ACM SIGIR Conference on Research and Development in Information Retrieval, ACM, New York, N. Y., 1996, pages 279-287.

Huffman-95 – Huffman, S. and M. Damashek, "Acquaintance: A Novel Vector Space N-Gram Technique for Document Categorization", In D.K. Harman, editor, Overview of the Third Text Retrieval Conference (TREC-3), NIST Special Publication 500-225, April 1995, pp. 305-310

Hyman-82 – Hyman, Richard. Shelf Access in Libraries, Chicago, ALA, 1982.

HYMAN-89 – Hyman, R. J., Information Access , American Library Association, Chicago, 1989.

Ide-69 – Ide, E, "Relevance Feedback in an Automatic Document Retrieval System", Report No. ISR-15 to National Science Foundation from Department of Computer Science, Cornell University.

Ide-71 – Ide, E., "New Experiments in Relevance Feedback", in The SART Retrieval System, ed. G. Salton, , Englewod, N. J., Prentice-Hall, 1971, pages 337-54.

IETF-96 – "Uniform Resource Names, a Progress Report", in the February 1996 issue of D-Lib Magazine.

Ingwersen-92 – Ingwersen, P., Information Retrieval Interaction, ISBN:0-947568-54-9, London, England, 1992.

Iyengar-80 – Iyengar, S. and V. Alia, "A String Search Algorithm", Applied Math. Computation., 6, 1980, pages 123-31.

Johnson-91, "Tree Maps, A Space Filling Approach to the Visualization of Hierarchical Information Structures", IEEE Visualization '91 Conference Proceedings, IEEE Computer Society Press, Los Alamitos, Ca., 1991, pages 284-91.

Jones-71 – Jones, K. Sparck, Automatic Keyword Classification for Information Retrieval, Buttersworths, London, 1971.

Kaiser-96 – Kaiser, Mary K., http://vision.arc.nasa.gov/AFH/Brief/Vision.S.T./Perceptually.T.html, as of November 2, 1996.

Karp-87 – Karp, R. and M. Rabin, "Efficient Randomized Pattern Matching Algorithms", IBM Journal of Research and Development, 31, 1987, pages 249-60.

Katzer-82 – Katzer, J., McGill, M., Tessier, J., Frakes, W., and P. Gupta, "A Study of the Overlap Among Document Representations", Information Technology: Research and Development, 1(2), 1982, pages 261-274.

Keen-71 – Keen, E."Evaluation Parameters", in The SMART Retrieval System - Experiments in Automatic Document Processing, G. Salton (ed.), Prentice-Hall, Inc., Englewood, New Jersey, 1971, Chapter 5.

Kellog-96 – Kellog, R. and M. Subhas, "Text to Hypertext: Can Clustering Solve the Problem in Digital Libraries", Proceedings of the 1ST ACM International Conference on Digital Libraries, E. Fox and G. Marchionini (eds), March 1996, pages 144-148.

Kowalski-83 – Kowalski, G., "High Speed Multi-Term String Matching Algorithms", Dissertation for Doctor of Science, The George Washington University, May 1983.

Kracsony-81 – Kracsony, P. and G. Kowalski and A. Meltzer, "Comparative Analysis of Hardware versus Software Text Search", Information Retrieval Research, edited by Oddy, R. N., 1981, pp. 268-309.

Knuth-77 – Knuth, D.E., Morris, J. and V. Pratt, "Fast Pattern Matching in Strings", SIAM Journal of Computing, Vol. 6, No. 2, June 1977, pages 323-350.

Krohn-95 – Krohn, U., "Visualization of navigational retrieval in virtual information spaces", in Proceedings of the Workshop on New Paradigms in Information Visualization and Manipulation, Baltimore, Md., 1995, pages 26-32.

Krovetz-93 – Krovetz, Robert, "Viewing Morphology as an Inference Process", Proceeding of the ACM-SIGIR Conference on Research and Development in information retrieval, 1993, pp. 191-202.

Kstem-95 – Information from the Kstem.doc file distributed with INQUERY search system, Applied Computing Systems Institute of Massachusetts, Inc (ACSIOM), 1995.

Kupiec-95 – Kupiec, J., Pedersen, J. and Chen, F., "A Trainable Document Summarizer", in Proceeding of the 18th Annual International ACM SIGIR Conference on Research and Development in Information Retrieval, 1995, pages 68-74.

Kunze-95 – Kunze, John J. and R.P.C. Rodgers, "Z39.50 in a Nutshell", Lister Hill National Center for Biomedical Communications, National Library of Medicine, July 1995.

Kwok-95 – Kwok, K. and L. Grunfeld, "TREC-3 Ad-Hoc Routing Retrieval and Thresholding Experiments using PIRCS", In D.K. Harman, editor, Overview of the Third Text Retrieval Conference (TREC-3), NIST Special Publication 500-225, April 1995, pages 247-255.

Kwok-96 – Kwok, K. and L. Grunfeld, "TREC-4 Ad-Hoc Routing Retrieval and Filtering Experiments using PIRCS", In D.K. Harman, editor, Overview of the Fourth Text Retrieval Conference (TREC-4), NIST, 1996.

Lamping-95 – Lamping, J., Rao, R. and P. Pirolli, "A Focus + Context Technique Based on Hyperbolic Geometry for Visualizing Large Hierarchies", in CHI 95, Proc. ACM Conference on Human Factors in Computing Systems, ACM Press, New York, 1995, pages 401-408.

Lance-66 – Lance, G.N. and W. Williams, "A General Theory of Classificatory Sorting Strategies. 1. Hierarchical Systems", Computer Journal, 9, 1966, pages 373-80.

Lee-85 – Lee, D.L.,"The Design and Evaluation of a Text Retrieval Machine for Large Databases", Ph.D. Thesis, University of Toronto, September 1985.

Lee-90 – Lee, D.L. and F. Lochovsky, "HYTREM - A Hybird Text-Retrieval Machine for Large Databases", IEEE Transactions on Computers, 39(1), 1990, pages 111-123.

Lee-88 – Lee, W.C. and E.A. Fox, "Experimental Comparison of Schemes for Interpreting Boolean Queries", Virginia Tech M.S. Thesis, Technical Report TR-88-27,Department of Computer Science, 1988.

Lee-89 – Lee, D.L. and C.W. Leng, "Partitioned Signature Files: Design and Performance Evaluation", ACM Transactions on Information Systems, 7 (2), 1989, pp. 158-80.

Lehnert-91 – Lehnert, w. and Beth Sundheim, A performance evaluation of text-analysis technologies", A.I. Magazine, Vol. 12, No. 3, Fall 1991, pages 81-93.

Lewis-92 – Lewis, D., "An Evaluation of Phrasal and Clustered Representations on a Text Categorization Task", In Proceedings of the Fifteenth Annual ACM SIGIR Conference on Research and Development in Information Retrieval, 1992, pages 37-50.

Lewis-94 – Lewis, D. and W. Gale, "A Sequential Algorithm for Training Text Classifiers", In Proceedings of the Seventeenth Annual ACM SIGIR Conference on Research and Development in Information Retrieval, ACM, New York, N. Y., 1994, pages 11-22.

Lewis-94a – Lewis, D., and M. Ringuette, "A Comparison of Two Learning Algorithms for Text Categorization", in Symposium on Document Analysis and Information Retrieval, University of Las Vegas, 1994.

Lewis-95 – Lewis, D., "Evaluating and Optimizing Autonomous Text Classification Systems", in E.Fox, P.Ingwersen, and R. Fidel (eds.), SIGIR'95: Proceedings of the 18th Annual International ACM SIGIR Conference on Research and Development in Information Retrieval, ACM, New York, 1995, pages 246-254

Lewis-96 – Lewis, D., "The TREC-4 Filtering Track", paper to be included in the Overview of the Fifth Text Retrieval Conference (TREC-5), NIST Special Publications.

Liddy-93 – Liddy, Elizabeth D. and Sung H. Myaeng, "DR-LINK's Linguistic-Conceptual Approach to Document Detection, The First Text Retrieval Conference (TREC-1), NIST Special Publication 500-207, NIST, Gaithersburg, Md., March 1993, pages 113-129

Lin-88 – Lin, Z. and C. Faloutsos, "Frame Sliced Signature Files", CS-TR-2146 and UMI-ACS-TR-88-88, Department of Computer Science, University of Maryland, 1988.

Lin-91 – Lin, X., Liebscher, and G. Marchionini, "Graphic Representation of Electronic Search Patterns", J. Am. Society for Information Science, Vol. 42, No. 7, 1991, pages 469-478.

Lin-92—Lin, X., "Visualization for the Document Space", Proceedings of Visualization '92, Boston, Ma., Oct. 1992, pages 274-281.

Lin-96 – Lin, Xia, "Graphical Table of Contents", Proceedings of the 1ST ACM International Conference on Digital Libraries, E. Fox and G. Marchionini (eds), March 1996, pages 45-53.

Lochbaum-89 – Lochbaum, K.E. and L.A. Streeter, "Comparing and Combining the Effectiveness of Latent Semantic Indexing and the Ordinary Vector Space Model for Information Retrieval", Information Processing and Management, 25(6), 1989, pages 665-76.

Lovins-68 – Lovins, J.B., "Development of a Stemming Algorithm.", Mechanical Translation and Computational Linguistics, 11(1-2), 1968, 22-31.

Lennon-81 – Lennon, M.D., D. Pierce, B. Tarry, and P. Willett, 1981. "An Evaluation of Some Conflation Algorithms for Information Retrieval." Journal of Information Science 3, 1981, pages 177-83.

Levine-94 – Levine, John R. and Carol Baroudi, The Internet for Dummies, IDG Books, San Mateo, Ca., 1994, pp. 261-262.

Lovins-68 – Lovins, J.B., "Development of a Stemming Algorithm", Mechanical Translation and Computational Linguistics, 11, 1968, pp. 22-31.

Luhn-58 – H.P.Luhn, The Automatic Creation of Literature Abstracts, IBM Journal of Research and Development, Vol. 2, No. 2, April 1958, pages 159-165.

Marchionini-88 – Marchionini, G. and B. Shneiderman, "Finding Facts vs. Browsing Knowledge in Hypertext Systems", Computer, January 1988, pages 70-80.

Maron-60 – Maron, M. E. and J. L. Kuhns, "On relevance, probabilistic indexing, and information retrieval", J. ACM, 1960, pages 216-244.

Masand-92 – Masand, B., Linoff, G. and D. Waltz, "Classifying News Stories Using Memory Based Reasoning", In Proceedings of the Fifteenth Annual ACM SIGIR Conference on Research and Development in Information Retrieval, 1992, pages 59-65.

Mayper-80 – Mayper, V., Nagy, A., Bird R., J. Tu, and L. Michaels, "Finite State Automation with Multiple State Types", U.S. Patent 4, 241, 402, December 23, 1980.

McIllroy-82 – McIlroy, M. Douglas, "Development of a Spelling List", IEEE Transaction on Communications, Vol. Com-30, 1982, pp. 91-99.

McCullagh-89 – McCullagh, P. and J. Nelder, Generalized Linear Models, chapter 4, pages 101-123, Chapman and Hall, 2nd edition, 1989.

McCulloch-43 – McCulloch,W. and W. Pitts, " A Logical Calculus of the Ides Immanent in Nervous Activity", Bulletin of Mathematical Biophysics, No. 5, 1943, pages 115-137.

Mettler-93 – Mettler, M., "Text Retrieval with the TRW Fast Data Finder", The First Text Retrieval Conference (TREC-1), NIST Special Publication 500-207, NIST, Gaithersburg, Md., March 1993, pages 309-317.

Miike-94 – Miike, S., Itoh, E., Ono, K., and K. Sumita, "A full text retrieval system with a dynamic abstract generation function", Proceedings of the Seventeenth Annual ACM SIGIR Conference on Research and Development in Information Retrieval, ACM, New York, N. Y., 1994, pages 152-161.

Minker-77 – Minker, J., "Information Storage and Retrieval - A Survey and Functional Description", SIGIR Forum, Association for Computer Machinery, Vol. 12., No. 2, Fall 1977, pages 1-108.

Mitkas-89 – Mitkas, P., Berra, P., and P. Guilfoyle, "An Optical System for Full Text Search", Proceedings of SIGIR 89.

Moller-Nielsen-84 – Mollier-Nielsen, P. and J. Staunstrup, "Experiments with a Fast String Searching Algorithm", Inf. Proc. Letters, 18, 1984, pages 129-35.

Mooers-49 – Mooers, C., "Application of Random Codes to the Gathering of Statistical Information", Bulletin 31, Zator Co., Cambridge, Mass., 1949.

Morris-75 – Morris, Robert and Lorinda Cherry, "Computer Detection of Typographical Errors", IEEE Transactions on Professional Communications, Vol. 18, No. 1, March 1975, pp. 54-56.

Morris-92 – Morris, A., Kasper, G. and D. Adams, "The effects and limitations of automated text condensing on reading comprehension performance", Information Systems research, March 1992, pages 17-35.

Mukherjea -95 – Mukherjea, S. and J. D. Foley,"Visualizing the WorldWide Web with Navigational View Builder", Computer Networks and ISDN Systems, 27, 1995, pages 1075-087.

Munzer-95 – Munzer, T. and P. Burchard, "Visualizing the Structure of the World Wide Web in 3D Hyperbolic Space", The Geometry Center, University of Minnesota, 1995. (see http://www.geom.umn.edu/docs/research/webviz/ current November 1996)

Murtagh-83 – Murtagh, F., "A Survey of Recent Advances in Hierarchical Clustering Algorithms", Computer Journal, 26, 1983, pages 354-359.

Murtagh-85 – Murtagh, F., Multidimensional Clustering Algorithms, Vienna:Physica-Verlag (COMP-STAT Lectures 4), 1985.

Nelson-65 – Nelson T., "A File Structure for the complex, the changing, the indeterminate", Proceedings of the ACM 20th National Conference, 1965, pages 84-100.

Nelson-74 – Nelson, T., Computer Lib/Dream Machine, first edition self-published in 1974 (revised edition published by Microsoft Press in 1987).

Norman-90 – Norman, D. A.,"Why Interfaces Don't Work", in The Art of Human Computer Interface Design, Brenda Laurel (ed.), Addison Wesley, 1990, pages 209-219.

Norris-69 – Norris, Dorthy May, A History of Cataloguing and Cataloguing Methods 1100-1850, (1939; reprint ed., Detroit: Gale, 1969)

Nowell-96 – Nowell, L., France, R., Hix, D., Heath, L., and E. Fox,"Visualzing Search results: Some Alternatives to Query-Document Similarity", In Proceedings of the Nineteenth Annual ACM SIGIR Conference on Research and Development in Information Retrieval, ACM, New York, N. Y., 1996, pages 66-75.

Olsen-93 – Olsen, K.A. et. al., "Visualization of a Document Collection: the VIBE System", Information Processing and Management, Vol. 29, No. 1, 1993, pages 69-81.

ORION-93 – ORION White Paper, Wide-Area Information Server (WAIS) Evaluation, Orion Scientific, Inc., 1993.

Paice-84 – Paice, C. "Soft Evaluation of Boolean Search Queries in Information Retrieval Systems", Information Technology, Research and Development Applications, 3(1), 1983, pages 33-42.

Paice-90 – Paice, C. "Another Stemmer," ACM SIGIR Forum, 24(3), 1990, pages 56-61.

Paice-93 – Paice,C. and P. Jones, "The identification of important concepts in highly structured technical papers, in the Sixteenth Annual International ACM SIGIR Conference on Research and Development in Information Retrieval, ACM Press, June 1993, pages 69-78.

Paice-94 – Paice, C., "An Evaluation Method for Stemming Algorithms", Proceedings of the Seventeenth Annual International ACM-SIGIR Conference, Springer-Verlag, London, 1994, pp. 42-50.

Paracel-96 – Biology Tool Kit Software Manual, Revision 1, Paracel Inc., Pasadena, Ca.

Pearl-88 – Pearl, J., Probabilistic Reasoning in Intelligent Systems, Morgan Kaufmann, San Mateo, Ca., 1988.

Peterson-80 – Peterson, James L., "Computer Programs for Detecting and Correcting Spelling Errors", Communications of the ACM, Vol. 23., No. 12, December 1980, pp. 676-687.

Pirolli-96 – Pirolli, P., Schank, P., Hearst, M. and C. Diehl, "Scatter/gather browsing communicates the topic structure of a very large text collection", in Proceedings of the ACM SGCHI Conference on Human Factors in Computing Systems, Vancouver, Wa., May 1996.

Porter-80 – Porter, M.F., "An Algorithm for Suffix Stripping.", Program, 14(3), 1980. pages 130-137.

Pratt-42 – Pratt, Fletcher, Secret and Urgent, Blue Ribbon Books, Garden City, N.J., 1942, page 50.

Rather-77 – Rather, Lucia, "Exchange of Bibliographic Information in Machine Readable Form", Library Trends 25, Jan 1977. pages 625-643.

Rearick-91 – Rearick, T."Automating the conversion of text into hypertext", InBerk & Devlin, Eds., Hypertext/Hypermedia Handbook, MacGraw-Hill Inc., New York, 1991, pages 113-140.

Reimer-88 – Reimer, U. and U. Hahn, "Text condensation as knowledge base abstraction", in IEEE Conference on AI Applications, 1988, pages 338-344.

RETRIEVALWARE-95 – CONQUEST Software Manual, The ConQuest Semantic Network, 1995.

Ribeiro-96 – Ribeiro, B. and R. Muntz, "A Belief Network Model for IR", In Proceedings of the Nineteenth Annual ACM SIGIR Conference on Research and Development in Information Retrieval, ACM, New York, N. Y., 1996, pages 253-260.

Rivest-77 – Rivest, R., "On the Worst-Case Behavior of String Searching Algorithms", SIAM Journal on Computing, 6, 1977, pages 669-74.

Rijsbergen-79 – van Rijsbergen, C.J., Information Retrieval, 2nd Edition, Buttersworths, London, 1979.

Roberts-78 – Roberts, D.C., "A Specialized Computer Architecture for Text Retrieval", Fourth Workshop on Computer Architecture for NonNumeric Processing, Syracuse, N.Y. (published as SIGIR Vol. 13, no. 2: SIGARCH Vol. 7, No. 2; and SIGMOD 10., no. 1), pages 51-59.

Roberts-79 – Roberts,C.S., "Partial-Match Retrieval via the Method of Superimposed Codes", Proc. IEEE, 67 (12), 1979, pp. 1624-1642.

Robertson-69 – Robertson, S.E., "The Parametric Description of Retrieval Tests, Part I: The Basic Parameters", Journal of Documentation, Vol. 25, No. 1, March 1969, pages 1-27.

Robertson-76 – Robertson, S.E. and K. Spark Jones, "Relevance Weighting of Search Terms," J. American Society for Information Science, 27(3), 1976, pages 129-46.

Robertson-77 – Robertson, S.E., "The probability ranking principle in IR", Journal of Documentation, No. 33, 1977, pages 294-304.

Robertson-93 – Robertson G.G., "Information Visualization Using 3-D Interactive Animation", Communications of the ACM, Vol. 36, N0. 4, April 1993, pages 57-71.

Rocchio-71 – Rocchio, J. J., "Relevance Feedback in Information Retrieval", in Salton G. (ed.), The SMART Retrieval Storage and Retrieval System, Englewood Cliffs, N.J., Prentice Hall, Inc., 1971, pages 313-23.

Rock-90 – Rock, I and S. Palmer,"The legacy of Gestalt psychology", Scientific American, December, 1990, pages 84-90.

Rose-95 – Rose, R. ed., P1000 Science and Technology Strategy for Information Visualization, Version 1.6, August 1995.

Rose-96 – Rose, R. ed., P1000 Science and Technology Strategy for Information Visualization, Version 2, 1996.

Roseler-94 – Roseler, M. and D. Hawkins, "Gent Agents: Software Servants for an Electronic Information World (and More!)", ONLINE, July 1994, pages 19-32.

Rumelhart-95 – Rumelhart, D., Durbin, R., Golden, R., and Y. Chauvin, "Learning Internal Representation by Error Propagation", in Back-propagation: Theory, Architectures and Applications, Lawrence Erlbaum, Hillsdale, N.J., 1995.

Rumelhart-95a – Rumelhart, D., Durbin, R., Golden, R., and Y. Chauvin, "Backpropagation: The Basic Theory", in Back-propagation: Theory, Architectures and Applications, Lawrence Erlbaum, Hillsdale, N.J., 1995.

Rush-71 – Rush, J., Salvador, R., and A Zamora, "Automatic Abstracting and Indexing II, Production of Indicative Abstracts by Application of Contextual Inference and Syntactic Coherence Criteria", Journal of the ASIS, Vol. 22, No. 4., 1971, pages 260-274.

Rytter-80 – Rytter, W. "A Correct Preprocessing Algorithm for Boyer-Moore String Searching", SIAM Journal on Computing, Vol 9., No. 3, August 1980, pages 509-512.

Sacks-Davis-83 – Sacks-Davis, R. and K. Ramamohanarao, "A Two Level Superimposed Coding Scheme for Partial Match Retrieval", Information Systems,8 (4), 1983, pp. 273-80.

Sacks-Davis-87 – Sacks-davis, R., Kent, A. and K. Ramamohanarao, "Multikey Access Methods Based on Superimposed Coding Techniques", ACM Transactions on Database Systems, 12 (4), pp. 655-96.

Salton-68 – Salton, G. Automatic Information Organization and Retrieval. New York: McGraw-Hill, 1968.

Salton-72 – Salton G. Experiments in Automatic Thesaurus Construction for Information Retrieval, Information Processing 71, North Holland Publishing Co., Amsterdam, 1972, pp. 115-123

Salton-73 – Salton, g. and C.S. Yang, "On the specification of Term Values in Automatic Indexing", Journal f Documentation, 29(4), 351-72.

Salton-75 – Salton, G., Dynamic Information and Library Processing, Prentice-Hall Inc., Englewod, New Jersey, 1975.

Salton-83 – Salton, G. and M. McGill, Introduction to Modern Information Retrieval, McGraw-Hill, 1983.

Salton-83a – Salton, G.E., E.A. Fox, and H. Wu, "Extended Boolean Information Retrieval", Communications of the ACM, 26(12), 1983, pages 1022-36

Salton-88 – Salton, G. and C.Buckley, "Term-Weighting Approaches in Automatic Text Retrieval," Information Processing and Management, 24(5), 513-23.

Salton-89 – Salton, G.E., Automatic Text Processing, Addison-Wesley, Reading, Mass, 1989, pages 260-265.

Saracevic-91 – Saracevic,T., "Individual Differences in Organizing, Searching and Retrieving Information", ASIS '91: Proceedings of the American Society for Information Science (ASIS) 54th Annual Meeting, Vol. 28, 1991, pages 82-86.

Saracevic-95 – Saracevic, T., "Evaluation of Evaluation in Information Retrieval", Proceeding of the 18th Annual International ACM SIGIR Conference on Research and Development in Information Retrieval, 1995, pages 138-145.

Schamber-90 – Schamber, L., Eisenberg, M. and M. Nilan, "A Re-examination of Relevance: Toward a Dynamic, Situational Definition", Information Processing and Management, 26(6), 1990, pages 755-776.

Schuster-79 – Schuster, S., Nguyen, H., Ozkarahan, E., and K. Smith, "RAP2 - An Associative Processor for Databases and Its Application", IEEE Transactions on Computers, Vol. C-28, No. 6., June 1979, pages 446-458.

Schek-78 – Schek, H.J., The Reference String Indexing Method, Research report, IBM Scientific Center, Heidelberg, Germany, 1978.

Schuegraf-76 – Schuegraf, E.J. and H.S. Heaps, Query Processing in a Retrospective Document Retrieval System That Uses Word Fragments as Language Elements, Information Processing and Management, Vol. 12, No. 4, 1976, pp. 283-292.

Schuster-79 – Schuster, S., Nguyen, H., Ozkarahan, E., and K. Smith, "RAP2 - An Associative Processor for Databases and Its Application", IEEE Transactions on Computers, Vol. C-28, No. 6., June 1979, pages 446-458.

Schutze-95 – Schutze, H., Hull, D and J. Pedersen, "A Comparison of Classifiers and Document Representations for the Routing Problem", Proc. of the 18th Annual International ACM SIGIR Conference on Research and Development in Information Retrieval, Seattle Washington, July 1995, pp.229-237.

Sedgewick-88 – Sedgewick, R., Algorithms, Second Edition, Addison-Wesley, 1988 .

Shannon-51 – Shannon, C.E., Predication and Entropy of Printed English, Bell Technical Journal, Vol. 30, No. 1, January 1951, pages 50-65.

Singhal-95 – Singhal, A., Salton, G., Mitra, M. and Chris Buckley, Document length normalization, Technical Report TR95-1529, Cornell University, 1995.

Smit-82 – Smit, G, "A Comparison of Three String Matching Algorithms", Software Practice and Experience, Vol.. 12, 1982, pages 57-66.

Sparck Jones-71 – Sparck Jones, K. Sparck, Automatic Keyword Classification for Information Retrieval, Buttersworths, London, 1971.

Sparck Jones-75 – Sparck Jones, K., and C. van Rijisbergen, "Report on the Need for and Provision of an "Ideal" Information Retrieval Test Collection, British Library Research and Development Report 5266, Computer Laboratory, University of Cambridge, England, 1975.

Sparck Jones-79 – Sparck Jones, K. and Webster, Research in Relevance Weighting, British Library Research and Development Report 5553, Computer Laboratory, University of Cambridge, 1979.

Sparck Jones-81 – Sparck Jones, K., Information retrieval Experiment, Butterworths, London, England, 1981.

Sparck Jones-93 – Sparck Jones, K.,"Discourse Modeling for Automatic Summarizing", Technical Report 29D, Computer Laboratory, University of Cambridge, 1993.

Spoerri-93 – Spoerri, A.,"Visual Tools for Information Retrieval", in Proc. IEEE Symposium on Visual Languages, IEEE CS Press, Los Alamitos, Ca., 1993, pages 160-168.

Stirling-77 – Stirling, K.H., The effect of document ranking on retrieval system performance: a search for an optimal ranking rule, Ph.D. thesis, University of California, Berkley, 1977.

Sundheim-92 – Sundheim, Beth M., Overview of the Fourth Message Understanding Evaluation and Conference, Proceedings Fourth Message Understanding Conference (MUC), Morgan Kaufmann Publishers, Inc., 1992, pages 3-21.

Thesuarus-93 – Microsoft Word Version 6.0a, 1983-1994 Microsoft Corporation, Thesaurus, Soft-Art Inc., 1984-1993.

Thorelli-62 – Thorelli, Lars Erik, "Automatic Correction of Errors in Text", BIT, Vol. 2, No. 1, 1962, pp. 45-62

Thorelli-90 – Thorelli, L.G. and W.J. Smith, Using Computer Color Effectively, Prentice Hall, 1990.

Tong-94 – Tong, R. and L. Appelbaum, "Machine Learning for Knowledge Based Document Routing", in The Second Text Retrieval Conference (TREC-2) Proceedings, NIST publications, 1993, pages 253-264.

Turner-95 – Turner, Fay, "An Overview of the Z39.50 Information Retrieval Standard", UDT Occasional paper #3, National Library of Canada, July 1995.

Van Dam-88 – van Dam, A., Hypertext'87 keynote address, Communications of the ACM, 31, 7, July 1988, pp. 887-895.

Veerasamy-96 – Veerasamy, A. and N. Belkin, "Evaluation of a Tool for Information Visualization of Information Retrieval Results", In Proceedings of the Nineteenth Annual ACM SIGIR Conference on Research and Development in Information Retrieval, ACM, New York, N. Y., 1996, pages 85-93.

Vickery-70 – B.C. Vickery, Techniques of Information Retrieval, Archon Books, Hamden, Conn., 1970.

Voorhees-86 – Voorhees, E.M. The Effectiveness and Efficiency of Agglomerative Hierarchic Clustering in Document Retrieval, Ph.D. thesis, 1986, Cornell University.

Voorhees-96 – Voorhees, E. and P. Kantor, "TREC-5 Confusion Track" , paper to be included in the Overview of the Fifth Text Retrieval Conference (TREC-5), NIST Special Publications.

Wade-89 – Wade, S.J., J. P. Willet and D. Bawden, "SIBRIS: the Sandwich Interactive Browsing and Ranking Information System", J. Information Science, 15, 1989, pages 249-260.

Wang-77 – Wang, C.H.C, Mitchell, P.C., Rugh, J.S. and B.W. Basheer, "A Statistical Method for Detecting Spelling Errors in Large Databases", IEEE Proceedings of the 14th International Computer Society Conference, 1977, pp. 124-128.

Wang-85 – Wang, Y-C, Vandenthorpe, J. and M. Evans, "Relationship Thesauri in Information Retrieval", J. American Society of Information Science, pp. 15-27, 1985.

Waltz-85 – Waltz, D.L., J. B. Pollack, "Massively Parallel Parsing: A Strongly Interactive Model of Natural Language Interpretation", Cognitive Science, 9, 1985, pages 51-74.

Ward-63 – Ward, J. H., "Hierarchical Grouping to Optimize an Objective Function", J. American Statistical Association, 58(301), 1963, pages 235-44.

Wiederhold-95 – Wiederhold, G., "Digital Libraries, Value, and productivity", Communications of the ACM, Vol. 38, No. 4, April 1995, pages 85-96.

Weiner-95 – Weiner, Michael L. and Elizabeth D. Liddy, "Intelligent text processing and intelligence tradecraft", Journal of the AGSI, July 1995.

Wilkinson-95 – Wilkinson, R., "Effective Retrieval of Structured Documents", Proceedings of the Seventh Annual International ACM SIGIR Conference on Research and Development in Information Retrieval, Dublin, Ireland, July 1994.

Wilkenson-95 – Wilkenson, Ross and Justin Zobel. Comparison of Fragment Schemes for Document Retrieval. In D.K. Harman, editor, Overview of the Third Text Retrieval Conference (TREC-3), pages 81-84, NIST Special Publication 500-225, April 1995.

Willet-88 – Willet, P., "Recent Trends in Hierarchic Document Clustering: A Critical Review", Information Processing & Management, 24(5), 1988, pages 577-97.

Wise-95 – Wise, J.A et. al. "Visualizing the Nonvisual: Spatial Analysis and Interaction with Information from Text Documents", Proceeding of Information Visualization Symposium, IEEE Computer Society Press, Los Alamitos, Ca., 1995, pages 51-58.

Wu-92 –Wu, S. and U Manber, "Fast Text Searching Allowing Errors", Communications of the ACM, Vol. 35, No. 10, October 992, pages 83-89.

Yang-94 – Yang, Y.,"Expert Network: Effective and Efficient Learning from Human Decisions in Text Categorization and Retrieval", in Proceedings of the Seventeenth Annual ACM SIGIR Conference on Research and Development in Information Retrieval, ACM, New York, N. Y., 1994, pages 13-22.

Yochum-85 – Yochum, Julian, "A High-Speed Text Scanning Algorithm Utilizing Least Frequent Trigraphs", IEEE Proceedings New Directions in Computing Symposium, Trondheim, Norway, 1985, pp. 114-121.

Yochum-95 – Yochum, Julian, "Research in Automatic Profile Creation and relevance Ranking with LMDS", In D.K. Harman, editor, Overview of the Third Text Retrieval Conference (TREC-3), NIST Special Publication 500-225, April 1995, pp. 289-298.

Yu-86 – Yu, K., Hsu, S., Heiss, R. and L. Hasiuk, "Pipelined for Speed: The Fast Data Finder System", Quest, Technology at TRW, 9(2), Winter 1986/87, 4-19.

Zadeh-65 – Zadeh, L.A, "Fuzzy Sets", Information and Control, 8, 1965, pages 338-53.

Zamora-81 – Zamora, E.M, Pollack, J.J., and Antonio Zamora, "Use of Trigram Analysis of Spelling Error Detection", Information Processing and Management, Vol. 17, No. 6, 1981, pp. 305-316.

Zaremba-95 – Zaremba, Donald,http://www.europe.digital.com/.i/info/DTJ102 /DTJ102sc.TXT, current as of November 21, 1996.

Ziph-49 – G.K. Ziph, Human Behavior and the Principle of Least Effort, Adson Wesley Publishing, Reading, Massachusetts, 1949.

Zizi-96 – Hascoet-Zizi, M. and N. Pediotakis, "Visual Relevance Analysis", Proceedings of the 1ST ACM International Conference on Digital Libraries, E. Fox and G. Marchionini (eds), March 1996, pages 54-62

Zloof-75 – "Query By Example", Proc. NCC 44, Anaheim, Ca., AFIPS Press, Montvale, N.J., 1975.

Author Index

Subject Index

Printed in the United Kingdom
by Lightning Source UK Ltd.
124080UK00006B/177/A

LANCASTER UNIVERSITY LIBRARY

Due for return by end of service on date below
(or earlier if recalled)

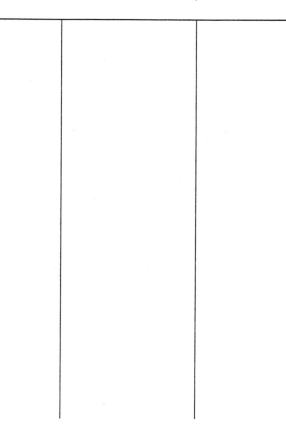